PRENTICE HALL

Algebra 1

Daily Cumulative Review Masters

Needham, Massachusetts
Upper Saddle River, New Jersey
Glenview, Illinois

Overview

Daily Cumulative Review Masters provides a continuous review of skills and concepts from *Prentice Hall Algebra 1*. A Daily Review worksheet is provided for each lesson in the Student Edition.

The first section of each worksheet reviews a key objective from the previous lesson. The second section of each worksheet reviews material covered two lessons prior to the current lesson. The third section provides a Mixed Review of problems from previous lessons or chapters. Lesson references are provided with each exercise in Mixed Review.

Daily Review worksheets for Chapter 1 review key concepts from the previous year as well as from Chapter 1.

The Daily Review format helps students solidify and retain math skills learned throughout the school year.

ISBN 0-13-044392-1

1 2 3 4 5 6 7 8 9 10 04 03 02 01 00

Daily Cumulative Review

Contents

Daily Cumulative Review

Contents (continued)

Name ______________________ Class ______________ Date ____________

Daily Cumulative Review 1-1

Mixed Review *(From Last Year)*

Tell whether each expression is a numerical or a variable expression. For a variable expression, name the variable.

1. $9c - 8$

____

2. $4 - 2(5 + 9)$

____

3. $48 \div (2 \times 3) + 4$

____

4. $8 \cdot 5 - 2x + 4$

____

5. $5h - 4 + 2(3 + 5)$

____

6. $8 + 3 - 5(1 + b)$

____

Simplify each expression.

7. $5 + 2 \cdot 4$

____

8. $17 - 12 \div 2$

____

9. $3 \times 6 + 8 \div 4$

____

10. $9 \times 2 + 7$

____

11. $10 - 2 \cdot 5 + 11$

____

12. $1 + 6 \div 3 \cdot 4$

____

Name each property.

13. $2 + 3 = 3 + 2$ ______________________

14. $(6 + 10) + 14 = 6 + (10 + 14)$ ______________________

15. $5(3 + 6) = 5 \cdot 3 + 5 \cdot 6$ ______________________

16. $4(2 \cdot 5) = (4 \cdot 2) \cdot 5$ ______________________

State whether each number is divisible by 2, 3, 5, 9, or 10. Write *yes* or *no* for each.

	2?	**3?**	**5?**	**9?**	**10?**
17. 25,743	______	______	______	______	______
18. 84,510	______	______	______	______	______
19. 41,825	______	______	______	______	______
20. 78,354	______	______	______	______	______

Name ______________________ Class ______________ Date __________

Daily Cumulative Review 1-2

Evaluate. *(Lesson 1-1)*

1. $t + 17$ for $t = 8$
2. $9 - h$ for $h = 6$
3. $8m$ for $m = 7$
4. $\frac{n}{3p}$ for $n = 24$ and $p = 2$
5. $\frac{63}{a}$ for $a = 9$
6. $19 - b$ for $b = 8$
7. $x + y$ for $x = 5$ and $y = 7$
8. $2pq$ for $p = 12$ and $q = 5$
9. $\frac{d}{13}$ for $d = 65$

Mixed Review *(From Last Year)*

Find each product.

10. $3 \cdot 3 \cdot 3$
11. $2 \cdot 2 \cdot 2 \cdot 2 \cdot 2$
12. $(4.3)(5.1)$
13. $1000(0.042)$
14. $\frac{3}{4} \cdot \frac{8}{9}$
15. $2\frac{1}{2} \cdot \frac{3}{5}$
16. $100(\frac{3}{25})$
17. $(0.1)(3.53)$
18. $\frac{1}{3} \cdot \frac{1}{3} \cdot \frac{1}{3}$

Find each difference.

19. $2.7 - 1.9$
20. $8.6 - 0.91$
21. $\frac{3}{4} - \frac{3}{8}$
22. $3\frac{1}{2} - 1\frac{3}{4}$
23. $4.7 - 2.06$
24. $\frac{5}{9} - \frac{1}{3}$
25. $55.5 - 16.25$
26. $2\frac{5}{8} - 1\frac{1}{4}$
27. $\frac{13}{14} - \frac{1}{7}$

Name ______________________ Class ______________ Date __________

Daily Cumulative Review 1-3

Simplify. *(Lesson 1-2)*

1. $\frac{20}{48}$

2. $\frac{56}{4}$

3. $\frac{11a}{14a}$

4. $\frac{40xy}{5x}$

5. $\frac{45m}{15mn}$

6. $\frac{7hz}{12ah}$

Simplify. *(Lesson 1-1)*

7. $28 \div 7 + 3 \times 5$

8. $9 \times 4 \div 3 + 5$

9. $4 + 5 \times 2 - 3$

10. $6 + 24 \div 3 - 9$

11. $5 + 3 \times 4 \div 2$

12. $7 \div 2 \times 4 - 5$

Mixed Review *(From Last Year)*

Find each sum.

13. $348 + 295$

14. $0.41 + 4.1$

15. $\frac{2}{3} + \frac{3}{4}$

16. $2\frac{3}{5} + 1\frac{4}{5}$

17. $7.53 + 6.48$

18. $\frac{1}{6} + \frac{1}{7}$

Find each quotient.

19. $1222 \div 47$

20. $4.9 \div 125$

21. $6 \div \frac{1}{7}$

22. $3\frac{1}{3} \div \frac{5}{6}$

23. $4.8 \div 0.6$

24. $\frac{5}{9} \div \frac{2}{3}$

25. $5.6 \div 1.4$

26. $\frac{1}{3} \div 2$

27. $\frac{5}{6} \div 2\frac{1}{2}$

Name ______________________ Class ______________ Date ______________

Daily Cumulative Review 1-4

Evaluate each expression. *(Lesson 1-3)*

1. n^4 for $n = 2$ ______

2. $3y^2$ for $y = 5$ ______

3. $(2x)^2$ for $x = 3$ ______

4. j^{12} for $j = 1$ ______

5. $(7h)^8$ for $h = 0$ ______

6. $b^2 - 5$ for $b = 9$ ______

Write an equivalent expression using a commutative property. *(Lesson 1-2)*

7. xy ______

8. $5 + h$ ______

9. $de + f$ ______

Mixed Review

Evaluate.

10. *(1-1)* $b + 6 - b$ for $b = 11$ ______

11. *(1-1)* $\frac{c}{7}$ for $c = 35$ ______

12. *(1-1)* $4 + 2x$ for $x = 5$ ______

13. *(1-1)* $\frac{ab}{9}$ for $a = 12$ and $b = 3$ ______

14. *(1-1)* $2x + 3y$ for $x = 6$ and $y = 3$ ______

15. *(1-1)* $\frac{w}{3z}$ for $w = 12$ and $z = 2$ ______

Name the coefficients, any like terms, and any constants. *(From Last Year)*

16. $5a + 6 + 7a$

coefficients: ______

like terms: ______

constants: ______

17. $7x + 4y + 3y + 2x$

coefficients: ______

like terms: ______

constants: ______

18. $5m + 3n + 5 + 15m + 7n + 8$

coefficients: ______

like terms: ______

constants: ______

19. $3b + 4c + a + 5c + b$

coefficients: ______

like terms: ______

constants: ______

Name ______________________ Class ______________ Date __________

Daily Cumulative Review 1-5

Calculate. *(Lesson 1-4)*

1. $9 - 2^2$ ______

2. $(9 - 2)^2$ ______

3. $2 \cdot 5^2$ ______

4. $(2 \cdot 5)^2$ ______

5. $(6 + 3)^2$ ______

6. $6 + 3^2$ ______

Write using exponential notation. *(Lesson 1-3)*

7. $8 \cdot 8 \cdot 8 \cdot 8 \cdot 8$ ______

8. $b \cdot b \cdot b \cdot b$ ______

9. $7 \cdot h \cdot h \cdot h$ ______

Mixed Review

Simplify.

10. *(1-2)* $\frac{8}{72}$ ______

11. *(1-2)* $\frac{45n}{9n}$ ______

12. *(1-2)* $\frac{8jp}{11pq}$ ______

13. *(1-1)* $8 + 2 \cdot 3$ ______

14. *(1-1)* $15 - 3 \cdot 3$ ______

15. *(1-1)* $4 + 5 \times 7 - 10$ ______

Write a number expression and use it to find each amount. *(From Last Year)*

16. 8 less than 12

______

17. 5 more than twice 3

______

18. 9 more than 7

______

19. the sum of 6 and the quantity 3 times 10

______

Name ______________________ Class ______________ Date ________

Daily Cumulative Review 1-6

Collect like terms. *(Lesson 1-5)*

1. $8x + 12x$

2. $3m + 5n + 6m$

3. $5y^2 + 2y + 7y + 6y^2$

4. $\frac{1}{8}y + \frac{3}{8}y + \frac{1}{8}y$

5. $3z + 4z^2 + 10z + 1$

6. $\frac{1}{2}a + b + 2a + b$

Evaluate each expression. *(Lesson 1-4)*

7. $4x^2 - 3$ for $x = 3$

8. $5(a + 6)$ for $a = 4$

9. $(15 - b)^2$ for $b = 7$

10. $(n - 3)(n + 7)$ for $n = 6$

11. $3(2m - 1)$ for $m = 9$

12. $5x^3 + 1$ for $x = 2$

Mixed Review

Write an equivalent expression using a commutative property.

13. *(1-2)* $7 + x$

14. *(1-2)* pq

15. *(1-2)* $y + xz$

Evaluate each expression.

16. *(1-3)* a^3 for $a = 4$

17. *(1-3)* $2y^2$ for $y = 7$

18. *(1-3)* $(3y)^2$ for $y = 2$

19. *(1-3)* c^{20} for $c = 0$

20. *(1-1)* $m + 11$ for $m = 8$

21. *(1-1)* $3x + y$ for $x = 5$ and $y = 2$

Tell whether each pair of expressions is equivalent.

22. *(1-2)* $2t + 5$ and $2 \cdot 5 + t$

23. *(1-2)* $pq + 4r$ and $p \cdot 4 + qr$

24. *(1-2)* $abc + d$ and $bac + d$

Name ____________________ Class ____________ Date ____________

Daily Cumulative Review 1-7

Write as an algebraic expression. *(Lesson 1-6)*

1. the product of 15 and h ____________

2. 12 more than x ____________

3. five less than b ____________

4. c divided by 7 ____________

5. the sum of y and 9 ____________

6. the quotient of 16 and d ____________

Factor. *(Lesson 1-5)*

7. $12p + 21q$ ____________

8. $18m + 30$ ____________

9. $8p + 24q + 72$ ____________

10. $9 + 54r + 63t$ ____________

11. $10y + 210z$ ____________

12. $14 - 49r + 7s$ ____________

Mixed Review

Write using exponential notation.

13. $5 \cdot 5 \cdot 5 \cdot 5 \cdot 5 \cdot 5 \cdot 5$ *(1-3)* ____________

14. $a \cdot a \cdot a \cdot a$ *(1-3)* ____________

15. $6n \cdot n \cdot n \cdot n \cdot n$ *(1-3)* ____________

Write with a single exponent.

16. $\frac{16^4}{16^2}$ *(1-3)* ____________

17. $\frac{8^7}{8^3}$ *(1-3)* ____________

18. $\frac{9^3}{9}$ *(1-3)* ____________

Simplify.

19. $8 - 2 \times 3 + 7$ *(1-1)* ____________

20. $9 + 6 \div 3$ *(1-1)* ____________

21. $15 \div 3 + 4 \times 4$ *(1-1)* ____________

Calculate.

22. $(3 + 4)^2$ *(1-4)* ____________

23. $3 + 4^2$ *(1-4)* ____________

24. $3^2 + 4$ *(1-4)* ____________

25. $3 \cdot 4^2$ *(1-4)* ____________

26. $(3 \cdot 4)^2$ *(1-4)* ____________

27. $4 \cdot 3^2$ *(1-4)* ____________

Name ______________________ Class ______________ Date __________

Daily Cumulative Review 1-8

Solve for the given replacement set. *(Lesson 1-7)*

1. $x - 9 = 20$ $\{11, 29, 35\}$

2. $2y + 5 = 19$ $\{4, 6, 7\}$

3. $15 + n = 4n$ $\{5, 6, 7\}$

4. $m + 15 = 3m + 1$ $\{5, 7, 8\}$

Write as an algebraic expression. *(Lesson 1-6)*

5. Let d be the amount Shauna had before buying a CD. The CD cost \$9. Write an expression for the amount Shauna had after buying the CD.

6. Kyle lives twice as far from school as Shequille. Let d be the distance Shequille lives from school. Write an expression for the distance Kyle lives from school.

Mixed Review

Use the associative properties to write an equivalent expression.

7. *(1-4)* $5 + (p + q)$

8. *(1-4)* $(3m)n$

9. *(1-4)* $(9 + h) + j$

Collect like terms.

10. *(1-5)* $9b + 8b$

11. *(1-5)* $4j + 3h + 2j$

12. *(1-5)* $\frac{1}{5}z + \frac{3}{5}z$

What is the meaning of each expression?

13. *(1-3)* 7^4

14. *(1-3)* j^5

15. *(1-3)* $2m^3$

16. *(1-3)* $4h^6$

Name ______________________ Class ______________ Date __________

Daily Cumulative Review 1-9

Solve by drawing a diagram. *(Lesson 1-8)*

1. Misty has a long piece of chain she needs cut into 5 pieces. It costs $2.50 for each cut. How much will it cost in all?

____

2. Marcus ran 12 km in 3 days to train for a race. He ran twice as far the second day as the first. The third day he ran as far as he did the first two days together. How far did he run each day?

____

Solve mentally. The replacement set is all whole numbers. *(Lesson 1-7)*

3. $y + 4 = 19$ ________

4. $\frac{x}{7} = 5$ ________

5. $10p = 60$ ________

6. $a - 6 = 8$ ________

7. $\frac{b}{9} = 4$ ________

8. $j + 3 = 21$ ________

9. $5c = 35$ ________

10. $\frac{z}{4} = 6$ ________

11. $d - 15 = 20$ ________

Mixed Review

Evaluate each expression.

12. *(1-4)* $9y^2 - 7$ for $y = 3$ ________

13. *(1-4)* $(x + 4)^2$ for $x = 6$ ________

14. *(1-4)* $z^2 + 16$ for $z = 4$ ________

Write with a single exponent.

15. *(1-3)* $\frac{10^8}{10^5}$ ________

16. *(1-3)* $\frac{6^9}{6^2}$ ________

17. *(1-3)* $\frac{9^7}{9^2}$ ________

Factor.

18. *(1-5)* $21 + 28h$ ________

19. *(1-5)* $40x + 15y + 45$ ________

20. *(1-5)* $32a + 20b + 8$ ________

Name ______________________ Class ______________ Date ____________

Daily Cumulative Review 1-10

Find each. *(Lesson 1-9)*

1. Find the amount of interest (I) paid on a principal (p) amount of $1200 at a rate ($r$) of 0.03 (3%) for a term (t) of 4 years using the formula $I = prt$. ____________

2. Find the approximate stopping distance (d) in feet for an automobile driving 60 mi/h, using the formula $d = x + \frac{x^2}{20}$, where x is the speed in mi/h. ____________

Solve by drawing a diagram. *(Lesson 1-8)*

3. An iceberg rises 330 ft above the surface of the ocean. The distance from the bottom of the iceberg to the water's surface is 940 ft. What is the height of the iceberg?

____

Mixed Review

Use the distributive property to write an equivalent expression.

4. $3(m + 7)$ *(1-5)* ____________

5. $(4 + b)8$ *(1-5)* ____________

6. $2(5h + 9)$ *(1-5)* ____________

7. $5(n + 6)$ *(1-5)* ____________

8. $9(2x + 7)$ *(1-5)* ____________

9. $4(3a + 11)$ *(1-5)* ____________

Write as an algebraic expression.

10. 9 fewer than x *(1-6)* ____________

11. twice b *(1-6)* ____________

12. 10 more than y *(1-6)* ____________

Use the commutative and associative properties to write three equivalent expressions.

13. $(r + s) + t$ *(1-4)* ____________ ____________ ____________

14. $(b \cdot c)7$ *(1-4)* ____________ ____________ ____________

15. $(9x + y) + 4$ *(1-4)* ____________ ____________ ____________

Name ______________________ Class ______________ Date __________

Daily Cumulative Review 2-1

Solve using the *Try, Test, Revise* strategy. *(Lesson 1-10)*

1. $\frac{3 \cdot \square - 6}{3} = 6$

2. $\frac{5 \cdot \square + 1}{4} = 9$

3. $4(5 + \square) = 28$

4. $6 \cdot \square + 2 = 8 \cdot \square - 4$

5. $\frac{10}{3 + \square} = 2$

6. $\frac{3 \cdot 4 + \square}{6} = 3$

The formula below gives the approximate stopping distance (*d*) in feet for an automobile driving at *x* miles per hour. Find the approximate stopping distance for each speed given. *(Lesson 1-9)*

$$d = x + \frac{x^2}{20}$$

7. 15 mi/h ________ **8.** 60 mi/h ________ **9.** 45 mi/h ________

10. 20 mi/h ________ **11.** 65 mi/h ________ **12.** 5 mi/h ________

Mixed Review

Write each as an improper fraction. *(From Last Year)*

13. $2\frac{3}{4}$ ________ **14.** $1\frac{5}{8}$ ________ **15.** 3.5 ________

16. $12\frac{1}{5}$ ________ **17.** $6\frac{1}{7}$ ________ **18.** 10.71 ________

Write each set of numbers in order from least to greatest. *(From Last Year)*

19. $\frac{1}{4}, \frac{3}{8}, \frac{1}{2}, \frac{1}{8}, \frac{3}{16}$ ______________________________

20. $\frac{8}{5}, \frac{3}{5}, \frac{3}{10}, \frac{7}{10}, \frac{4}{5}$ ______________________________

Write using exponential notation.

21. $8 \cdot 8 \cdot 8 \cdot 8 \cdot 8 \cdot 8$ ______ *(1-3)*

22. $h \cdot h \cdot h \cdot h \cdot h$ ______ *(1-3)*

23. $7 \cdot m \cdot m \cdot m$ ______ *(1-3)*

24. $10 \cdot 10 \cdot 10 \cdot 10$ ______ *(1-3)*

25. $2 \cdot x \cdot x$ ______ *(1-3)*

26. $3 \cdot y \cdot y \cdot y \cdot y$ ______ *(1-3)*

Simplify each expression.

27. $6 + 5 \cdot 9$ ______ *(1-1)*

28. $18 - 12 \div 3$ ______ *(1-1)*

29. $4 \cdot 7 + 3 \cdot 2$ ______ *(1-1)*

30. $21 - 4^2$ ______ *(1-4)*

31. $(4 + 5)^2$ ______ *(1-4)*

32. $3 \cdot 4^2$ ______ *(1-4)*

33. $3 + 8 \cdot 5 - 7$ ______ *(1-1)*

34. $(40 - 35)^2$ ______ *(1-4)*

35. $2 + 6^2$ ______ *(1-4)*

Name ______________________ Class ______________ Date ____________

Daily Cumulative Review 2-2

Evaluate. *(Lesson 2-1)*

1. $|-8| + |-7|$ ____ **2.** $|6| \cdot |-6|$ ____ **3.** $|-3| \cdot |2| \cdot |-4|$ ____

4. $|2| \cdot |-5| + |-4|$ ____ **5.** $|9| \cdot |-3| - |5|$ ____ **6.** $|-8| \cdot |-12| \cdot |0|$ ____

Solve using the *Try, Test, Revise* strategy. *(Lesson 1-10)*

7. The sum of the measures of the interior angles of a quadrilateral is 360°. Two angles have the same measure. The other two angles are each twice as big as one of the smaller angles. What are the measures of the angles of the quadrilateral?

____

8. Consecutive numbers are numbers that follow each other when counting. For example, 5, 6, and 7 are consecutive numbers. Find three consecutive numbers whose sum is 66.

____

9. The sum of two numbers is 25. Their product is 154. What are the numbers? ____________

Mixed Review

Evaluate each expression.

10. m^5 for $m = 2$ *(1-3)* ____________

11. $4a^2$ for $a = 10$ *(1-3)* ____________

12. $(3b)^2$ for $b = 4$ *(1-3)* ____________

13. j^1 for $j = 37$ *(1-3)* ____________

14. y^{12} for $y = 0$ *(1-3)* ____________

15. $d^2 - 4$ for $d = 7$ *(1-3)* ____________

16. $37 - h$ for $h = 9$ *(1-1)* ____________

17. $6n$ for $n = 7$ *(1-1)* ____________

18. $\frac{x}{7y}$ for $x = 42$ and $y = 3$ *(1-1)* ____________

Find each sum or difference. *(From Last Year)*

19. $3.7 + 0.56$ ____ **20.** $9.8 - 2.14$ ____ **21.** $16.5 - 4.32$ ____

22. $\frac{2}{3} + 1\frac{1}{3}$ ____ **23.** $\frac{5}{8} - \frac{1}{4}$ ____ **24.** $1\frac{1}{6} - \frac{2}{3}$ ____

25. $\frac{7}{8} + \frac{3}{8}$ ____ **26.** $\frac{4}{5} - \frac{1}{10}$ ____ **27.** $2\frac{1}{2} + 1\frac{3}{4}$ ____

Name ______________________ Class ______________ Date __________

Daily Cumulative Review 2-3

Graph each rational number. *(Lesson 2-2)*

1. $\frac{5}{4}$ 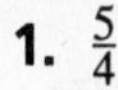

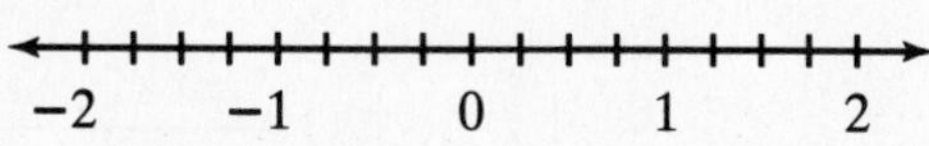

2. $-\frac{3}{4}$

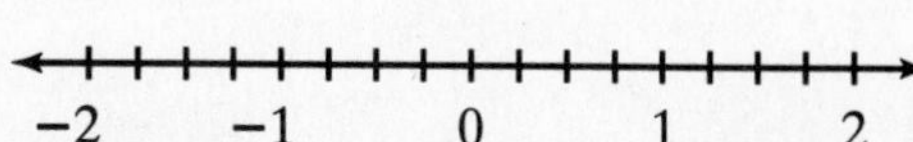

3. −0.5

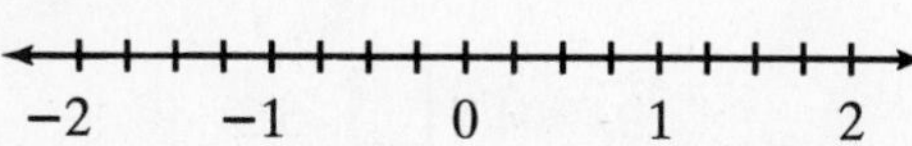

4. 1.2

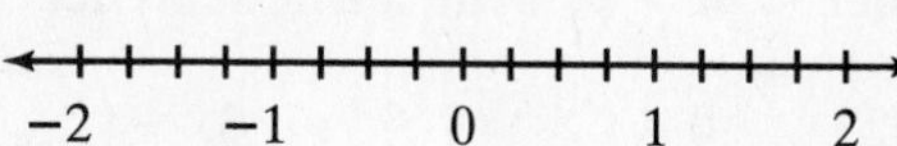

5. 0.75

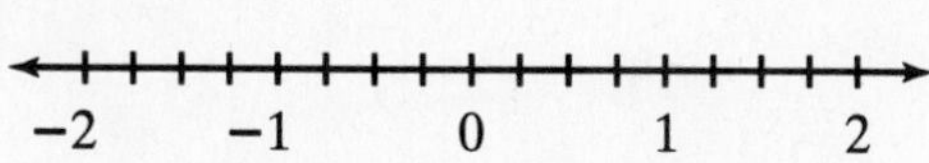

6. $-\frac{15}{8}$

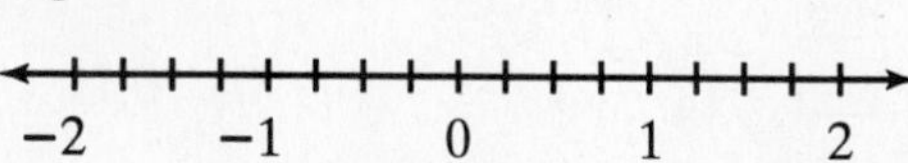

Write the following integers in order from least to greatest. *(Lesson 2-1)*

7. –12, –17, 15, –8, –3 ______________________

8. –35, 27, –28, –5, –16, –31 ______________________

Mixed Review

Write as an algebraic expression.

9. half of b *(1-6)* ______________

10. 7 more than twice h *(1-6)* ______________

11. the number m increased by the quantity 3 times n *(1-6)* ______________

Calculate.

12. $(4 + 3)^2$ *(1-4)* ______________

13. $5 \cdot 2^2$ *(1-4)* ______________

14. $30 - 4^2$ *(1-4)* ______________

Write with a single exponent.

15. $9 \cdot 9 \cdot 9 \cdot 9$ *(1-3)* ______________

16. $p \cdot p \cdot p \cdot p \cdot p \cdot p \cdot p$ *(1-3)* ______________

17. $15 \cdot n \cdot n \cdot n \cdot n \cdot n$ *(1-3)* ______________

Solve for the given replacement set.

18. $4m - 7 = 5$; {3, 4, 5} *(1-7)* ______________

19. $3h^2 - 1 = 11$; {1, 2, 4} *(1-7)* ______________

20. $d + 7 = 2d - 5$; {10, 11, 12} *(1-7)* ______________

21. $2j + 4 = 3j - 1$; {4, 5, 6} *(1-7)* ______________

Name ______________________ Class ______________ Date ____________

Daily Cumulative Review 2-4

Add without using a number line. *(Lesson 2-3)*

1. $16 + (-12)$ ________ **2.** $-3.1 + (-1.7)$ ________ **3.** $-5.8 + 5.8$ ________

4. $-\frac{4}{9} + \left(-\frac{2}{9}\right)$ ________ **5.** $-\frac{7}{10} + \frac{3}{5}$ ________ **6.** $-\frac{5}{7} + \left(-\frac{1}{3}\right)$ ________

Use either < or > to write a true sentence. *(Lesson 2-2)*

7. 0.923 ☐ 0.932 **8.** $-\frac{2}{3}$ ☐ $-\frac{5}{6}$ **9.** – 4.7 ☐ –5.3

10. −11.5 ☐ 1.15 **11.** $\frac{4}{7}$ ☐ $\frac{5}{8}$ **12.** 2.5 ☐ −0.25

13. $\frac{9}{13}$ ☐ $-\frac{1}{10}$ **14.** 0.11 ☐ 0.111 **15.** −125 ☐ −124

Mixed Review

Evaluate.

16. $3h$ for $h = 8$ *(1-1)* ________

17. $15 - x$ for $x = 6$ *(1-1)* ________

18. $\frac{b}{9}$ for $b = 63$ *(1-1)* ________

19. $p + q$ for $p = 5$ and $q = 11$ *(1-1)* ________

20. mn for $m = 2$ and $n = 12$ *(1-1)* ________

21. $\frac{x}{y}$ for $x = 48$ and $y = 8$ *(1-1)* ________

Simplify.

22. $\frac{15}{35}$ *(1-2)* ________ **23.** $\frac{7h}{13h}$ *(1-2)* ________ **24.** $\frac{12ab}{4a}$ *(1-2)* ________

25. $\frac{6xy}{8yz}$ *(1-2)* ________ **26.** $\frac{9pq}{3qr}$ *(1-2)* ________ **27.** $\frac{14m}{21n}$ *(1-2)* ________

Find each product. *(From Last Year)*

28. $7 \cdot 5 \cdot 9$ ________ **29.** $\frac{2}{3} \cdot \frac{6}{7} \cdot \frac{1}{2}$ ________

30. $\frac{1}{4} \cdot \frac{7}{9} \cdot \frac{3}{14}$ ________ **31.** 0.08(4)(6) ________

32. 0.03(5)(1.4) ________ **33.** 3.5(0.02)(1.3) ________

34. (0.82)(1.03)(0.05) ________ **35.** $\frac{5}{9} \cdot \frac{3}{10} \cdot \frac{8}{9}$ ________

36. $\frac{2}{3} \cdot \frac{5}{8} \cdot \frac{4}{15}$ ________ **37.** 0.5(0.6)(0.7) ________

Name ______________________ Class ______________ Date ____________

Daily Cumulative Review 2-5

Subtract. *(Lesson 2-4)*

1. $-5 - 6$ ________
2. $0.41 - 0.41$ ________
3. $248 - 312$ ________
4. $-12 - (-17)$ ________
5. $\frac{3}{7} - \left(-\frac{1}{7}\right)$ ________
6. $-8 - 7.2$ ________

Find the additive inverse of each. *(Lesson 2-3)*

7. 54 ________
8. –39 ________
9. $-\frac{5}{3}$ ________
10. 0.517 ________
11. 451 ________
12. −3.7 ________
13. 0 ________
14. −8 ________
15. $\frac{2}{9}$ ________

Mixed Review

Use the distributive property to write an equivalent expression.

16. $9(y + 6)$ *(1-5)* ________
17. $3(5m + 8)$ *(1-5)* ________
18. $(4p + 7q + 10)4$ *(1-5)* ________
19. $2(9 + j)$ *(1-5)* ________
20. $8(11z + 10)$ *(1-5)* ________
21. $7(6v + 5w + 5)$ *(1-5)* ________

Find each quotient. *(From Last Year)*

22. $7 \div \frac{1}{4}$ ________
23. $\frac{5}{6} \div \frac{5}{9}$ ________
24. $\frac{108}{12}$ ________
25. $\frac{12}{1.5}$ ________
26. $4.8 \div 0.6$ ________
27. $1\frac{3}{4} \div \frac{7}{8}$ ________
28. $\frac{16}{0.4}$ ________
29. $9.5 \div 0.05$ ________
30. $2\frac{1}{3} \div \frac{7}{9}$ ________

Evaluate each expression.

31. $|x| + 30$ for $x = -8$ *(2-1)* ________
32. $|a| + |b|$ for $a = 19$ and $b = -4$ *(2-1)* ________
33. $2a - |b|$ for $a = 7$ and $b = -5$ *(2-1)* ________
34. $3|y| + |y|$ for $y = 9$ *(2-1)* ________

Name ______________ Class ______________ Date ______________

Daily Cumulative Review 2-6

Multiply. *(Lesson 2-5)*

1. $-7 \cdot 9$ ________

2. $-8(-4)$ ________

3. $0.3(-1.2)$ ________

4. $-\frac{5}{7} \cdot \left(-\frac{7}{15}\right)$ ________

5. $-4.2(5)$ ________

6. $\frac{4}{5}\left(-\frac{15}{16}\right)\left(-\frac{2}{3}\right)$ ________

Simplify. *(Lesson 2-4)*

7. $14 - (-8) - 5 - (-2)$ ________

8. $-28 - 12 - (-3) - (-10)$ ________

9. $25 - 30 + (-8) - (-16)$ ________

10. $6 - (-2x) + 7x - (-13)$ ________

Mixed Review

Collect like terms.

11. $6x + 8x$ *(1-5)* ________

12. $9y^2 + y + 3y + 4y^2$ *(1-5)* ________

13. $\frac{1}{2}h + \frac{3}{4}h$ *(1-5)* ________

14. $9a + 5a + 12b$ *(1-5)* ________

15. $4b + 7 + 8b + 8$ *(1-5)* ________

16. $14m + 7m + 19n$ *(1-5)* ________

Factor.

17. $18x + 16$ *(1-5)* ________

18. $7a + 21b + 63$ *(1-5)* ________

19. $30p + 35q + 45$ *(1-5)* ________

Solve for the given replacement set.

20. $4y - 3 = 17; \{3, 5, 6\}$ *(1-7)* ________

21. $2x + 5 = 25; \{9, 10, 12\}$ *(1-7)* ________

22. $4 - n = 3n; \{1, 2, 3\}$ *(1-7)* ________

23. $2m^2 + 1 = 19; \{2, 3, 4\}$ *(1-7)* ________

24. $3b - 5 = 2b + 1; \{5, 6, 7\}$ *(1-7)* ________

25. $x^2 = 3x + 10; \{3, 4, 5\}$ *(1-7)* ________

The formula $P = 2(l + w)$ gives the perimeter of a rectangle with length l and width w. Find the perimeter of the rectangle for each set of dimensions given.

26. $l = 15$ m, $w = 9$ m *(1-9)*

$P =$ ________

27. $l = 28$ ft, $w = 16$ ft *(1-9)*

$P =$ ________

28. $l = 112$ mm, $w = 75$ mm *(1-9)*

$P =$ ________

Name ______________________ Class ______________ Date ____________

Daily Cumulative Review 2-7

Divide. Check your answer. *(Lesson 2-6)*

1. $-36 \div 3$ ________
2. $\frac{-56}{-8}$ ________
3. $\frac{0}{-25}$ ________
4. $\frac{-6.5}{-5}$ ________
5. $\frac{3}{5} \div \left(-\frac{3}{10}\right)$ ________
6. $-\frac{2}{7} \div -\frac{3}{7}$ ________

Simplify. *(Lesson 2-5)*

7. $-3[5 + (-4)]$ ________
8. $-12(-19 + 14)\left(-\frac{1}{3}\right)$ ________
9. $(-2)^4$ ________
10. $-(4^2) \cdot [-(2^4)]$ ________
11. $8[(-10) + 6]$ ________
12. $(-1)^{33}$ ________

Mixed Review

Evaluate each expression.

13. $5(a + 7)$ for $a = 2$ *(1-4)* ________
14. $(x + 3)^2$ for $x = 7$ *(1-4)* ________
15. $\frac{3y}{4 + y}$ for $y = 8$ *(1-4)* ________
16. $(9 - x)(x + 5)$ for $x = 4$ *(1-4)* ________
17. $4a^2 - 6$ for $a = 3$ *(1-4)* ________
18. $\frac{3x + 7}{x}$ for $x = 7$ *(1-4)* ________
19. $\frac{45}{a}$ for $a = 3$ *(1-1)* ________
20. $16 - x$ for $x = 3$ *(1-1)* ________
21. mn for $m = 4$ and $n = 9$ *(1-1)* ________

Find the additive inverse of each.

22. -48 *(2-3)* ________
23. -1.56 *(2-3)* ________
24. $\frac{3}{2}$ *(2-3)* ________

Write as an algebraic expression.

25. 5 times j *(1-6)* ________
26. 7 more than n *(1-6)* ________
27. half the product of b and h *(1-6)* ________
28. 2 less than the quantity 3 times h *(1-6)* ________
29. the sum of p and q *(1-6)* ________
30. the number a decreased by the quantity 4 times c *(1-6)* ________

Name ______________________ Class ______________ Date __________

Daily Cumulative Review 2-8

Multiply. *(Lesson 2-7)*

1. $5(y - 6)$ ______
2. $-4(x - 3y - 8)$ ______
3. $\frac{3}{4}(4a - 8b - 40)$ ______
4. $2\left(6x - \frac{1}{2}y - \frac{7}{2}\right)$ ______
5. $-\frac{3}{5}\left(\frac{5}{9}a - \frac{10}{27}\right)$ ______
6. $-1.5(3.4 - 8x - 7y)$ ______

Find the reciprocal. All variables represent nonzero rational numbers.
(Lesson 2-6)

7. -12 ______
8. $3\frac{1}{5}$ ______
9. -0.7 ______
10. $\frac{a}{b}$ ______
11. $\frac{l}{m}$ ______
12. $\frac{2x}{5y}$ ______
13. $\frac{3w}{-4u}$ ______
14. $\frac{1}{2b}$ ______
15. $\frac{-1}{9z}$ ______

Mixed Review

Solve by drawing a diagram.

16. (1-8) Half the cars on a train are flat cars. The train has half as many coal cars as flat cars and one-fifth as many passenger cars as coal cars. The remaining 28 cars include engines, a caboose, cattle cars, and others. How many cars does the train have? ______

Solve using the *Try, Test, Revise* strategy.

17. (1-10) $\frac{9 \cdot \square - 3}{6} = 7$
18. (1-10) $\frac{4 \cdot \square + 4}{6} = 6$
19. (1-10) $6 \cdot \square - 2 = 5 \cdot \square + 5$
20. (1-10) $3(10 + \square) = 36$

Use either < or > to write a true sentence.

21. (2-2) $2.35 \square 2.53$
22. (2-2) $-4.3 \square -3.4$
23. (2-2) $-9.8 \square -10$
24. (2-2) $\frac{1}{5} \square \frac{3}{10}$
25. (2-2) $-\frac{7}{8} \square -\frac{5}{8}$
26. (2-2) $-\frac{2}{3} \square -\frac{2}{5}$
27. (2-1) $14 \square 0$
28. (2-1) $-8 \square -9$
29. (2-1) $-7 \square 0$
30. (2-1) $4 \square -5$
31. (2-1) $-15 \square -12$
32. (2-1) $-6 \square -1$

Name ____________________ Class ______________ Date ____________

Daily Cumulative Review 2-9

Simplify. *(Lesson 2-8)*

1. $10m - (3m + 7)$ ____________

2. $5x + 4x - 2(3x - 1)$ ____________

3. $(4a - 5b) + (3a + 2b)$ ____________

4. $8m - 4n - 5n - (12m - 3n)$ ____________

Factor. *(Lesson 2-7)*

5. $9h - 63j$ ____________

6. $48 - 4m$ ____________

7. $\frac{1}{3}m - \frac{2}{3}n - \frac{5}{3}$ ____________

8. $ax - ay$ ____________

9. $7x - ax$ ____________

10. $bx - by + 3bz$ ____________

Mixed Review

Write an equivalent expression using a commutative property.

11. *(1-2)* $y + 9$ ____________

12. *(1-2)* pq ____________

13. *(1-2)* $7m + n$ ____________

Use the associative properties to write an equivalent expression.

14. *(1-4)* $(x + y) + 17$ ____________

15. *(1-4)* $(14m)n$ ____________

16. *(1-4)* $5x^2 + (x + 9)$ ____________

Subtract.

17. *(2-4)* $8 - 37$ ____________

18. *(2-4)* $11 - (-4)$ ____________

19. *(2-4)* $-10 - (-27)$ ____________

20. *(2-4)* $-\frac{4}{5} - \left(-\frac{2}{5}\right)$ ____________

21. *(2-4)* $3.09 - 5.12$ ____________

22. *(2-4)* $0 - (-7.4)$ ____________

Use the distributive property to write an equivalent expression.

23. *(1-5)* $6(x + 5)$ ____________

24. *(1-5)* $(1 + y)5$ ____________

25. *(1-5)* $2(a + b + 7)$ ____________

Name ______________________ Class ______________ Date __________

Daily Cumulative Review 2-10

Write an equation that can be used to solve the problem. *(Lesson 2-9)*

1. The Bears scored 23 points in a football game, which was 14 more points than the Panthers. How many points did the Panthers score? ______________

2. The Jean Shack is having a sale. Five T-shirts cost \$9. How much does one T-shirt cost? ______________

Rename each additive inverse without parentheses. *(Lesson 2-8)*

3. $-(3x + 19)$ ______________

4. $-(5a - 6b)$ ______________

5. $-(-2x - 7y + 8z)$ ______________

6. $-(4a - 5b + 11)$ ______________

7. $-(-7x - 8y)$ ______________

8. $-(13x + 2y + 15)$ ______________

Mixed Review

Solve mentally. The replacement set is all whole numbers.

9. $x + 12 = 22$ ______________ *(1-7)*

10. $y - 8 = 12$ ______________ *(1-7)*

11. $8y = 56$ ______________ *(1-7)*

12. $\frac{x}{4} = 7$ ______________ *(1-7)*

13. $x + 9 = 14$ ______________ *(1-7)*

14. $d - 15 = 3$ ______________ *(1-7)*

The formula $A = \frac{1}{2}bh$ gives the area of a triangle with base length b and height h. Find the area of the triangle for each set of dimensions given.

15. $b = 16$ ft, $h = 9$ ft *(1-9)*

$A =$ ______________

16. $b = 25$ cm, $h = 18$ cm *(1-9)*

$A =$ ______________

17. $b = 35$ in., $h = 27$ in. *(1-9)*

$A =$ ______________

Evaluate each expression.

18. $|h| + 19$ for $h = -8$ *(2-1)*

____

19. $|s| - 12$ for $s = 25$ *(2-1)*

____

20. $|x| + |y|$ for $x = -7$ and $y = -4$ *(2-1)*

____

21. $2|p| - 5$ for $p = -6$ *(2-1)*

____

22. $15 - |m|$ for $m = 7$ *(2-1)*

____

23. $4c - |d| + 5$ for $c = 5$ and $d = -8$ *(2-1)*

____

Name ______________________ Class ______________ Date ____________

Daily Cumulative Review 3-1

Which axiom or property guarantees the truth of each statement? *(Lesson 2-10)*

1. $-5h + 5h = 0$ ____________

2. $x(2x - 4) = 2x^2 - 4x$ ____________

3. $4(m - n) = (m - n)4$ ____________

4. $(5y + 9) + 2 = 5y + (9 + 2)$ ____________

Write an equation that can be used to solve the problem. *(Lesson 2-9)*

5. Maurice bought 4 CDs at the same sale price. The CDs cost a total of $33.20 before tax. What was the price of each CD? ____________

6. Sound travels at 1087 feet per second. How long does it take the sound of thunder to reach you when it is 16,000 ft away? ____________

7. A basketball player attempted 50 baskets and made 39 of them. How many baskets did she miss? ____________

Mixed Review

Multiply.

8. $-6 \cdot 7$ ____________ *(2-5)*

9. $(-2.5)(-8)$ ____________ *(2-5)*

10. $(0.3)(-0.6)$ ____________ *(2-5)*

11. $-\frac{1}{2}\left(-\frac{4}{7}\right)$ ____________ *(2-5)*

12. $\frac{3}{5}\left(-\frac{4}{9}\right)$ ____________ *(2-5)*

13. $(1.1)(-4)(-0.2)$ ____________ *(2-5)*

Find the reciprocal.

14. -25 ____________ *(2-6)*

15. $2\frac{3}{4}$ ____________ *(2-6)*

16. -0.9 ____________ *(2-6)*

Calculate.

17. $5 \cdot 3^2$ ____________ *(1-4)*

18. $(6 \cdot 2)^2$ ____________ *(1-4)*

19. $8 + 4^2$ ____________ *(1-4)*

20. $20 - 2^2$ ____________ *(1-4)*

21. $(2 + 5)^2$ ____________ *(1-4)*

22. $30 - 3^3$ ____________ *(1-4)*

Write with a single exponent.

23. $\frac{8^5}{8^3}$ ____________ *(1-3)*

24. $\frac{10^4}{10}$ ____________ *(1-3)*

25. $\frac{5^9}{5^5}$ ____________ *(1-3)*

Name ______________________ Class ______________ Date __________

Daily Cumulative Review 3-2

Solve. *(Lesson 3-1)*

1. $y + 8 = 3$ ________

2. $-4 + s = 7$ ________

3. $h - 6 = -15$ ________

4. $2.5 = m + 4.8$ ________

5. $x - 3.4 = -1$ ________

6. $j - \frac{1}{2} = -\frac{2}{3}$ ________

Which axiom or property guarantees the truth of each statement? *(Lesson 2-10)*

7. $\frac{1}{5}(5h) = h$

____

8. $1 \cdot (6n - 7) = 6n - 7$

____

9. $13(3x + 1) = 39x + 13$

____

10. $8(w + z) = (w + z)8$

____

Mixed Review

Collect like terms.

11. $6a + 5a$
(1-5)

____

12. $25x + 4x$
(1-5)

____

13. $5y + 7y + 9$
(1-5)

____

14. $2x^2 + 6x + 5x^2$
(1-5)

____

15. $7m + 4n + 3m + 2n$
(1-5)

____

16. $8 + 6a + 2b + 8a + 3$
(1-5)

____

Use the distributive property to write an equivalent expression.

17. $5(a + 6)$
(1-5)

____

18. $7(2y + 7)$
(1-5)

____

19. $(x + 9)4$
(1-5)

____

20. $-4(b - 6)$
(2-7)

____

21. $-3(-2x + y - 5)$
(2-7)

____

22. $\frac{1}{3}(9m - 5n + 18)$
(2-7)

____

23. $-5(-4x + 2y - 8)$
(2-7)

____

24. $-3(x - 9)$
(2-7)

____

25. $\frac{1}{2}(8a + 4b - 7)$
(2-7)

____

Write using exponential notation.

26. $4 \cdot 4 \cdot 4 \cdot 4 \cdot 4 \cdot 4$
(1-3)

____

27. $3 \cdot y \cdot y \cdot y \cdot y$
(1-3)

____

28. $8 \cdot n \cdot n \cdot n \cdot n \cdot n$
(1-3)

____

Name ________________ Class ________________ Date ________________

Daily Cumulative Review 3-3

Solve. *(Lesson 3-2)*

1. $7x = -42$ ________ **2.** $-5y = -45$ ________ **3.** $\frac{m}{-4} = 6$ ________

4. $-z = 38$ ________ **5.** $\frac{2}{3}h = 12$ ________ **6.** $-4.8n = 33.6$ ________

Solve. *(Lesson 3-1)*

7. $c + 7 = 1$ ________ **8.** $n - 3 = -14$ ________ **9.** $5.4 = y + 2.3$ ________

10. $-6 + t = -12$ ________ **11.** $x - \frac{5}{6} = \frac{3}{4}$ ________ **12.** $8.1 = z - 3.5$ ________

Mixed Review

Write as an algebraic expression.

13. 7 more than a *(1-6)* ________

14. 5 times h *(1-6)* ________

15. 4 less than n *(1-6)* ________

Factor.

16. $3x + 36$ *(1-5)* ________

17. $7y + 56$ *(1-5)* ________

18. $4x + 8y + 24$ *(1-5)* ________

19. $4x - 36$ *(2-7)* ________

20. $bx - 12b$ *(2-7)* ________

21. $\frac{2}{3}y - \frac{1}{3}z + \frac{4}{3}$ *(2-7)* ________

Find the additive inverse of each.

22. -57 *(2-3)* ________

23. 3.59 *(2-3)* ________

24. $-\frac{2}{7}$ *(2-3)* ________

The formula below gives a rule for determining the amount of medicine a child should take if you know the age of the child (*a*) and the dosage (*D*) of the medicine an adult would take. Find the child's dosage (*d*) for the given values of *a* and *D*. Round to the nearest tenth.

$$d = \frac{a}{a + 12} \cdot D$$

25. $a = 7$ yr, $D = 3.5$ mL *(1-9)* ________

26. $a = 3$ yr, $D = 6$ mL *(1-9)* ________

27. $a = 9$ yr, $D = 5$ mL *(1-9)* ________

Name ____________ Class ____________ Date ____________

Daily Cumulative Review 3-4

Solve. *(Lesson 3-3)*

1. $3x + 7 = 25$ ______

2. $5x - 9 = 11$ ______

3. $-2x + 15 = 3$ ______

4. $4x + x = 30$ ______

5. $-2.6y - 3.4y = 4.2$ ______

6. $3(4x - 5) = 33$ ______

Solve. *(Lesson 3-2)*

7. $9x = 36$ ______

8. $-\frac{a}{3} = 7$ ______

9. $\frac{4}{5}y = 24$ ______

10. $5.7z = 17.1$ ______

11. $-6.5b = 39$ ______

12. $-\frac{7}{8}s = -\frac{3}{16}$ ______

13. $\frac{1}{15} = -\frac{x}{8}$ ______

14. $\frac{-a}{12} = 3$ ______

15. $32.8x = 295.2$ ______

Mixed Review

Simplify.

16. $-4[(-3) + (-5)]$ *(2-5)* ______

17. $(-1)^{19}$ *(2-5)* ______

18. $-\frac{2}{3}[14 - (-4)]$ *(2-5)* ______

Use the associative properties to write an equivalent expression.

19. $3 + (x + y)$ *(1-4)* ______

20. $(m \cdot n) \cdot 8$ *(1-4)* ______

21. $7x + (x + z)$ *(1-4)* ______

Rename each additive inverse without parentheses.

22. $-(5m + 3)$ *(2-8)* ______

23. $-(4x - 9)$ *(2-8)* ______

24. $-(-3a - 7b + 11)$ *(2-8)* ______

Simplify.

25. $\frac{25}{75}$ *(1-2)* ______

26. $\frac{6a}{30ab}$ *(1-2)* ______

27. $\frac{14pq}{19pqr}$ *(1-2)* ______

28. $11 + 35 \div 5$ *(1-1)* ______

29. $4 \times 6 \div 2$ *(1-1)* ______

30. $8 + 6 \div 2 - 1$ *(1-1)* ______

31. $9 - 12 \div 2$ *(1-1)* ______

32. $8 \times 5 \div 4$ *(1-1)* ______

33. $2 + 5 \times 3 - 4$ *(1-1)* ______

Name ______ Class ______ Date ______

Daily Cumulative Review 3-5

Write as an algebraic expression. *(Lesson 3-4)*

1. 17 less than the quantity 5 times a number ______

2. 9 more than the quotient of a number and 3 ______

3. twice the difference of a number and 7 ______

4. 3 times the difference of a number and 5 ______

5. 8 greater than half a number ______

6. a third the sum of a number and 5 ______

Solve. *(Lesson 3-3)*

7. $9x - 5 = -59$ ______

8. $-2x + 9 = -17$ ______

9. $6y + y = -63$ ______

10. $-3z - 15 = -60$ ______

11. $4z - 24 = 24$ ______

12. $-8y + 62 = 46$ ______

Mixed Review

Multiply.

13. *(2-5)* $-3(-12)$ ______

14. *(2-5)* $0.5(-20)$ ______

15. *(2-5)* $\left(-\frac{2}{7}\right)\left(\frac{5}{6}\right)$ ______

16. *(2-5)* $(0.6)(-0.4)$ ______

17. *(2-5)* $-\frac{1}{8}\left(-\frac{2}{3}\right)\left(-\frac{3}{5}\right)$ ______

18. *(2-5)* $(2.1)(-3.5)(-1)$ ______

Divide.

19. *(2-6)* $48 \div (-6)$ ______

20. *(2-6)* $-85 \div (-5)$ ______

21. *(2-6)* $-\frac{2}{3} \div \left(-\frac{4}{9}\right)$ ______

22. *(2-6)* $\frac{-500}{-4}$ ______

23. *(2-6)* $\frac{0}{-8}$ ______

24. *(2-6)* $-\frac{5}{6} \div \frac{5}{9}$ ______

Simplify.

25. *(2-8)* $4x - (3x + 5)$ ______

26. *(2-8)* $5n - (11n - 12)$ ______

27. *(2-8)* $4a + 6a - (5a - 4)$ ______

28. *(2-8)* $3m - (10m + 17)$ ______

29. *(2-8)* $8y - (2y - 7)$ ______

30. *(2-8)* $9b + 2b - (7b - 6)$ ______

Write the following integers in order from least to greatest.

31. *(2-1)* $-14, 12, -16, -11, 5$ ______

32. *(2-1)* $-24, -35, -10, -21, -2$ ______

Name ______________________ Class ______________ Date __________

Daily Cumulative Review 3-6

Solve. *(Lesson 3-5)*

1. $9x - 11 = 8x$

2. $7x + 3 = 5x - 9$

3. $4x - 7 = 9x + 8$

4. $3y - (5y - 9) = 1$

5. $-2(4a - 5) + 3a = 18$

6. $6(t - 3) = 3(t - 2)$

Write as an algebraic expression. *(Lesson 3-4)*

7. 6 more than the product of 3 and a number

8. 5 less than half a number

9. 3 times the sum of a number and 8

Mixed Review

Evaluate.

10. *(1-1)* $14 + x$ for $x = 10$

11. *(1-1)* $20 - x$ for $x = 6$

12. *(1-1)* $5h$ for $h = 9$

13. *(1-1)* $p + q$ for $p = 6$ and $q = 15$

14. *(1-1)* $\frac{x}{y}$ for $x = 28$ and $y = 7$

15. *(1-1)* $2(a + 6)$ for $a = 2$

16. *(1-3)* m^4 for $m = -2$

17. *(1-3)* $(3x)^2$ for $x = 5$

18. *(1-3)* $y^2 - 20$ for $y = 7$

The formula $A = \frac{1}{2}h(b + c)$ gives the area of a trapezoid with base lengths b and c and height h. Find the area of the trapezoid for each set of dimensions given.

19. *(1-9)* $b = 9$ in., $c = 12$ in., $h = 8$ in.

$A =$ ______________

20. *(1-9)* $b = 12$ cm, $c = 15$ cm, $h = 9$ cm

$A =$ ______________

21. *(1-9)* $b = 30$ ft, $c = 32$ ft, $h = 25$ ft

$A =$ ______________

Subtract.

22. *(2-4)* $8 - (-8)$

23. *(2-4)* $7 - 12$

24. *(2-4)* $-3 - 11$

25. *(2-4)* $2.4 - (-3.6)$

26. *(2-4)* $-2 - (-12)$

27. *(2-4)* $\frac{2}{3} - \left(-\frac{5}{6}\right)$

Name ______________________ Class ______________ Date __________

Daily Cumulative Review 3-7

Solve. Clear the fractions first if necessary. *(Lesson 3-6)*

1. $\frac{2}{3} + \frac{1}{6}n = 2n - \frac{1}{2}$ ________

2. $\frac{5}{9} + \frac{1}{3}t = \frac{2}{9}$ ________

3. $\frac{1}{4}x - \frac{1}{8} + \frac{5}{8} = \frac{3}{4} + x$ ________

4. $0.4y - 0.3 + 0.1y = 1.2$ ________

5. $\frac{1}{3} - \frac{5}{6}h = \frac{1}{4} - \frac{1}{2}h$ ________

6. $0.5m - 0.1 = 0.15m + 0.6$ ________

Solve. *(Lesson 3-5)*

7. $15y - 7 = 14y$ ________

8. $2x - 11 = 5x + 4$ ________

9. $4(2t - 5) = 3(3t - 7)$ ________

10. $6z - 5 = 30 - z$ ________

11. $8 - 3(2x - 5) = 35$ ________

12. $9c - 10 = 2(c - 19)$ ________

Mixed Review

Evaluate each expression.

13. *(2-1)* $|a| + 5$ for $a = -4$ ________

14. *(2-1)* $|x| - 20$ for $x = -32$ ________

15. *(2-1)* $3|h|$ for $h = -9$ ________

16. *(2-1)* $|m| + |n|$ for $m = -7$ and $n = 8$ ________

17. *(2-1)* $2|x| - |y|$ for $x = 5$ and $y = -11$ ________

18. *(2-1)* $|t| - 17$ for $t = 21$ ________

Solve using the *Try, Test, Revise* strategy. *(Lesson 1-10)*

19. *(1-10)* $\frac{3 \cdot \square + 12}{6} = 4$ ________

20. *(1-10)* $\frac{\square \cdot 5 + 9}{2} = 12$ ________

21. *(1-10)* $8(17 - \square) = 48$ ________

22. *(1-10)* $7(4 + \square) = 63$ ________

Solve for the given replacement set.

23. *(1-7)* $8n + 3 = 7; \{\frac{1}{2}, 2, 1\}$ ________

24. *(1-7)* $x - 4 = 10; \{0, 6, 14\}$ ________

25. *(1-7)* $15 - n = 4n; \{2, 3, 4\}$ ________

26. *(1-7)* $2m^2 - 4 = 14; \{3, 2, 5\}$ ________

27. *(1-7)* $9y - 8 = 28; \{2, 4, 5\}$ ________

28. *(1-7)* $t + 6 = 2t - 8; \{9, 12, 14\}$ ________

Name ______________________ Class ______________ Date __________

Daily Cumulative Review 3-8

Solve. *(Lesson 3-7)*

1. $I = Prt$ for r ______________
2. $A = \frac{a + b + c + d}{4}$ for d ______________
3. $A = lw$ for w ______________
4. $\sigma = \frac{f}{A}$ for A ______________
5. $V = \frac{4}{3}\pi r^3$ for r^3 ______________
6. $m = \frac{y_2 - y_1}{x_2 - x_1}$ for y_2 ______________

Solve. Clear the fractions first if necessary. *(Lesson 3-6)*

7. $\frac{4}{5} + \frac{1}{2}y = \frac{1}{10}$ ______________
8. $\frac{1}{9}n - \frac{3}{2} = \frac{1}{3}n - \frac{5}{6}$ ______________
9. $0.6x - 2.4 = 0.5x$ ______________

Mixed Review

Solve.

10. $8z = 56$ ______________ *(3-2)*
11. $-4x = 44$ ______________ *(3-2)*
12. $\frac{3}{2}m = 15$ ______________ *(3-2)*
13. $\frac{n}{2} = -5$ ______________ *(3-2)*
14. $\frac{-P}{6} = 7$ ______________ *(3-2)*
15. $\frac{t}{12} = \frac{1}{4}$ ______________ *(3-2)*

Write an equation that can be used to solve the problem.

16. Shequille earned \$330 working 40 hours last week. How much did he earn per hour? *(2-9)*

____

Find the additive inverse of each.

17. -63 ______________ *(2-3)*
18. $\frac{4}{3}$ ______________ *(2-3)*
19. -2.8 ______________ *(2-3)*

Multiply.

20. $-5(x - 4)$ *(2-7)* ______________
21. $-6(2n - 3m - 8)$ *(2-7)* ______________
22. $-1.6(2.5y - 3)$ *(2-7)* ______________
23. $-7(y - 9)$ *(2-7)* ______________
24. $-\frac{1}{2}(4m - 8n - 16)$ *(2-7)* ______________
25. $-2.4(5x - 1.5)$ *(2-7)* ______________

Name ______________________ Class ______________ Date ____________

Daily Cumulative Review 3-9

Solve. *(Lesson 3-8)*

1. $|x| = 37$ ____________

2. $|y| + 4 = 15$ ____________

3. $4|n| = 36$ ____________

4. $-3|a| = -7$ ____________

5. $-5|b| + 7 = -3$ ____________

6. $8|h| - 6 = 18$ ____________

Solve. *(Lesson 3-7)*

7. $V = lwh$ for h ____________

8. $y = mx + b$ for x ____________

9. $s = 2\pi rh + 2\pi r^2$ for h ____________

Mixed Review

Simplify.

10. *(1-2)* $\frac{7m}{7}$ ____________

11. *(1-2)* $\frac{24}{36}$ ____________

12. *(1-2)* $\frac{12ab}{23a}$ ____________

13. *(1-2)* $\frac{35xyz}{5xy}$ ____________

14. *(1-2)* $\frac{n}{6mn}$ ____________

15. *(1-2)* $\frac{45cd}{15c}$ ____________

Solve.

16. *(3-2)* $11m = -77$ ____________

17. *(3-2)* $\frac{a}{-9} = 6$ ____________

18. *(3-2)* $-\frac{2}{5}b = 6$ ____________

19. *(3-2)* $0.6n = 0.75$ ____________

20. *(3-2)* $0.25p = 9$ ____________

21. *(3-2)* $0.09t = 2.88$ ____________

Show that each number can be written as the ratio of two integers.

22. *(2-2)* -5 ____________

23. *(2-2)* 3.6 ____________

24. *(2-2)* $-2\frac{1}{8}$ ____________

25. *(2-2)* -0.17 ____________

26. *(2-2)* $4\frac{1}{3}$ ____________

27. *(2-2)* -5.5 ____________

Name ______ Class ______ Date ______

Daily Cumulative Review 3-10

Solve. *(Lesson 3-9)*

1. A preschool has a policy of having 2 teachers for every 6 babies under 2 years old. How many teachers does the school need for 15 babies? ______

2. A car travels 161 km on 14 L of gasoline. How many liters are needed to travel 575 km? ______

Solve. *(Lesson 3-8)*

3. $|y| = 25$ ______

4. $|x| + 6 = 16$ ______

5. $-4|n| + 5 = -11$ ______

Mixed Review

Write as an algebraic expression.

6. *(3-4)* 15 less than the quantity 4 times a number ______

7. *(3-4)* 6 more than the quotient of a number and 5 ______

8. *(3-4)* half the sum of a number and 12 ______

Solve.

9. *(3-3)* $6x - 9 = 15$ ______

10. *(3-3)* $4x + 3x = -77$ ______

11. *(3-3)* $5(2y - 7) = 15$ ______

12. *(3-3)* $-3y - 5y = 40$ ______

13. *(3-3)* $2.7x + 8.1 = -2.7$ ______

14. *(3-3)* $1.5(4y - 8) = 6$ ______

Evaluate each expression.

15. *(1-3)* a^3 for $a = 5$ ______

16. *(1-3)* $3x^2$ for $x = 10$ ______

17. *(1-3)* $(2n)^2$ for $n = 3$ ______

18. *(1-4)* $4x^2 - 6$ for $x = 3$ ______

19. *(1-4)* $(2y)^2 - 7$ for $y = 4$ ______

20. *(1-4)* $(9 - m)^2$ for $m = 5$ ______

21. *(1-4)* $(x - 3)(x + 2)$ for $x = 5$ ______

22. *(1-4)* $\frac{b^2 + b}{4}$ for $b = 8$ ______

23. *(1-4)* $\frac{3y - 2}{y}$ for $y = 4$ ______

Name ________________ Class ________________ Date ________________

Daily Cumulative Review 3-11

Solve. *(Lesson 3-10)*

1. A basketball team won 9 out of 15 games played. What percent of the games played did the team win? ____________

2. A meal for 3 people cost $23.40. How much is a 15% tip? ____________

3. The sales tax rate in San Jose is $8\frac{1}{4}$%. What would be the sales tax on an automobile that cost $20,000? What is the total cost for the the automobile, including tax? ____________ ____________

4. A family spends $1200 per month for rent. This is 40% of its income. What is its monthly income? ____________

Solve these proportions. *(Lesson 3-9)*

5. $\frac{m}{6} = \frac{35}{42}$ ____________ **6.** $\frac{25}{y} = \frac{10}{6}$ ____________ **7.** $\frac{10}{4} = \frac{n}{14}$ ____________

8. $\frac{5}{8} = \frac{15}{b}$ ____________ **9.** $\frac{7}{9} = \frac{5}{k}$ ____________ **10.** $\frac{h}{40} = \frac{21}{12}$ ____________

Mixed Review

Solve by drawing a diagram.

11. *(1-8)* A farmer is fencing a 270 ft by 330 ft rectangular pasture. Posts are to be placed every 6 ft. How many posts are needed? ____________

Subtract.

12. $4 - 19$ *(2-4)* ____________

13. $2.7 - (-1.3)$ *(2-4)* ____________

14. $-9 - (-19)$ *(2-4)* ____________

15. $-\frac{3}{8} - \frac{1}{2}$ *(2-4)* ____________

16. $-17 - (-6)$ *(2-4)* ____________

17. $-5.4 - 2.3$ *(2-4)* ____________

Solve.

18. $y + 5 = 18$ *(3-1)* ____________ **19.** $b + 23 = 8$ *(3-1)* ____________ **20.** $j - 2.5 = 1.4$ *(3-1)* ____________

21. $s - 11 = -7$ *(3-1)* ____________ **22.** $n + 4 = -15$ *(3-1)* ____________ **23.** $-17 = m - 5$ *(3-1)* ____________

Write an equivalent expression using a commutative property.

24. $x + 9$ *(1-2)* ____________

25. pq *(1-2)* ____________

26. $7m + 9$ *(1-2)* ____________

Name ______ Class ______ Date ______

Daily Cumulative Review 3-12

Solve. *(Lesson 3-11)*

1. The sum of three consecutive odd integers is 111. What are the integers? ______

2. Ms. Garofalo deposited some money in a bank at 5% simple interest. At the end of the year, she had $1260 in the account. How much did she deposit originally? ______

3. The perimeter of a rectangle is 38 ft. The width is 7 ft less than the length. What are the length and width of this rectangle? ______ ______

Solve. *(Lesson 3-10)*

4. What percent of 8 is 5? ______

5. What is 30% of 24? ______

6. 12.5 is 25% of what number? ______

7. What percent of 48 is 16.8? ______

Mixed Review

Graph each rational number.

8. -2.5 *(2-2)* — number line: −4 −3 −2 −1 0 1 2 3 4

9. $-\frac{13}{4}$ *(2-2)* — number line: −4 −3 −2 −1 0 1 2 3 4

10. $1\frac{1}{8}$ *(2-2)* — number line: −4 −3 −2 −1 0 1 2 3 4

Use either < or > to write a true sentence.

11. $5.43 \square 5.34$ *(2-2)*

12. $-0.61 \square -0.59$ *(2-2)*

13. $4.7 \square 0.47$ *(2-2)*

14. $-\frac{5}{8} \square \frac{3}{11}$ *(2-2)*

15. $\frac{4}{5} \square \frac{3}{10}$ *(2-2)*

16. $-\frac{2}{3} \square -\frac{5}{6}$ *(2-2)*

17. $-15 \square 0$ *(2-1)*

18. $-6 \square -7$ *(2-1)*

19. $-8 \square -4$ *(2-1)*

20. $-9 \square 5$ *(2-1)*

21. $-3 \square -1$ *(2-1)*

22. $-25 \square -30$ *(2-1)*

Which axiom or property guarantees the truth of each statement?

23. If $y = 2x$ and $2x = 3z$, then $y = 3z$ *(2-10)* ______

24. $(4 + 3x) + 5 = 4 + (3x + 5)$ *(2-10)* ______

25. $5(x + y) = 5(y + x)$ *(2-10)* ______

26. $5(x + y) = 5x + 5y$ *(2-10)* ______

Name ________________ Class ________________ Date ________________

Daily Cumulative Review 4-1

Solve using one or more problem solving strategies. *(Lesson 3-12)*

1. Two long-distance buses leave a station on Monday. One bus returns every 4 days and the other returns every 5 days. How many days will it be before both buses return to the station at the same time? What day of the week will it be? ________ ________

2. There are 25 tennis players in a single-elimination tournament. (Each player is eliminated after one loss.) How many tennis matches are played in the tournament? ________

Solve. *(Lesson 3-11)*

3. A store wants to sell soccer balls for $14.99 after a 40% mark up. How much can the store afford to pay for each ball? ________

4. A taxi costs $3.00 per ride plus $.75 per mile. How much does it cost to take a taxi for a 17-mile trip? ________

Mixed Review

Add.

5. $8 + (-24)$ ________ *(2-3)*

6. $-32 + (-26)$ ________ *(2-3)*

7. $-\frac{7}{8} + \frac{3}{8}$ ________ *(2-3)*

8. $-\frac{3}{4} + \frac{2}{3}$ ________ *(2-3)*

9. $-0.6 + 0.04$ ________ *(2-3)*

10. $-2.5 + (-0.47)$ ________ *(2-3)*

Subtract.

11. $-5 - 17$ ________ *(2-4)*

12. $3 - (-18)$ ________ *(2-4)*

13. $-\frac{5}{9} - \frac{1}{3}$ ________ *(2-4)*

14. $\frac{3}{8} - \frac{5}{4}$ ________ *(2-4)*

15. $-2.9 - 5.2$ ________ *(2-4)*

16. $-0.46 - (-3.1)$ ________ *(2-4)*

Solve.

17. $b + 9 = -6$ *(3-1)* ________

18. $m - 21 = -4$ *(3-1)* ________

19. $x + 4.7 = 1.5$ *(3-1)* ________

20. $a - 3 = -1.2$ *(3-1)* ________

21. $n + \frac{2}{3} = \frac{1}{6}$ *(3-1)* ________

22. $y - \frac{4}{5} = \frac{1}{2}$ *(3-1)* ________

Collect like terms.

23. $7x + 9x$ *(1-5)* ________

24. $\frac{3}{4}b + \frac{1}{8}b + \frac{2}{3}$ *(1-5)* ________

25. $6m^2 + 5m + 2m^2$ *(1-5)* ________

Name ______________ Class ______________ Date ______________

Daily Cumulative Review 4-2

Write the inequality shown by each graph. *(Lesson 4-1)*

1. −5 −4 −3 −2 −1 0 1 2 3 4 5 ______________

2.  −5 −4 −3 −2 −1 0 1 2 3 4 5 ______________

3. −5 −4 −3 −2 −1 0 1 2 3 4 5 ______________

Solve using one or more problem solving strategy. *(Lesson 3-12)*

4. Carson has 140 m of fencing to enclose a field. He wants to use sides that are only whole meter lengths. What dimensions should he use to enclose the greatest possible area? ______________

5. The sum of three consecutive integers is 378. What are the integers? ______________

Mixed Review

Multiply.

6. $-7 \cdot 7$ ________ *(2-5)*

7. $-6(-12)$ ________ *(2-5)*

8. $(-0.5)(-3)$ ________ *(2-5)*

9. $(3.5)(-4.6)$ ________ *(2-5)*

10. $-5(14)$ ________ *(2-5)*

11. $-9(1.6)(-4)$ ________ *(2-5)*

12. $-\frac{5}{7} \cdot \frac{7}{15}$ ________ *(2-5)*

13. $-\frac{6}{11} \cdot \left(-\frac{11}{12}\right)$ ________ *(2-5)*

14. $\frac{2}{3}\left(-\frac{3}{5}\right)\left(-\frac{5}{8}\right)$ ________ *(2-5)*

Divide.

15. $-39 \div (-13)$ ________ *(2-6)*

16. $-\frac{300}{4}$ ________ *(2-6)*

17. $-5 \div 0$ ________ *(2-6)*

18. $5.7 \div (-0.3)$ ________ *(2-6)*

19. $-\frac{7}{8} \div \left(-\frac{3}{4}\right)$ ________ *(2-6)*

20. $-\frac{5}{9} \div \frac{7}{6}$ ________ *(2-6)*

Solve.

21. $\frac{n}{-4} = -15$ *(3-2)* ________

22. $-3h = 36$ *(3-2)* ________

23. $-\frac{4}{5}r = -\frac{8}{15}$ *(3-2)* ________

24. What is 35% of 18? *(3-10)* ________

25. What percent of 76 is 15.2? *(3-10)* ________

26. 138 is 75% of what number? *(3-10)* ________

Name ______________________ Class ______________ Date __________

Daily Cumulative Review 4-3

Solve. *(Lesson 4-2)*

1. $5x - 4x + 8 > 4$ ______
2. $-8y + 9y + 7 \leq 12$ ______
3. $12n - 4 - 11n \geq 3$ ______
4. $4(r + 5) - 3r > 12$ ______
5. $7(z - 4) - 6z < -20$ ______
6. $-3(a - 4) + 4a \leq 2$ ______

Determine whether each number is a solution of the inequality $x < -1$. *(Lesson 4-1)*

7. 0 ______
8. -5 ______
9. -1 ______
10. 3 ______

Mixed Review

Multiply.

11. $9(x - 11)$ *(2-7)* ______
12. $-4(y - 8)$ *(2-7)* ______
13. $3(2x + 5y - 8)$ *(2-7)* ______
14. $\frac{3}{4}\left(8m - 6n + \frac{1}{9}\right)$ *(2-7)* ______
15. $-1.5(3c - 4d)$ *(2-7)* ______
16. $\frac{1}{2}\left(4a - 8b + \frac{4}{5}\right)$ *(2-7)* ______

Solve.

17. $7x = -35$ *(3-2)* ______
18. $\frac{n}{-8} = -10$ *(3-2)* ______
19. $-4h = 52$ *(3-2)* ______
20. $-\frac{2}{3}m = -14$ *(3-2)* ______
21. $2.4h = -9.6$ *(3-2)* ______
22. $-\frac{6}{7}y = -\frac{2}{21}$ *(3-2)* ______
23. $6x - 7 = 5x$ *(3-5)* ______
24. $9x - 10 = 5x - 22$ *(3-5)* ______
25. $6x + 8 + 5x = 8x - 10$ *(3-5)* ______
26. $12x + 16 = 11x$ *(3-5)* ______
27. $15y - 11 = 10y + 24$ *(3-5)* ______
28. $9y + 4 + 6y = 11y - 36$ *(3-5)* ______

Solve. Clear the fractions first, if necessary.

29. $\frac{1}{2}y + \frac{3}{4} = \frac{1}{4}y - \frac{1}{4}$ *(3-6)* ______
30. $\frac{3}{5}t - \frac{1}{2} = \frac{7}{10}$ *(3-6)* ______
31. $\frac{5}{6}x + \frac{2}{3}x - \frac{1}{4} = \frac{3}{4}x + \frac{1}{6}$ *(3-6)* ______

Name ______________________ Class ______________ Date __________

Daily Cumulative Review 4-4

Solve. *(Lesson 4-3)*

1. $9x < -54$ ______________

2. $3x \geq -10$ ______________

3. $-4y < 44$ ______________

4. $-2y > -7$ ______________

5. $8x \leq -4.8$ ______________

6. $-5y \leq 6.25$ ______________

Solve and graph the solution. *(Lesson 4-2)*

7. $y + 4 > 1$ ______________

−5 −4 −3 −2 −1 0 1 2 3 4 5

8. $x + 9 \leq 10$ ______________

−5 −4 −3 −2 −1 0 1 2 3 4 5

9. $3x - 6 - 2x < -8$ ______________

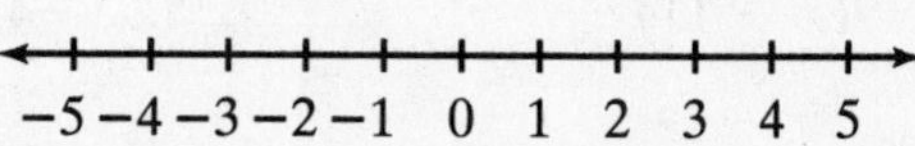

Mixed Review

Write as an algebraic expression.

10. *(1-6)* the sum of 9 and n ______________

11. *(1-6)* 5 times x ______________

12. *(1-6)* 18 less than m ______________

13. *(3-4)* 8 more than the product of 19 and a number ______________

14. *(3-4)* half the difference of a number and 17 ______________

15. *(3-4)* 11 more than the quotient of a number and 4 ______________

Use the associative properties to write an equivalent expression.

16. *(1-4)* $8x + (x + y)$ ______________

17. *(1-4)* $9 \cdot (7x)$ ______________

18. *(1-4)* $4 \cdot [3(x + y)]$ ______________

Write a true sentence using < or >.

19. *(2-1)* 18 ☐ 0

20. *(2-1)* −14 ☐ −8

21. *(2-1)* −26 ☐ −29

22. *(2-2)* 8.14 ☐ 8.014

23. *(2-2)* −5.04 ☐ −5.4

24. *(2-2)* $-\frac{2}{3}$ ☐ $-\frac{5}{12}$

25. *(2-2)* 0.35 ☐ 0.305

26. *(2-2)* −2.61 ☐ −2.16

27. *(2-2)* $-\frac{3}{4}$ ☐ $-\frac{7}{8}$

Name ______________________ Class ______________ Date __________

Daily Cumulative Review 4-5

Solve. *(Lesson 4-4)*

1. $5 + 3x > 32$ ______

2. $6y - 9 < -27$ ______

3. $7 - 2x \leq 11$ ______

4. $15 - 8y + 5y \geq 12$ ______

5. $9 - 10y + 9y > 2$ ______

6. $4 - 15x < 5 - 9x$ ______

Solve and graph the solution. *(Lesson 4-3)*

7. $12x < -24$ ______ −5 −4 −3 −2 −1 0 1 2 3 4 5

8. $-7x < 21$ ______ −5 −4 −3 −2 −1 0 1 2 3 4 5

9. $-11x \geq -33$ ______ −5 −4 −3 −2 −1 0 1 2 3 4 5

Mixed Review

Factor.

10. $8 + 40a$ *(1-5)* ______

11. $14x + 7y$ *(1-5)* ______

12. $6m + 9n + 15$ *(1-5)* ______

13. $5y - 35$ *(2-7)* ______

14. $-6m - 48$ *(2-7)* ______

15. $ax - 17a$ *(2-7)* ______

16. $\frac{3}{5}n - \frac{2}{5}m + \frac{4}{5}$ *(2-7)* ______

17. $dx - dy + 3d$ *(2-7)* ______

18. $-15h - 18j$ *(2-7)* ______

Solve using one or more problem solving strategies.

19. *(3-12)* A vending machine needs to be programmed to accept any combination of coins totalling 75¢, excluding pennies and half-dollars. How many combinations are possible? ______

Solve.

20. $4x - 9 = 7$ *(3-3)* ______

21. $-8x + 17 = -47$ *(3-3)* ______

22. $2(3y + 8) = -14$ *(3-3)* ______

23. $|y| = 45$ *(3-8)* ______

24. $-4|m| = -48$ *(3-8)* ______

25. $3|x| - 7 = 7$ *(3-8)* ______

Name ______________________ Class ______________ Date __________

Daily Cumulative Review 4-6

Translate to an inequality. *(Lesson 4-5)*

1. 15 is less than a number n.

____

2. Half a number x is at least 16.

____

3. 8 more than twice a number m is greater than the opposite of the number.

____

Solve. *(Lesson 4-4)*

4. $8 + 5x < -22$ ______________

5. $10 - 7x < 45$ ______________

6. $6 - 8y \geq 11 - 7y$ ______________

Mixed Review

Write using exponential notation.

7. *(1-3)* $8 \cdot 8 \cdot 8$ ______________

8. *(1-3)* $y \cdot y \cdot y \cdot y \cdot y \cdot y \cdot y$ ______________

9. *(1-3)* $6 \cdot m \cdot m \cdot m \cdot m$ ______________

Simplify.

10. *(2-5)* $-8[(-7) + 9]$ ______________

11. *(2-5)* $(-1)^{31}$ ______________

12. *(2-5)* $11[(-4) - 8]$ ______________

Calculate.

13. *(1-4)* $6 \cdot 2^2$ ______________

14. *(1-4)* $(6 \cdot 2)^2$ ______________

15. *(1-4)* $18 - 4^2$ ______________

16. *(1-4)* $(18 - 4)^2$ ______________

17. *(1-4)* $3 + 5^2$ ______________

18. *(1-4)* $(3 + 5)^2$ ______________

The formula $A = s^2$ gives the area of a square with side lengths s. Find the area of the square for each side length given.

19. *(1-9)* $s = 7$ in.

$A =$ ______________

20. *(1-9)* $s = 15$ m

$A =$ ______________

21. *(1-9)* $s = 2.5$ cm

$A =$ ______________

Name ______________________ Class ______________ Date ________

Daily Cumulative Review 5-1

Solve using one or more strategies. *(Lesson 4-6)*

1. You can win a new car in a game show if you can put 4 balls in 4 cups in the right order. The cups are lettered A, B, C, and D and the balls are lettered the same. One ball goes in each cup but no ball goes in a cup with the same letter. You try ball C in cup A, D in B, A in C, and B in D and find none of these are correct. The show's host gives you a hint that ball D does not go in cup A and ball A does not go in cup B. Which balls go in which cups?

____

2. Area codes in the United States used to have 3 digits with the middle digit being 0 or 1. In addition, the first digit could not be 0, and an area code could not end with 00 or 11. Now, area codes can have any digit in the middle position. (The first digit still cannot be 0, and an area code still cannot end with 00 or 11.) How many different area codes were there under the old rules? How many are there now?

____

Solve. *(Lesson 4-5)*

3. The perimeter of a rectangle is less than or equal to 42 m. The length of the rectangle is twice the width. What is the greatest the width can be? ________

4. Maria and her husband James must save $15,000 to put a down payment on a house. Maria earns 10% more than James, so she will contribute 10% more than James will to their savings. How much must each save? ________ ________

Mixed Review

Evaluate each expression.

5. h^4 for $h = -2$ *(2-5)* ________

6. $3n^2$ for $n = -3$ *(2-5)* ________

7. $(3n)^2$ for $n = -3$ *(2-5)* ________

8. $(4y)^2$ for $y = 5$ *(1-3)* ________

9. $4y^2$ for $y = 5$ *(1-3)* ________

10. $x^3 + 6$ for $x = 2$ *(1-3)* ________

Solve.

11. $x + 21 = -8$ *(3-1)* ________

12. $y - 2.6 = 5.4$ *(3-1)* ________

13. $a + \frac{2}{7} = \frac{3}{14}$ *(3-1)* ________

14. $\frac{y}{-4} = 11$ *(3-2)* ________

15. $435 = -x$ *(3-2)* ________

16. $-10m = -35$ *(3-2)* ________

Name ____________________ Class ____________ Date ____________

Daily Cumulative Review 5-2

Simplify. Express using exponents. *(Lesson 5-1)*

1. $m^9 \cdot m^4$ ________ **2.** $(a^3b^2)(a^7b^9)$ ________ **3.** $(x^2y^3z)(x^4y^5z^3)$ ________

4. $\frac{h^6}{h^3}$ ________ **5.** $\frac{x^5y^6}{x^2y^2}$ ________ **6.** $\frac{m^7 \cdot n^{-2}}{m^6n^3}$ ________

Solve using one or more strategies. *(Lesson 4-6)*

7. Kara, Leonardo, Marcus, and Nina are running for Student Council president, vice president, secretary, and treasurer on one ticket. Nina does not want to be vice president. Kara does not want to be vice president or president. Marcus likes money, so he wants to be the treasurer. Who should run for which office so everyone is happy?

____

8. Two competitors in a cross-country bike race were tied for the lead going into the last 4 stages of the race. Mark finished the last four stages in 6 h 23 min, 7 h 5 min, 5 h 57 min, and 6 h 2 min, respectively. Luc finished the last four stages in 6 h 24 min, 6 h 59 min, 6 h, and 6 h 3 min, respectively. No one finished ahead of Mark or Luc in the last four stages. Who won the race, and by how much time?

____

Mixed Review

Multiply.

9. $-9 \cdot 8$ ________ *(2-5)* **10.** $(-12)(-6)$ ________ *(2-5)* **11.** $-7(-0.5)$ ________ *(2-5)*

12. $3.2(-4.1)$ ________ *(2-5)* **13.** $-\frac{2}{9} \cdot \frac{5}{8}$ ________ *(2-5)* **14.** $-\frac{9}{4} \cdot \left(-\frac{2}{3}\right)$ ________ *(2-5)*

Divide.

15. $-\frac{42}{21}$ ________ *(2-6)* **16.** $\frac{0}{-46}$ ________ *(2-6)* **17.** $\frac{-305}{-5}$ ________ *(2-6)*

18. $-5.7 \div (-3)$ ________ *(2-6)* **19.** $-\frac{6}{11} \div \left(-\frac{8}{11}\right)$ ________ *(2-6)* **20.** $\frac{5}{6} \div \left(-\frac{7}{4}\right)$ ________ *(2-6)*

Solve.

21. $\frac{n}{6} = \frac{24}{36}$ *(3-9)* ________ **22.** $\frac{7}{5} = \frac{a}{10}$ *(3-9)* ________ **23.** $\frac{9}{x} = \frac{6}{8}$ *(3-9)* ________

24. $|x| = 206$ *(3-8)* ________ **25.** $7 + |n| = 25$ *(3-8)* ________ **26.** $\frac{|y|}{-3} = -15$ *(3-8)* ________

Name ____________ Class ____________ Date ____________

Daily Cumulative Review 5-3

Simplify. *(Lesson 5-2)*

1. $(3^4)^2$ ________ **2.** $(y^7)^3$ ________ **3.** $(6x^5)^2$ ________

4. $\left(\frac{n^3}{2}\right)^5$ ________ **5.** $\left(\frac{a^6}{b^2}\right)^3$ ________ **6.** $\left(\frac{3x^9y^5}{z^4}\right)^2$ ________

Simplify. Express without using exponents. *(Lesson 5-1)*

7. 9^{-2} ________ **8.** $(-7)^0$ ________ **9.** 2^{-5} ________

10. 1^{-6} ________ **11.** y^0 ________ **12.** 3^{-4} ________

Mixed Review

Solve.

13. $8y < -96$ *(4-3)* ________

14. $-4n < 56$ *(4-3)* ________

15. $-5x > -\frac{1}{4}$ *(4-3)* ________

16. $7m - 6m > 25$ *(4-3)* ________

17. $3h - 4h \geq 23$ *(4-3)* ________

18. $6y \leq -72$ *(4-3)* ________

19. $5 + 3x < 20$ *(4-4)* ________

20. $8 - y \leq 7$ *(4-4)* ________

21. $12n - 7 - 11n \leq 3$ *(4-4)* ________

22. $4y - 7 > 3y - 12$ *(4-4)* ________

23. $3x - 9 > 7x + 3$ *(4-4)* ________

24. $4(2y - 6) < 9(y - 1)$ *(4-4)* ________

Determine whether each number is a solution of the inequality $x < -3$.

25. 0 *(4-1)* ________ **26.** −3 *(4-1)* ________ **27.** −1 *(4-1)* ________ **28.** −7 *(4-1)* ________

Write a true sentence using < or >.

29. $-28 \square -30$ *(2-1)*

30. $-42 \square -45$ *(2-1)*

31. $|-12| \square |-15|$ *(2-1)*

32. $-9 \square -11$ *(2-1)*

33. $-6 \square 0$ *(2-1)*

34. $|-5| \square -5$ *(2-1)*

35. $3.05 \square 3.5$ *(2-2)*

36. $-2.9 \square -2.09$ *(2-2)*

37. $-\frac{4}{5} \square -\frac{3}{10}$ *(2-2)*

Name ____________ Class ____________ Date ____________

Daily Cumulative Review 5-4

Multiply or divide. *(Lesson 5-3)*

1. $(8x^5)7$ ________ **2.** $(-x^4)(x^5)$ ________ **3.** $(-9y^3)(-2y^6)$ ________

4. $\frac{a^{12}}{a^4}$ ________ **5.** $\frac{6n^7}{9n^8}$ ________ **6.** $\frac{10a^{11}b^4}{25a^3b^6}$ ________

Simplify. *(Lesson 5-2)*

7. $(5m^6)^3$ ________ **8.** $\left(\frac{2x^3}{y^7}\right)^4$ ________ **9.** $\left(\frac{a^2b^4}{5c^9}\right)^2$ ________

Mixed Review

What are the terms of each expression?

10. $5x + 3y$ *(2-7)* ________

11. $8a - 4b + 7$ *(2-7)* ________

12. $5m - \frac{2}{3}n - 8p + q$ *(2-7)* ________

Collect like terms.

13. $6a + 15a$ *(1-5)* ________

14. $9x^2 + 5x + 2x^2$ *(1-5)* ________

15. $4 + 6m + 3n + 5n + 4m$ *(1-5)* ________

16. $y - 8y$ *(2-7)* ________

17. $4x - 15x$ *(2-7)* ________

18. $6y - 3x - y$ *(2-7)* ________

19. $2.7m - 4.8n + 1.6n$ *(2-7)* ________

20. $\frac{1}{9}a + \frac{2}{3}b - \frac{4}{9}a$ *(2-7)* ________

21. $1.7x - 3.5y - 2.1y - 0.6x$ *(2-7)* ________

Solve.

22. $7x - 9 = 40$ *(3-3)* ________

23. $-5x + 3 = 18$ *(3-3)* ________

24. $6x - 8x = 48$ *(3-3)* ________

25. $12y - 6 = 11y$ *(3-5)* ________

26. $3y - 5 = y + 9$ *(3-5)* ________

27. $8x + 7 = 5x - 14$ *(3-5)* ________

28. $10x + 4 = 8x$ *(3-5)* ________

29. $x - 6 = 5x + 18$ *(3-5)* ________

30. $2x + 11 = 12x - 39$ *(3-5)* ________

Name ______________________ Class ______________ Date ________

Daily Cumulative Review 5-5

Write using scientific notation. *(Lesson 5-4)*

1. 46,000 ________

2. 0.000807 ________

3. 0.000000049 ________

Simplify. *(Lesson 5-3)*

4. $(a^3b^8)(a^2b^2)$ ________

5. $\frac{-6x^3y^7}{12x^8y^2}$ ________

6. $(-3m^6n)(-7mn^4)$ ________

Mixed Review

Evaluate each expression.

7. *(1-1)* $m - 7$ for $m = 18$ ________

8. *(1-1)* $5x$ for $x = 11$ ________

9. *(1-1)* $\frac{18}{a}$ for $a = 2$ ________

10. *(1-4)* $3x^2 - 6$ for $x = 4$ ________

11. *(1-4)* $(9 - w)^3$ for $w = 7$ ________

12. *(1-4)* $(y - 4)(y + 5)$ for $y = 6$ ________

13. *(1-4)* $2a^3 - 5$ for $a = 3$ ________

14. *(1-4)* $(x + 3)^2$ for $x = 8$ ________

15. *(1-4)* $(m + 3)(m - 7)$ for $m = 9$ ________

The formula below gives the approximate stopping distance (d) in feet for an automobile driving at x miles per hour. Find the stopping distance for each speed given.

$$d = x + \frac{x^2}{20}$$

16. *(1-9)* 55 mi/h ________

17. *(1-9)* 42 mi/h ________

18. *(1-9)* 25 mi/h ________

Solve.

19. *(3-10)* What is 45% of 125? ________

20. *(3-10)* What percent of 58 is 29? ________

21. *(3-10)* 17.36 is 7% of what number? ________

22. *(3-10)* What percent of 320 is 208? ________

23. *(3-10)* 79.8 is 95% of what number? ________

24. *(3-10)* What is 83% of 60? ________

Name ______________________ Class ______________ Date ___________

Daily Cumulative Review 5-6

Identify the degree of each term and the degree of the polynomial. *(Lesson 5-5)*

1. $3x - 9$ ______________

2. $x^3 - 2x^2 + 7$ ______________

3. $-6x^2y + 2xy + 5x$ ______________

4. $7x^3y^2 - 4x^2y^2 + 2x^2y + 5y$ ______________

Multiply or divide. Express your answer in scientific notation. *(Lesson 5-4)*

5. $(3.2 \times 10^5)(2.1 \times 10^{-3})$ ______________

6. $\frac{(8.0 \times 10^5)}{(2.0 \times 10^3)}$ ______________

7. $\frac{(4.8 \times 10^{12})}{(3.0 \times 10^4)}$ ______________

Mixed Review

Add.

8. $-15 + 28$ ________ *(2-3)*

9. $-64 + (-36)$ ________ *(2-3)*

10. $\frac{2}{9} + \left(-\frac{7}{9}\right)$ ________ *(2-3)*

11. $-8 + 3.1$ ________ *(2-3)*

12. $-\frac{3}{8} + \frac{1}{2}$ ________ *(2-3)*

13. $-26.9 + 26.9$ ________ *(2-3)*

Subtract.

14. $11 - 18$ ________ *(2-4)*

15. $-4 - 23$ ________ *(2-4)*

16. $-8 - (-2)$ ________ *(2-4)*

17. $-12 - 3.7$ ________ *(2-4)*

18. $2 - 3.85$ ________ *(2-4)*

19. $-\frac{3}{4} - \left(-\frac{1}{8}\right)$ ________ *(2-4)*

Simplify.

20. $5y - (3y - 6)$ ______________ *(2-8)*

21. $6a + 7a - (5a + 4)$ ______________ *(2-8)*

22. $[3(x + 7)] + [4(x - 9)]$ ______________ *(2-8)*

23. $[7(x - 3) - 8] - [5(x - 2) + 4]$ ______________ *(2-8)*

Solve. Clear the fractions first, if necessary.

24. $\frac{1}{4}x - \frac{1}{2} = \frac{1}{2}x + \frac{3}{4}$ *(3-6)* ______________

25. $\frac{1}{6} - \frac{1}{9}y = \frac{1}{3}y - \frac{2}{3}$ *(3-6)* ______________

26. $0.32x - 0.8 = 0.7x + 0.34$ *(3-6)* ______________

Name ______________________ Class ______________ Date __________

Daily Cumulative Review 5-7

Collect like terms and then arrange in descending order. *(Lesson 5-6)*

1. $3x^5 - 4x + 3x^2 + 5x$

2. $5m^3 + 3 - 2m^3 + 5m + 6$

3. $y^3 - 5 + 3y + 2y^3 - y^2$

4. $2x^3 + 3xy - 4xy + 8x^3 + y^2$

5. $9n + n^2 - 3n + 5 + n^2$

6. $b^5 - \frac{3}{4} + 2b^3 - b^5 - \frac{1}{2}$

Identify the terms. Give the coefficient of each term. *(Lesson 5-5)*

7. $3x^2 + 8x - 3$

8. $x^5y^3 - 3xy^2 + 8x^2y - 3$

9. $n^5 - 3n^2$

10. $-8b^5 + 3b - 9$

11. $x^5 - x^4 - x^3 - x^2 + 1$

12. $-5m^5 + m - 5$

Mixed Review

Translate to an inequality.

13. A number y is greater than -6.
(4-5)

14. Three times a number is less than 10.
(4-5)

Express using positive exponents.

15. $3x^{-3}$
(5-1)

16. $(3x)^{-3}$
(5-1)

17. ab^{-2}
(5-1)

18. $3n^{-1}$
(5-1)

Solve and graph the solutions.

19. $2x + 5 + 3x > 20$
(4-2)

20. $n - 5 < 6$
(4-2)

21. $y + \frac{1}{2} > \frac{3}{4}$
(4-2)

Name ______________________ Class ______________ Date ____________

Daily Cumulative Review 5-8

Add. *(Lesson 5-7)*

1. $2x - 5$ and $x + 3$ ____________

2. $(x^4 + x - 2) + (2x^4 + x^3 - 5)$ ____________

3. $(-x^5 + 2x^4 - x^2 + x) + (3x^5 - x^3 + x^2 + 5)$ ____________

4. $(5x^3 + 3x^2 + 4) + (x^3 - 2x^2 + 3x + 9)$ ____________

5. $(7x^5 - 3x^3 + x) + (3x^4 - 5x^2 + 6)$ ____________

6. $(7x^2 + 3x + 5) + (-4x + 6)$ ____________

Evaluate each polynomial for $x = 3$. *(Lesson 5-6)*

7. $x^4 - 5x^2 + 4$ ____________

8. $-4x^2 + 5x + 8$ ____________

9. $x^3 + 8x - 3$ ____________

10. $x^2 - 6x + 9$ ____________

11. $-2x^3 - x^2 + 11$ ____________

12. $x^4 - 3x + 8$ ____________

Mixed Review

Factor.

13. $5x + 10$ *(1-5)* ____________

14. $3a - 9b + 15$ *(1-5)* ____________

15. $8x - 20y$ *(1-5)* ____________

Show that each number can be written as a ratio of two integers.

16. -2.5 *(2-2)* ____________

17. 6.67 *(2-2)* ____________

18. -8 *(2-2)* ____________

19. 0.04 *(2-2)* ____________

Solve. Clear fractions first if necessary.

20. $5x + \frac{1}{2} = 2x - \frac{1}{4}$ *(3-6)* ____________

21. $\frac{1}{2}x - \frac{1}{3} = \frac{2}{3}$ *(3-6)* ____________

22. $1.6x + 0.5 = 2.6x$ *(3-6)* ____________

Solve for the given variable.

23. $PV = nRT$ for n *(3-7)* ____________

24. $PV = nRT$ for V *(3-7)* ____________

25. $A = \frac{1}{2}bh$ for b *(3-7)* ____________

Name ______________________ Class ______________ Date __________

Daily Cumulative Review 5-9

Subtract. *(Lesson 5-8)*

1. $(2x^2 + 3) - (x + 3)$ ______

2. $(-3n^4 + n^3 - 2n^2) - (2n^3 + 5n + 9)$ ______

3. $(b^3 + 8b^2 + 5b - 9) - (2b^3 - 8b + 6)$ ______

4. $(x^2y - 3xy^2 + 3x) - (2x^2y + 3x)$ ______

5.
$$\begin{array}{r} 2x^2 + 3x - 4 \\ \underline{-x^2 \qquad\quad + 3} \end{array}$$
______

6.
$$\begin{array}{r} 4x^2 + 3x + 6 \\ \underline{2x^2 - 5x + 2} \end{array}$$
______

Add. *(Lesson 5-7)*

7. $(b^2c - bc^2 + bc) + (c^2 + 2bc^2 + bc)$ ______

8. $(2x^2 + 3x - 5) + (x^2 - 3x + 10)$ ______

9. $(n^5 - 3n^3 + 2n^2 + 3) + (4n^5 - n^4 + 2n^2 + n)$ ______

10. $(y^2 - xy + 3x) + (x^2 + 2x)$ ______

Mixed Review

Simplify.

11. *(5-2)* $\left(\frac{xy^2}{z}\right)^{10}$ ______

12. *(5-2)* $\left(\frac{n}{m^2p^3}\right)^4$ ______

13. *(5-2)* $(4x^2)^3(3x)$ ______

14. *(5-2)* $\left(\frac{1}{x^5}\right)^2$ ______

Solve and graph the solution.

15. *(4-3)* $4y \leq -16$ ______

16. *(4-3)* $3x > 21$ ______

17. *(4-3)* $-4x < -8$ ______

Write as a decimal.

18. *(3-10)* 10% ______

19. *(3-10)* 5% ______

20. *(3-10)* 108% ______

21. *(3-10)* 0.9% ______

Name ______________________ Class ______________ Date ____________

Daily Cumulative Review 5-10

Multiply. *(Lesson 5-9)*

1. $4y(3y - 8)$

2. $3x^2(x - 5)$

3. $n^2(n^3 - 4n^2 + 3n + 8)$

4. $(x + 5)(x - 3)$

5. $(y^2 - 9)(y + 3)$

6. $(3m - 5)(m + 8)$

Simplify. *(Lesson 5-8)*

7. $(n + 6) - (3n + 5) + (8n + 18)$

8. $(x^2 + 5) - (3x + 8) + (5x^2 + 3x)$

9. $(5y^2 + 3y) + (y^2 + 4y + 4) - (2y - 3)$

10. $(x + 5) - (x - 3) - (2x + 1)$

Mixed Review

Write using scientific notation.

11. 285 *(5-4)*

12. 0.000598 *(5-4)*

13. six million *(5-4)*

14. 0.275 *(5-4)*

Divide.

15. $\frac{x^2}{x}$ *(5-3)*

16. $\frac{5y^5}{15y^2}$ *(5-3)*

17. $\frac{10y^2}{5}$ *(5-3)*

18. $\frac{a^2}{10a^4}$ *(5-3)*

Solve.

19. $|n + 5| = 3$ *(3-8)*

20. $5|x| + 3 = 23$ *(3-8)*

21. $\frac{|y|}{-5} = -6$ *(3-8)*

Simplify.

22. $-(3x - 9)$ *(2-8)*

23. $2y - (-3 + 4y)$ *(2-8)*

24. $2n + 5 - 3(n + 1)$ *(2-8)*

Name ______________________ Class ______________ Date __________

Daily Cumulative Review 5-11

Multiply. *(Lesson 5-10)*

1. $(2x + 3)^2$ ________

2. $(y + 5)(y - 5)$ ________

3. $(b - 2)(b - 2)$ ________

4. $(3n + 5)(3n - 5)$ ________

5. $(m + 8)(m + 8)$ ________

6. $(3x - 4)^2$ ________

Multiply. *(Lesson 5-9)*

7. $(2x + 3)(x - 7)$ ________

8. $(y - 8)(2y - 5)$ ________

9. $3m(m - 5)$ ________

10. $(y^2 + 3)(y - 2)$ ________

11. $-5x^2(2x + 8)$ ________

12. $(n + 5)(2n + 8)$ ________

Mixed Review

Find the reciprocal.

13. $\frac{2x}{3}$ *(2-6)* ________

14. $\frac{n}{m}$ *(2-6)* ________

15. 0.4 *(2-6)* ________

16. 10 *(2-6)* ________

Solve.

17. $8n + 5 > 3n - 2$ *(4-4)* ________

18. $\frac{2x}{5} \leq 8$ *(4-4)* ________

19. $\frac{y}{3} + 2 \geq \frac{2}{3}$ *(4-4)* ________

Identify the terms. Give the coefficient of each term.

20. $3x^2 - 5x + 8$ *(5-5)* ________

21. $y^2 - y - 20$ *(5-5)* ________

22. $3a^2b + 9ab^2 + 6b^2 - 5$ *(5-5)* ________

Solve each proportion.

23. $\frac{x}{5} = \frac{7}{15}$ *(3-9)* $x =$ ________

24. $\frac{n}{4} = \frac{20}{8}$ *(3-9)* $n =$ ________

25. $\frac{5}{4} = \frac{35}{y}$ *(3-9)* $y =$ ________

26. $\frac{8}{7} = \frac{4}{z}$ *(3-9)* $z =$ ________

Name ______________________ Class ______________ Date ____________

Daily Cumulative Review 5-12

Multiply. *(Lesson 5-11)*

1. $(y^2 + y + 1)(y - 1)$
2. $(2n^2 + 4n + 4)(n + 2)$
3. $(x^2 - 4)(x^2 + 4)$
4. $3b^2(b^2 + 8b + 16)$
5. $(3 - n^2)(3 - n^2)$
6. $(z^2 - z + 1)(z^2 - z + 1)$

Multiply. *(Lesson 5-10)*

7. $(b + 2)(b + 2)$
8. $(5x + 3)(5x + 3)$
9. $(2n - 5)(2n + 5)$
10. $(2y - 7)(2y - 7)$
11. $\left(m + \frac{1}{2}\right)\left(m - \frac{1}{2}\right)$
12. $(z^2 + 0.6)(z^2 - 0.6)$

Mixed Review

Write a formula for the area of each figure.

13. *(1-9)*

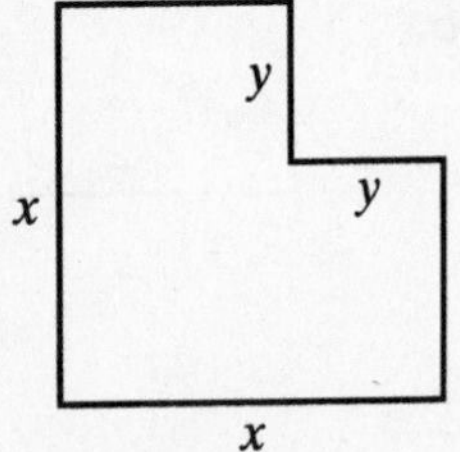

14. *(1-9)*

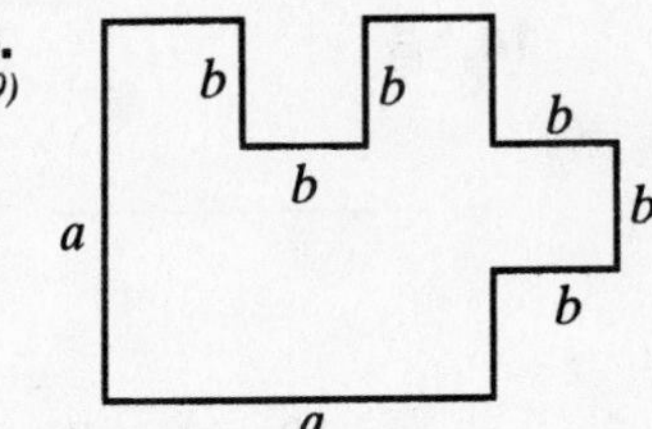

Each pair of equations is equivalent. Tell what was done to the first equation to get the second.

15. *(1-7)* $y - 8 = 13$
    $y = 21$
16. *(1-7)* $\frac{n}{3} = 8$
    $n = 24$
17. *(1-7)* $x + 5 = 3$
    $x - 5 = -7$

Evaluate.

18. *(2-1)* $|-3| - |2|$
19. *(2-1)* $|3.2| + |-1.8|$
20. *(2-1)* $|-5| \cdot |4|$

Name ______________________ Class ______________ Date ____________

Daily Cumulative Review 6-1

Solve. *(Lesson 5-12)*

1. Sue deposited money into her savings account every month for a year. The first month she deposited $20, the second month $40, the third month $60, and so on. How much money did she deposit in all? ________

2. 209 baseballs were divided among the members of a baseball team. Each player got the same number of balls. There were fewer than 15 players on the team. How many balls did each player receive? ________

Multiply. *(Lesson 5-11)*

3. $\left(\frac{3}{2} - x^2\right)\left(\frac{3}{2} - x^2\right)$ ________

4. $(2y^2 - y + 2)(y + 2)$ ________

5. $5n(-n^2 + 2n + 6)$ ________

6. $(y^3 + y^2 - y)(y^2 + y)$ ________

7. $(7 - 3x^2)(7 + 3x^2)$ ________

8. $(z^3 + z^2 + z + 1)(z - 1)$ ________

Mixed Review

Simplify.

9. *(5-2)* $(3y)^2$ ________

10. *(5-2)* $\left(\frac{-n}{m}\right)^3$ ________

11. *(5-2)* $(2x^2z^3)^5$ ________

12. *(5-2)* $\left(\frac{2a}{-b}\right)^4$ ________

Solve.

13. *(3-2)* $\frac{x}{-3} = 15$ ________

14. *(3-2)* $43 = -y$ ________

15. *(3-2)* $144 = 12n$ ________

Add.

16. *(2-3)* $12 + (-15)$ ________

17. *(2-3)* $-\frac{1}{2} + \left(-\frac{3}{4}\right)$ ________

18. *(2-3)* $21 + (-6) + 8 + (-15)$ ________

Write as an algebraic expression.

19. *(1-6)* 3 less than x ________

20. *(1-6)* n added to m ________

21. *(1-6)* half of y ________

22. *(1-6)* b greater than c ________

23. *(1-6)* x divided among 4 ________

24. *(1-6)* 6 multiplied by z ________

Name ______________________ Class ______________ Date __________

Daily Cumulative Review 6-2

Factor. *(Lesson 6-1)*

1. $3x^2 - 5x^4$
2. $3y^2 - 6y$
3. $2x^3y^2 - 7x^2y^5$
4. $n^5 - n^3 + n^2$
5. $7m^5 - 2m^4$
6. $3x^2 + 3x$

Solve. *(Lesson 5-12)*

7. Jim starts with one marble and doubles his marbles each week. Jill starts with 500 marbles and adds one marble each week. After how many weeks will Jim have more marbles than Jill?

8. In the above problem, how many marbles will Jim and Jill have altogether after 10 weeks?

Mixed Review

Multiply.

9. $(x^2 + 1)(x + 1)$ *(5-9)*
10. $5y^2(-3y + y^3)$ *(5-9)*
11. $(3n + 5)(n + 2)$ *(5-9)*
12. $-3(5a - 6b + 7c)$ *(2-7)*
13. $\frac{1}{2}(4x - 6y + 10)$ *(2-7)*
14. $2.5(4x + 2y)$ *(2-7)*

Simplify.

15. $2x - (6x + 5)$ *(2-8)*
16. $3y - 5y - 2(y - 8)$ *(2-8)*
17. $1 - (x + 8)$ *(2-8)*

Show that each number can be written as a ratio of two integers.

18. -8 *(2-2)*
19. $3\frac{1}{2}$ *(2-2)*
20. 2.4 *(2-2)*
21. -1.111 *(2-2)*

Solve.

22. $5x + 2 = 9x$ *(3-5)*
23. $7x + 5 = 8 - 8x$ *(3-5)*
24. $4n + 3 - n = 6 + 4n - 8$ *(3-5)*

Name ______________________ Class ______________ Date ______________

Daily Cumulative Review 6-3

Factor. *(Lesson 6-2)*

1. $3y^4 - 12$

2. $16 - x^2$

3. $1.92x^4 - 3$

4. $36 - y^2$

5. $9y^2 - 4x^2$

6. $169 - 25x^6$

Factor. *(Lesson 6-1)*

7. $3x^2 - 9x$

8. $2m^2 - 6m^4$

9. $y^5 - y^3 + y^4 + y^6$

10. $2x^2y + 4xy^2 + 8xy$

11. $a^2b + 3a^2b^2$

12. $5x^3 + x^2$

Mixed Review

Arrange each polynomial in descending order.

13. *(5-6)* $3x + 4x^2 - 3 + 2x^3$

14. *(5-6)* $5 + p^3 - p^2 + 8p$

15. *(5-6)* $2y^2 + 5y - 3y^3 + 8$

Simplify.

16. *(5-1)* $\frac{n^5}{n^3}$

17. *(5-1)* $\frac{x^5y^6}{x^2y^5}$

18. *(5-1)* y^0

19. *(5-1)* $\frac{x^3}{x^5}$

Solve and graph each inequality.

20. *(4-3)* $4x < -12$

21. *(4-3)* $5 \leq 7x + 3x$

22. *(4-3)* $-3y < -21$

Solve each proportion.

23. *(3-9)* $\frac{m}{8} = \frac{1}{2}$

24. *(3-9)* $\frac{15}{12} = \frac{5}{n}$

25. *(3-9)* $\frac{42}{x} = \frac{3}{5}$

26. *(3-9)* $\frac{40}{10} = \frac{x}{15}$

Name ____________ Class ____________ Date ____________

Daily Cumulative Review 6-4

Factor. *(Lesson 6-3)*

1. $2x^2 + 12x + 18$

2. $x^2 - 26x + 169$

3. $0.25x^2 + 10x + 100$

4. $x^2 + 10x + 25$

5. $5x^2 - 20x + 20$

6. $49x^2 - 56x + 16$

Factor. *(Lesson 6-2)*

7. $x^2 - 81$

8. $2.25y^2 - 0.64$

9. $18p^2 - 8y^2$

10. $n^{10} - 1$

11. $y^3 - 25y$

12. $5x^2 - \frac{1}{5}$

Mixed Review

Add.

13. $(-5x - 3) + (3x + 8)$
(5-7)

14. $(3y^5 + 2y^3 - y) + (y^4 + 8y^2 + y - 5)$
(5-7)

Solve.

15. $-5x - 2x + 5 > 19$
(4-4)

16. $4(3y + 2) \leq -16$
(4-4)

17. $\frac{2m}{3} < 14$
(4-4)

Express as a percent.

18. $\frac{1}{2}$
(3-10)

19. $\frac{3}{8}$
(3-10)

20. $\frac{19}{20}$
(3-10)

21. $\frac{6}{25}$
(3-10)

Write as an algebraic expression.

22. 2 more than the product of 3 and a number
(3-4)

23. 5 less than the quotient of a number and 3
(3-4)

Solve.

24. $-3(4x - 2) = 6$
(3-3)

25. $5(x - 3) = 15$
(3-3)

26. $2(y - 5) + 13 = -23$
(3-3)

Name ______________________ Class ______________ Date ____________

Daily Cumulative Review 6-5

Factor. *(Lesson 6-4)*

1. $x^2 + 8x + 12$ ____________
2. $y^2 - y - 30$ ____________
3. $m^2 - 3m + 2$ ____________
4. $x^2 + 6x - 55$ ____________
5. $m^2 + 20m + 75$ ____________
6. $x^2 - 18x + 56$ ____________

Factor. *(Lesson 6-3)*

7. $x^4 - 8x^2 + 16$ ____________
8. $y^2 + 18y + 81$ ____________
9. $5y^2 - 5y + \frac{5}{4}$ ____________
10. $4n^2 + 12n + 9$ ____________
11. $c^6 + 6bc^3 + 9b^2$ ____________
12. $2x^2 - 32x + 128$ ____________

Mixed Review

Divide.

13. *(2-6)* $72 \div (-8)$ ____________
14. *(2-6)* $\frac{-28}{7}$ ____________
15. *(2-6)* $-33 \div (-3)$ ____________
16. *(2-6)* $\frac{150}{-6}$ ____________

Multiply.

17. *(2-7)* $-3(y - 5)$ ____________
18. *(2-7)* $\frac{1}{3}(6y - 9x + 3)$ ____________
19. *(2-7)* $-5(3x - 8y + 2)$ ____________

Solve.

20. *(3-1)* $x - 5 = 21$ ____________
21. *(3-1)* $n - \frac{1}{4} = \frac{1}{2}$ ____________
22. *(3-1)* $6 + y = 15$ ____________

Subtract.

23. *(2-4)* $-3 - (-8)$ ____________
24. *(2-4)* $5 - 9$ ____________
25. *(2-4)* $-30 - (-80)$ ____________

Simplify.

26. *(5-2)* $(3n^5)^3$ ____________
27. *(5-2)* $\left(\frac{3}{x^3}\right)^2$ ____________
28. *(5-2)* $\left(\frac{x^2y}{z^3}\right)^4$ ____________
29. *(5-2)* $(y^8)^2$ ____________

Name ____________________ Class ____________ Date ________

Daily Cumulative Review 6-6

Factor. *(Lesson 6-5)*

1. $2x^2 + 5x - 3$

2. $4n^2 + 4n - 15$

3. $5y^2 - 36y - 32$

4. $7m^2 - 43m + 40$

5. $3x^2 - 21x + 36$

6. $6y^2 + 7y - 20$

Factor. *(Lesson 6-4)*

7. $x^2 + x - 20$

8. $y^2 - 9y + 18$

9. $a^2 + 10ab + 21b^2$

10. $n^2 - 3n - 10$

11. $x^2 + 15x + 26$

12. $56y^2 + 30yz + z^2$

Mixed Review

Subtract.

13. $5x^2 - (-3x^3 + x^2 - 5)$ *(5-8)*

14. $(4x^4 - 7x^3 + x + 5) - (x^5 + 3x^4 + x^2 - 8)$ *(5-8)*

Translate to an inequality.

15. 7.5 is less than a number *n*. *(4-5)*

16. Three more than a number *x* is less than -2. *(4-5)*

Solve and graph the solution.

17. $x - 5 \leq 13$ *(4-2)*

18. $2y + 5 + 3y > 10$ *(4-2)*

19. $-3(y + 8) + 5y < 0$ *(4-2)*

Solve.

20. $|x| + 12 = 19$ *(3-8)*

21. $\frac{|y|}{5} = 7$ *(3-8)*

22. $-5|z| + 10 = -5$ *(3-8)*

Name ____________ Class ____________ Date ____________

Daily Cumulative Review 6-7

Factor. *(Lesson 6-6)*

1. $2x^3 + 5x^2 - 6x - 15$ ____________

2. $5x^3 - 10x^2 + 4x - 8$ ____________

3. $na - ma + nb - mb$ ____________

4. $ya + 3a - yb - 3b$ ____________

5. $3y^5 - 15y^3 + 4y^2 - 20$ ____________

6. $6z^3 - 5z^2 + 18z - 15$ ____________

Factor. *(Lesson 6-5)*

7. $2x^2 - 11x - 40$ ____________

8. $6y^2 - 5y - 21$ ____________

9. $25 - 35b + 10b^2$ ____________

10. $6x^2 + 33x + 42$ ____________

11. $30x^2 + x - 14$ ____________

12. $2y^3 - 7y^2 - 72y$ ____________

Mixed Review

Factor.

13. *(6-1)* $2x^2 - 16x$ ____________

14. *(6-1)* $3a^2b + 9ab$ ____________

15. *(6-1)* $14x^2 + 7$ ____________

Multiply.

16. *(5-10)* $(x + 3)(x - 3)$ ____________

17. *(5-10)* $(2x + 5)(2x - 5)$ ____________

18. *(5-10)* $(n^2 + y)(n^2 - y)$ ____________

Write using standard notation.

19. *(5-4)* 5×10^5 ____________

20. *(5-4)* 2.56×10^{-3} ____________

21. *(5-4)* 5.0003×10^2 ____________

Write as a decimal.

22. *(3-10)* 250% ____________

23. *(3-10)* 16% ____________

24. *(3-10)* 0.5% ____________

25. *(3-10)* 3.6% ____________

Solve.

26. *(3-7)* $PV = nRT$ for R ____________

27. *(3-7)* $A = \frac{1}{2}bh$ for b ____________

28. *(3-7)* $V = \frac{4}{3}\pi r^3$ for π ____________

Name ______________________ Class ______________ Date __________

Daily Cumulative Review 6-8

Factor. *(Lesson 6-7)*

1. $3x^2 - 75$

2. $y^3 + 16y^2 + 64y$

3. $z^8 - 256$

4. $2x^2 - 4x - 30$

5. $15n^2 + 30n + 15$

6. $2y^5 - 11y^4 - 6y^3$

Factor. *(Lesson 6-6)*

7. $3y^3 - 15y^2 - 2y + 10$

8. $8b^3 + 28b^2 + 10b + 35$

9. $a^2 - 5a + ab - 5b$

10. $xz - 5x + yz - 5y$

11. $y^9 + 2y^5 + 3y^4 + 6$

12. $2x^3 + 7x^2 - 10x - 35$

Mixed Review

Multiply.

13. *(5-9)* $2n(-3n + 3)$

14. *(5-9)* $(2x^2 + 5)(x - 3)$

15. *(5-9)* $(x - 7)(x + 7)$

Collect like terms.

16. *(5-5)* $3x^2 + 5x - 8x + 2x^2$

17. *(5-5)* $m^2n + mn^2 - 3m^2n$

18. *(5-5)* $3y^3 - 6y^3 + 5$

Solve.

19. *(4-4)* $\frac{y}{6} - 8 \leq 2$

20. *(4-4)* $3(x + 3) > 5x - 7$

21. *(4-4)* $9 + 7z < -5$

22. *(3-5)* $3n = 4n - 7$

23. *(3-5)* $5x - 2 = 22 - x$

24. *(3-5)* $3y - 9y + 40 = 10 - 3y$

25. *(3-2)* $-5x = -75$

26. *(3-2)* $\frac{n}{5} = -3$

27. *(3-2)* $-\frac{2}{3}y = -\frac{5}{2}$

Name ______________________ Class ______________ Date __________

Daily Cumulative Review 6-9

Solve. *(Lesson 6-8)*

1. $(x + 3)(x - 8) = 0$ ______

2. $0 = y(y + 5)$ ______

3. $x^2 - 49 = 0$ ______

4. $x^2 - x - 20 = 0$ ______

5. $3x^2 + 9x = -6$ ______

6. $\left(\frac{1}{3} + 3x\right)\left(\frac{1}{2} - 5x\right) = 0$ ______

Factor. *(Lesson 6-7)*

7. $5x^2 - 20$ ______

8. $3x^2 + 30x + 75$ ______

9. $9y^3 + 24y^2 + 16y$ ______

10. $y^8 - 1$ ______

11. $n^4 - 8n^2 + 16$ ______

12. $3y^4 - 48$ ______

Mixed Review

Multiply.

13. *(5-11)* $(x + 2)(x^2 - 2x + 2)$ ______

14. *(5-11)* $(y^6 - 2y^4 + 3y^2)(3y^5 + 2y^3 - y)$ ______

Factor.

15. *(6-2)* $100x^2 - 49$ ______

16. *(6-2)* $2.25y^2 - 0.64$ ______

17. *(6-2)* $n^6 - 81$ ______

Classify each statement as true or false.

18. *(4-1)* $|-6| \leq 3$ ______

19. *(4-1)* $|-0.2| \leq 1.0$ ______

20. *(4-1)* $6 \geq 6$ ______

21. *(4-1)* $|-3| \geq 0$ ______

Solve.

22. *(3-3)* $3x - 8 = -2$ ______

23. *(3-3)* $-5n + 22 = -3$ ______

24. *(3-3)* $-4y - 5y = 45$ ______

25. *(3-1)* $y + \frac{5}{8} = \frac{3}{8}$ ______

26. *(3-1)* $x + 35 = -6$ ______

27. *(3-1)* $b - 0.6 = 7$ ______

Name ______________________ Class ______________ Date __________

Daily Cumulative Review 7-1

Translate to an equation and solve. *(Lesson 6-9)*

1. Roberta launched a model rocket upward at a speed of 60 meters per second. After how many seconds will Roberta's rocket reach a height of 177.5 meters? Use the formula $h = rt - 4.9t^2$ where h is the height in meters after t seconds of an object projected upward at a rate of r meters per second. ________ ________

2. The product of two consecutive even integers is 440. Find the integers. ________ ________

Solve. *(Lesson 6-8)*

3. $(y - 9)(y + 15) = 0$ ________

4. $5x(4x - 3) = 0$ ________

5. $x^2 - 2x - 24 = 0$ ________

6. $2x^2 + 5x = 12$ ________

Mixed Review

Evaluate each expression.

7. $2x - 9$ for $x = 3$ *(1-1)* ________

8. $-5x + 6$ for $x = 2$ *(1-1)* ________

9. $4x + 1$ for $x = -1$ *(1-1)* ________

10. $2x + 3y$ for $x = -1$ and $y = 2$ *(1-1)* ________

11. $4x - y$ for $x = -2$ and $y = -9$ *(1-1)* ________

12. $\frac{y - 3}{x - 5}$ for $x = 2$ and $y = -3$ *(1-1)* ________

Solve for the given replacement set.

13. $5n + 4 = 19$ $\{2, 3, 4\}$ *(1-7)* ________

14. $7m - 4 = 45$ $\{5, 6, 7\}$ *(1-7)* ________

15. $t + 6 = 2t + 5$ $\{0, 1, 2\}$ *(1-7)* ________

16. $3x - 2 = 22$ $\{8, 9, 10\}$ *(1-7)* ________

17. $6a + 1 = 43$ $\{6, 7, 8\}$ *(1-7)* ________

18. $5y - 8 = 4y + 2$ $\{8, 9, 10\}$ *(1-7)* ________

Evaluate each polynomial for $x = -1$.

19. $x^2 - 3x + 2$ ________ *(5-6)*

20. $6x + 9$ ________ *(5-6)*

21. $x^3 - x^4 + 2x - 4$ ________ *(5-6)*

22. $3x^4 + 2x^5$ ________ *(5-6)*

23. $4x^3 - x$ ________ *(5-6)*

24. $7x - 3$ ________ *(5-6)*

Name ______________________ Class ______________ Date ____________

Daily Cumulative Review 7-2

Plot these points. Write the ordered pair close to each point. *(Lesson 7-1)*

1. $(3, 4)$ **2.** $(-4, 5)$ **3.** $(0, 2)$

4. $(-1, -4)$ **5.** $(5, -1)$ **6.** $(-2, 0)$

7. $(-3, 3)$ **8.** $(-5, -5)$ **9.** $(2, -3)$

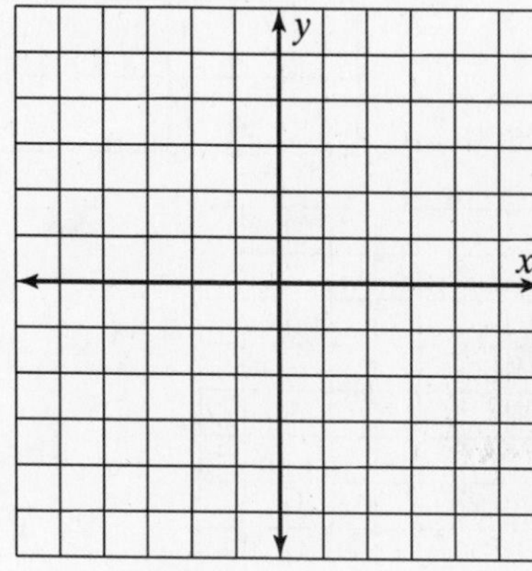

Translate to an equation and solve. *(Lesson 6-9)*

10. Leonardo is planning a rectangular garden. He wants it to be 10 m longer than it is wide and to have an area of 2475 m^2. What dimensions should Leonardo use? ____________

11. The height of a triangle is 5 in. less than the base. The area is 52 $in.^2$ Find the height and base. ____________ ____________

Mixed Review

Use either < or > to write a true sentence.

12. $0 \ \square\ -9$ *(2-1)*

13. $-8 \ \square\ -7$ *(2-1)*

14. $-6 \ \square\ 6$ *(2-1)*

15. $5 \ \square\ 0$ *(2-1)*

16. $-3 \ \square\ -10$ *(2-1)*

17. $-4 \ \square\ -2$ *(2-1)*

18. $-3.05 \ \square\ -3.5$ *(2-2)*

19. $-\frac{2}{3} \ \square\ -\frac{7}{9}$ *(2-2)*

20. $-\frac{1}{8} \ \square\ -\frac{1}{9}$ *(2-2)*

Solve.

21. $2x - 3 = 9$ ______ *(3-3)*

22. $5x - 2(3) = 4$ ______ *(3-3)*

23. $3(-2) + 4y = -10$ ______ *(3-3)*

24. $6x - 5(-1) = -7$ ______ *(3-3)*

25. $4(-1) - y = 3$ ______ *(3-3)*

26. $9(2) - (-3y) = 0$ ______ *(3-3)*

27. $3x - 5(0) = -12$ ______ *(3-2)*

28. $6 = \frac{1}{2}x$ ______ *(3-2)*

29. $-9 = \frac{3}{2}y$ ______ *(3-2)*

30. $y - 4 = 11$ ______ *(3-1)*

31. $x - 3 = 5$ ______ *(3-1)*

32. $x + 7 = 1$ ______ *(3-1)*

33. $y + 8 = 12$ ______ *(3-1)*

34. $x + 15 = 3$ ______ *(3-1)*

35. $y + 20 = 3$ ______ *(3-1)*

Name ______________________ Class ______________ Date ____________

Daily Cumulative Review 7-3

Make a table of solutions and graph each equation. *(Lesson 7-2)*

1. $y = -3x$

x	0	−1	1	2	−2
y					

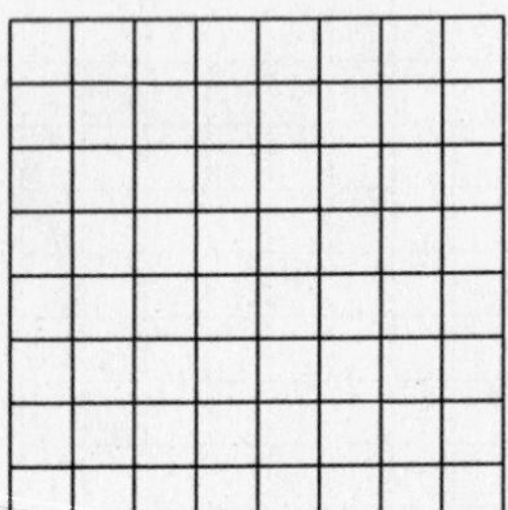

2. $y = 2x - 1$

x	0	1	−1	2	3
y					

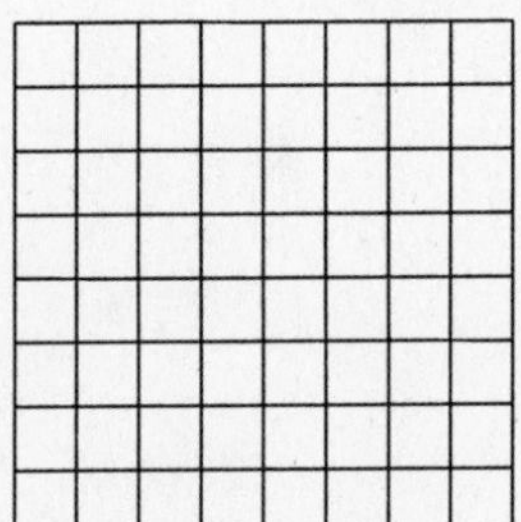

Find the coordinates of each point. *(Lesson 7-1)*

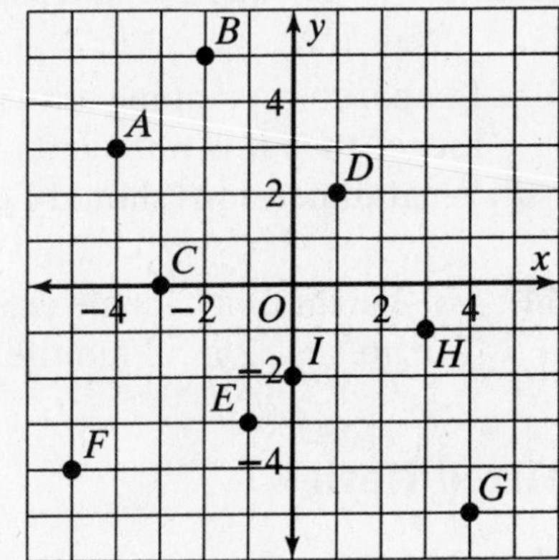

3. A _____ **4.** B _____ **5.** C _____

6. D _____ **7.** E _____ **8.** F _____

9. G _____ **10.** H _____ **11.** I _____

Mixed Review

Simplify.

12. $\frac{8}{24}$ ________ *(1-2)*

13. $\frac{6x}{48}$ ________ *(1-2)*

14. $\frac{15mn}{14n}$ ________ *(1-2)*

15. $\frac{56}{4}$ ________ *(1-2)*

16. $\frac{9y}{45}$ ________ *(1-2)*

17. $\frac{7pq}{8pqr}$ ________ *(1-2)*

18. $(5ab)^3$ ________ *(5-2)*

19. $\left(\frac{4}{xy^4}\right)^2$ ________ *(5-2)*

20. $\left(\frac{m^3n^4}{2}\right)^3$ ________ *(5-2)*

The formula below gives a rule for determining the amount of medicine a child should take if you know the age of the child (*a*) and the amount, or dosage (*D*) of the medicine an adult would take. Find the child's dosage (*d*) for the given values of *a* and *D*. Round answers to the nearest tenth.

$$d = \frac{a}{a + 12} \cdot D$$

21. $a = 6$ yr, $D = 3.5$ mL *(1-9)*

____

22. $a = 9$ yr, $D = 2$ mL *(1-9)*

____

23. $a = 4$ yr, $D = 4.5$ mL *(1-9)*

____

Name ______________________ Class ______________ Date __________

Daily Cumulative Review 7-4

Graph using intercepts. *(Lesson 7-3)*

1. $x - 4y = 4$

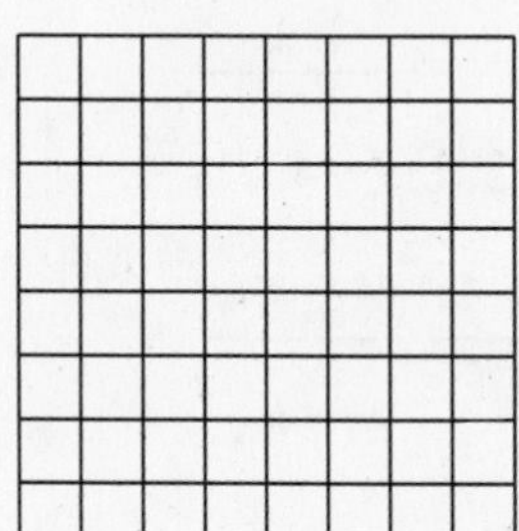

2. $2x - 3y = 6$

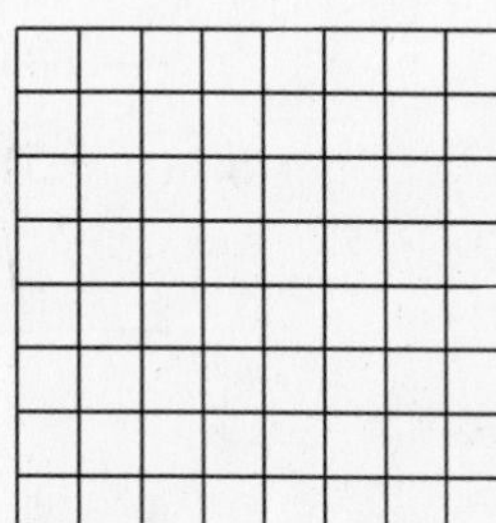

Determine whether the given point is a solution of the equation. *(Lesson 7-2)*

3. $y = 4x - 3$ $(1, -1)$ __________

4. $5x + 3y = 18$ $(3, 1)$ __________

5. $7x + 4y = 8$ $(4, -5)$ __________

6. $2x - 6y = 2$ $(5, 2)$ __________

Mixed Review

Write as an algebraic expression.

7. *(1-6)* 19 times a number n __________

8. *(1-6)* 16 less than h __________

9. *(1-6)* m divided by n __________

10. *(3-4)* 7 more than twice y __________

11. *(3-4)* 5 times the sum of x and 9 __________

12. *(3-4)* 15 less than half a __________

Factor.

13. *(6-1)* $3x^2 - 14x$ __________

14. *(6-1)* $10x^2 - 5x + 35$ __________

15. *(6-1)* $8mn^2 - 40m^2n^2 + 72m^2n$ __________

16. *(6-1)* $9y^2 - 23y$ __________

17. *(6-1)* $21n^2 - 7n + 28$ __________

18. *(6-1)* $12x^3y^2 - 6x^2y^2 + 42x^2y$ __________

19. *(6-2)* $x^2 - 100$ __________

20. *(6-2)* $9x^2 - 121$ __________

21. *(6-2)* $36y^4 - 25y^2$ __________

22. *(6-2)* $n^2 - m^2$ __________

23. *(6-2)* $16y^2 - 49$ __________

24. *(6-2)* $63x^2 - 7y^2$ __________

Name ______________________ Class ______________ Date ____________

Daily Cumulative Review 7-5

Find the slopes of the lines containing these points. *(Lesson 7-4)*

1. (3, 5) (2, 3)

2. (4, 0) (1, −1)

3. (8, −3) (5, −9)

4. (4, 7) (−2, −1)

5. (6, −5) (−2, 1)

6. (−3, 1) (−4, 7)

Graph. *(Lesson 7-3)*

7. $y = 2$

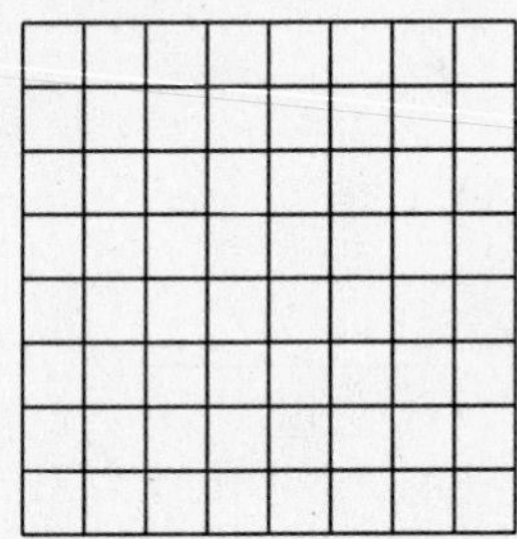

8. $x = -2$

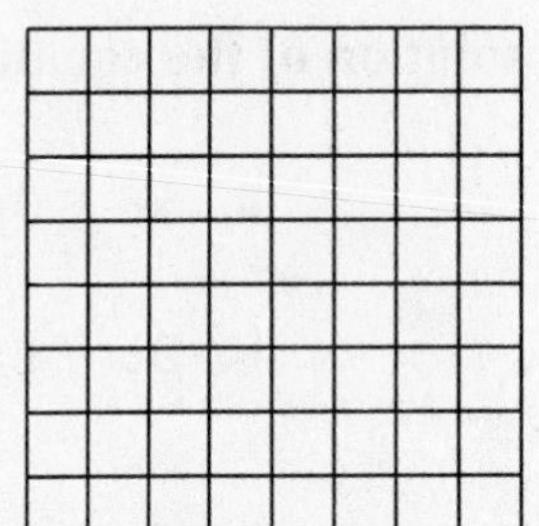

9. $y = -3$

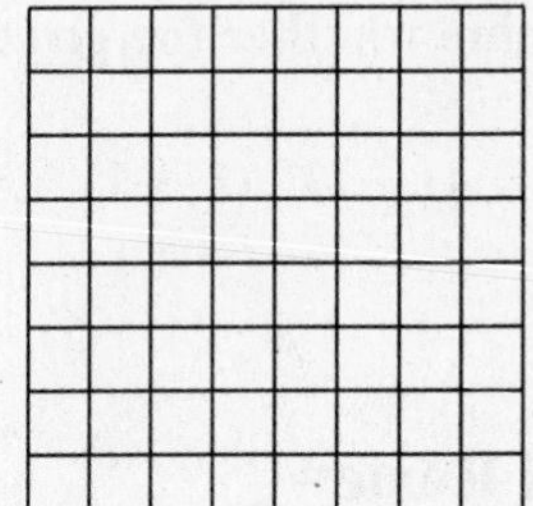

Mixed Review

Solve.

10. $x - 3 = 2(x + 7)$ *(3-5)*

11. $5(x - 2) = 4(x + 3)$ *(3-5)*

12. $8(x - 1) = 6(x - 5)$ *(3-5)*

13. $y - 9 = 3(y - 5)$ *(3-5)*

14. $7(x - 3) = 9(x - 1)$ *(3-5)*

15. $9(y - 2) = 4(y + 3)$ *(3-5)*

16. $y = mx + b$ for x *(3-7)*

17. $y - 3 = m(x - 2)$ for m *(3-7)*

18. $m = \frac{y + 7}{x - 8}$ for y *(3-7)*

19. $A = \frac{a + b + c + d}{4}$ for a *(3-7)*

20. $y - 7 = 3(x - 5)$ for x *(3-7)*

21. $2 = \frac{y - 4}{x + 3}$ for y *(3-7)*

Multiply.

22. $(x + 7)(x + 9)$ *(5-9)*

23. $3y(5y - 8)$ *(5-9)*

24. $(2x - 5)(x + 6)$ *(5-9)*

25. $(x - 4)(x - 11)$ *(5-9)*

26. $4x(12x + 7)$ *(5-9)*

27. $(3x - 1)(8x + 1)$ *(5-9)*

Name ______________________ Class ______________ Date ____________

Daily Cumulative Review 7-6

Find the slope of each line by solving for *y*. *(Lesson 7-5)*

1. $7x - 4y = 28$ ____________

2. $9x + y = 11$ ____________

3. $5y - 2x = 10$ ____________

4. $6x + 9y = 18$ ____________

5. $x - 3y = 6$ ____________

6. $8x + 4y = 16$ ____________

Find the slope of each line. *(Lesson 7-4)*

7.

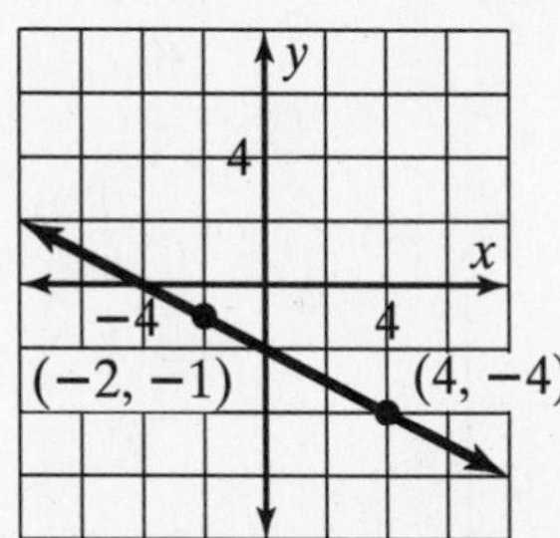

____

8.

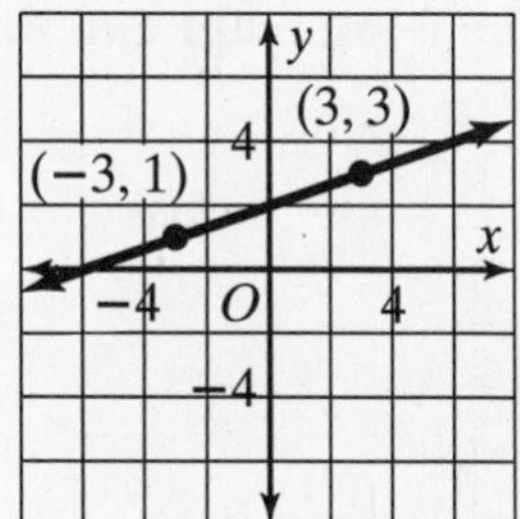

____

Mixed Review

Plot these points. Write the ordered pair close to each point.

9. (2, 1) *(7-1)*

10. (−5, 3) *(7-1)*

11. (4, 0) *(7-1)*

12. (−4, −2) *(7-1)*

13. (3, −4) *(7-1)*

14. (0, −5) *(7-1)*

15. (1, 5) *(7-1)*

16. (−2, 2) *(7-1)*

17. (1, −2) *(7-1)*

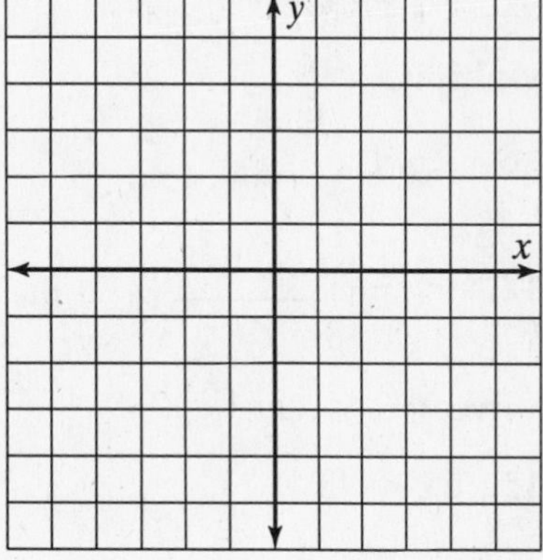

Factor.

18. $3x^2 + 19x - 14$ *(6-5)* ____________

19. $10x^2 + 13x - 3$ *(6-5)* ____________

20. $10x^2 + 35x - 20$ *(6-5)* ____________

21. $7x^2 - 15x + 2$ *(6-5)* ____________

22. $3x^2 - 17x + 20$ *(6-5)* ____________

23. $14x^2 + 77x + 63$ *(6-5)* ____________

24. $n^4 - 81$ *(6-7)* ____________

25. $5x^2 - 320$ *(6-7)* ____________

26. $8x^2 - 32x + 32$ *(6-7)* ____________

Name ______________________ Class ______________ Date __________

Daily Cumulative Review 7-7

Write an equation for each line with the given point and slope. Express the equation in slope-intercept form. *(Lesson 7-6)*

1. $(2, -4), m = 3$ ________

2. $(1, 2), m = -5$ ________

3. $(3, -4), m = \frac{2}{3}$ ________

4. $(7, -2), m = 1$ ________

5. $(4, 4), m = -\frac{3}{4}$ ________

6. $(-2, 5), m = \frac{4}{5}$ ________

Graph each line using the *y*-intercept and slope. *(Lesson 7-5)*

7. $y = -3x + 2$

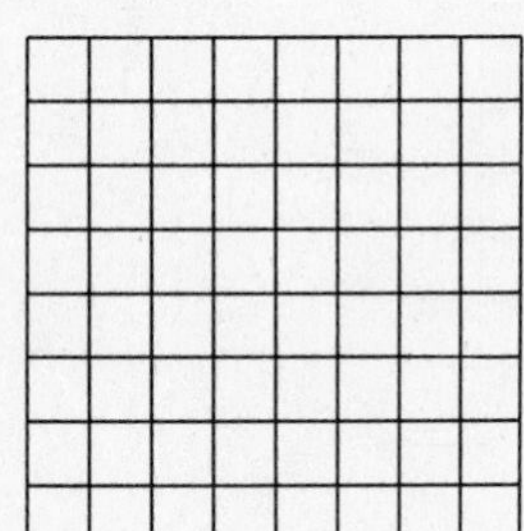

8. $y = -\frac{3}{2}x - 1$

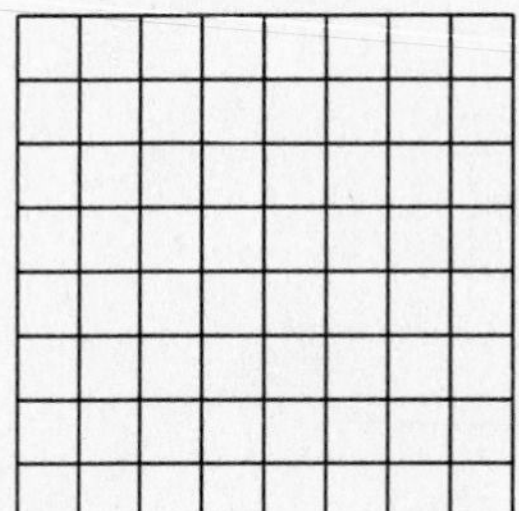

Mixed Review

Multiply.

9. $-9(11)$ ________ *(2-5)*

10. $-5(-12)$ ________ *(2-5)*

11. $1.1(-7)$ ________ *(2-5)*

12. $-\frac{2}{3}\left(-\frac{3}{2}\right)$ ________ *(2-5)*

13. $-4\left(\frac{1}{4}\right)$ ________ *(2-5)*

14. $\frac{7}{8}\left(-\frac{8}{7}\right)$ ________ *(2-5)*

Solve.

15. $6x < 48$ *(4-3)* ________

16. $-8y > 96$ *(4-3)* ________

17. $-11x \leq -77$ *(4-3)* ________

18. $5y \geq 4.5$ *(4-3)* ________

19. $-3x < -54$ *(4-3)* ________

20. $-4y \geq 64$ *(4-3)* ________

21. $3x - 7 \leq 11$ *(4-4)* ________

22. $8 - 5x > -22$ *(4-4)* ________

23. $9y - 7 < 10y + 5$ *(4-4)* ________

24. $(x - 12)(x + 11) = 0$ *(6-8)* ________

25. $x^2 + 4x - 21 = 0$ *(6-8)* ________

26. $3x^2 - 13x = 10$ *(6-8)* ________

Name ______________________ Class ______________ Date __________

Daily Cumulative Review 7-8

Solve. Assume a linear relationship fits each set of data. *(Lesson 7-7)*

1. The value of a used car is $8500. Two years later, the car has a value of $7150. Find the value of the car after 5 years. __________

2. The Morgans paid $50.40 for 1500 kilowatt hours (kwh) of electricity one month and $58.80 for 1680 kwh the next month. How much should they expect to pay for 1840 kwh? __________

Write an equation for each line that contains the given pair of points. *(Lesson 7-6)*

3. $(6, 2)\ (1, -3)$ __________

4. $(3, 2)\ (-3, -2)$ __________

5. $(2, 6)\ (-2, 8)$ __________

6. $(-1, 7)\ (-3, -3)$ __________

7. $(-4, 3)\ (4, 9)$ __________

8. $(3, 4)\ (-3, -6)$ __________

Mixed Review

Which axiom or property guarantees the truth of each statement?

9. *(2-10)* $\frac{2}{3} \cdot \frac{3}{4} = \frac{3}{4} \cdot \frac{2}{3}$ __________

10. *(2-10)* If $\frac{6}{9} = \frac{2}{3}$ then $\frac{2}{3} = \frac{6}{9}$. __________

11. *(2-10)* $\frac{4}{5}(x - x) = \frac{4}{5}(0)$ __________

12. *(2-10)* $5 + (4x + 17) = (5 + 4x) + 17$ __________

13. *(2-10)* $14(x + y) = 14(y + x)$ __________

14. *(2-10)* $3x + 6y = 3(x + 2y)$ __________

Add or subtract.

15. *(5-7)* $(9x^4 + 3x^3 - 7x^2 - 4x) + (2x^3 + 3x^2 - 8x + 5)$ __________

16. *(5-8)* $(6x^2y - 5xy - 2y + 4) - (5x^2y + 5xy - 7y + 15)$ __________

17. *(5-8)* $(7m^2n^2 - 8m^2n - 10mn^2) - (8m^2n^2 + 2mn^2 - 17mn)$ __________

Factor.

18. *(6-7)* $4x^2 - 44x + 120$ __________

19. *(6-7)* $10x^2 + 80x + 160$ __________

20. *(6-7)* $x^4 + 14x^2 + 49$ __________

Name ______________________ Class ______________ Date __________

Daily Cumulative Review 7-9

Determine whether the graphs of the equations are parallel lines. *(Lesson 7-8)*

1. $x + 9 = y$
$x + y = 8$

2. $2x + y = 8$
$-2x + 7 = y$

3. $3x - 2y = 4$
$4y = 6x - 9$

4. $5x - 4y = 3$
$8y = 10x - 6$

5. $\frac{2}{3}x + y = 6$
$8y - 12x = 12$

6. $8y = 7x - 8$
$16y - 14x = 5$

Solve. Assume a linear relationship fits the data. *(Lesson 7-7)*

7. Belle bought a savings bond for $64 that is valued at $100 after 10 years. If the value of the bond increases linearly, what should its value be after 6 years? ________

Mixed Review

Solve using one or more strategies.

8. *(5-12)* A salesperson earned a $100 bonus the first week she worked, a $125 bonus the second week, and a $150 bonus the third week. If she continues increases to her bonus the same amount each week, how much total will she earn in bonuses for the first 10 weeks she works? ________

Simplify. Express using exponents.

9. *(5-1)* $p^4 \cdot p^8$

10. *(5-1)* $a^8 \cdot a^0$

11. *(5-1)* $\frac{m^9}{m}$

12. *(5-1)* $(a^3b)(a^2b^6)$

13. *(5-1)* $\frac{y^{10}}{y^7}$

14. *(5-1)* $\frac{m^3n^4}{n^3}$

Simplify.

15. *(5-2)* $(x^4)^5$

16. *(5-2)* $\left(\frac{y^3}{2}\right)^4$

17. *(5-2)* $\left(\frac{3x^3y^2}{4}\right)^2$

18. *(5-2)* $(b^3)^7$

19. *(5-2)* $\left(\frac{a^7}{8}\right)^2$

20. *(5-2)* $\left(\frac{5x^4y^5}{6}\right)^2$

Name ______________________ Class ______________ Date __________

Daily Cumulative Review 7-10

Prove the following. *(Lesson 7-9)*

1. Prove that the x-intercept of the line with equation $ax + by = ab$ is b.

____

____

Determine whether the graphs of the equations are perpendicular lines. *(Lesson 7-8)*

2. $7x - 7y = 14$
   $8x + 8y = 16$

   ____

3. $y = -\frac{3}{5}x + 4$
   $3y = 6 - 5x$

   ____

4. $y = \frac{1}{4}x - 9$
   $4x + y = 3$

   ____

5. $x + y = 12$
   $y + 9 = x$

   ____

6. $y = \frac{1}{5}x + 3$
   $5x - y = 4$

   ____

7. $3x - 5y = 7$
   $5x - 3y = 4$

   ____

Mixed Review

Graph using intercepts.

8. $2x - 4y = 8$
(7-3)

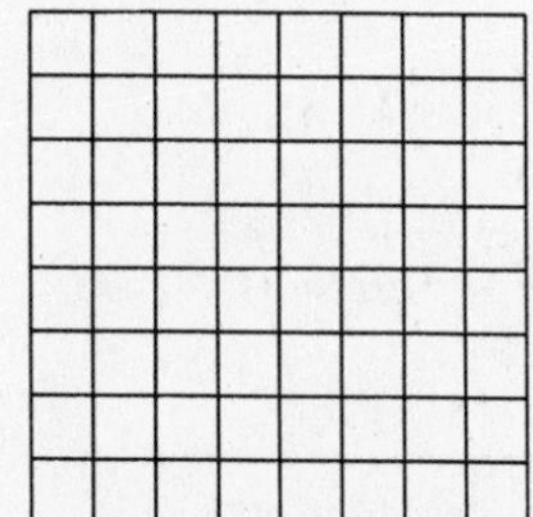

9. $5x - 4y = -20$
(7-3)

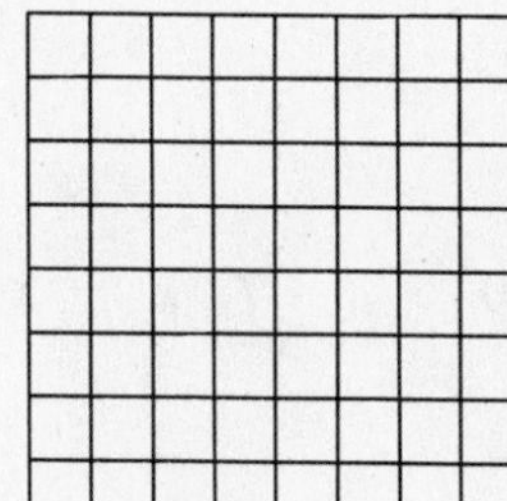

Determine whether the given point is a solution of the equation.

10. $(4, -6)$ $y = 6 - 3x$ ______
(7-2)

11. $(2, 3)$ $5x - 3y = -1$ ______
(7-2)

12. $(-1, -5)$ $y = 4x - 9$ ______
(7-2)

13. $(-6, 2)$ $2x + 7y = 2$ ______
(7-2)

Multiply.

14. $(x - 8)(x + 11)$
(5-10)

____

15. $(x - 9)^2$
(5-10)

____

16. $(5y^2 - 6)(2y^2 + 3)$
(5-10)

____

Name ______________________ Class ______________ Date __________

Daily Cumulative Review 8-1

Solve. *(Lesson 7-10)*

1. The figure at right was made with four triangles. An artist made a figure like this using 25 triangles. Each side of each triangle is 1 m long. What is the perimeter of the figure made with 25 triangles?

____

2. Sue built a 100 ft^3 sandbox for her daughter, Kelly. She is using a wheelbarrow to dump sand into the box in loads of 5 ft^3 each. Between each load Kelly throws 1 ft^3 of sand out of the box. How many loads will it take Sue to fill the box? ________

Follow the steps below to prove that if two non-vertical lines have the same slope and different *y*-intercepts, then they are parallel lines. *(Lesson 7-9)*

3. Use m for the slope, and b_1 and b_2 for the y-intercepts. Write the slope-intercept equation of each line. ________ ________

4. Suppose (x_0, y_0) is on the first line. Express y_0 in terms of x_0, m, and b_1, using the equation of the first line. ________

5. Show that (x_0, y_0) cannot be on the second line. (Hint: try to express y_0 in terms of x_0, m, and b_2, and show that this would require $b_1 = b_2$.)

____

Mixed Review

Solve.

6. $(x + 9)(x - 3) = 0$ *(6-8)* ________

7. $x^2 - x - 20 = 0$ *(6-8)* ________

8. $m^2 - 9m = 0$ *(6-8)* ________

Factor.

9. $x^3 + 8x^2 + 16x$ *(6-3)* ________

10. $9 - 12y^2 + 4y^4$ *(6-3)* ________

11. $m^2 + 26m + 169$ *(6-3)* ________

Multiply.

12. $(-x)(-x^4)$ *(5-3)* ________

13. $(3a^3b^4)(9a^2b)$ *(5-3)* ________

14. $(y^5)(8y)(2y^2)$ *(5-3)* ________

Name ______________________ Class ______________ Date __________

Daily Cumulative Review 8-2

Solve by graphing. *(Lesson 8-1)*

1. $2x + 3y = 12$
$x - y = 1$

______

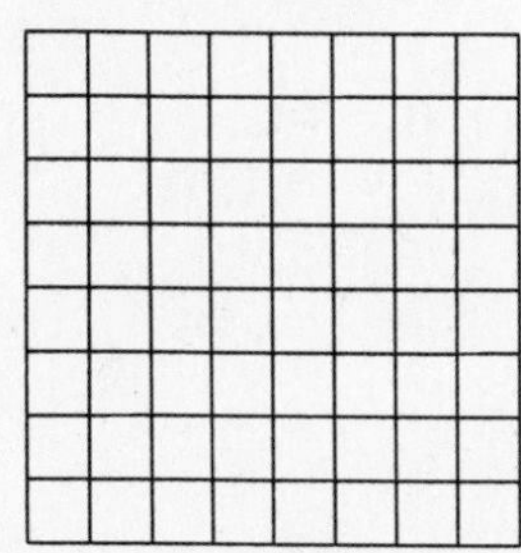

2. $y + 4 = x$
$3x + y = 0$

______

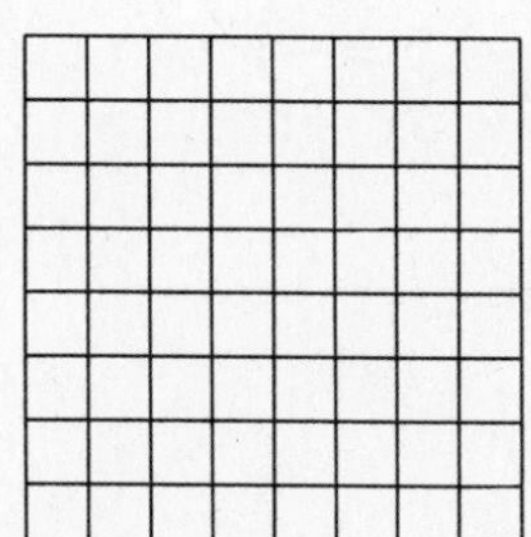

3. $y + x = 2$
$2y - x = 10$

______

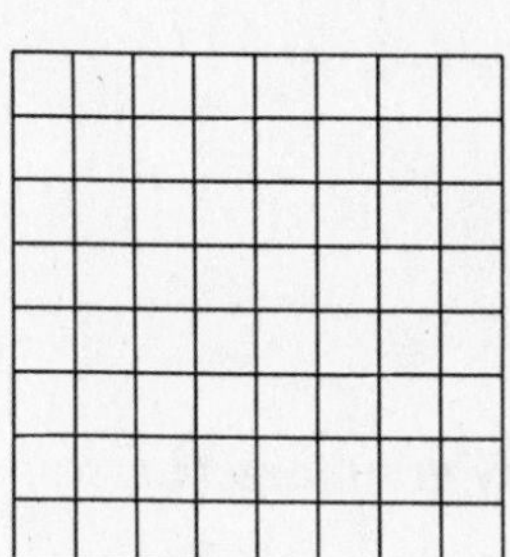

Solve. *(Lesson 7-10)*

4. Jim wants to buy a replica jersey of his favorite basketball team. The jersey comes in red or white. Jim can choose one of 15 numbers to be imprinted on the jersey; he can also have his own name or the name of one of the team's 12 players imprinted on the back. How many jersey combinations are possible? ______

5. In an 8-team soccer league, each team plays against all of the other teams once during the season. League rules require a different referee to be used for every league game. How many referees will be used during the season? ______

Mixed Review

Multiply.

6. *(5-11)* $(n^2 + 5)(n^2 + 5)$ ______

7. *(5-11)* $(x^3 + x^2 + x + 1)(x - 1)$ ______

8. *(5-11)* $3y(2y^2 - 8y + 5)$ ______

Simplify.

9. *(5-1)* $\frac{a^2b^3}{b}$ ______

10. *(5-1)* $x^5 \cdot x^3 \cdot x$ ______

11. *(5-1)* $(x^2yz^3)(xyz)$ ______

12. *(2-8)* $3x - (2x + 5)$ ______

13. *(2-8)* $2y + 6y - (2 + 5y)$ ______

14. *(2-8)* $a + b - 2(3a - b)$ ______

Add.

15. *(2-3)* $-5 + 18$ ______

16. *(2-3)* $9 + (-8)$ ______

17. *(2-3)* $-25 + 18$ ______

Name ______________________ Class ______________ Date __________

Daily Cumulative Review 8-3

Solve using the substitution method. *(Lesson 8-2)*

1. $y = -2 - 2x$
$2y + 4x = -4$

____

2. $y = x - 2$
$2x + y = 7$

____

3. $y = 2x + 3$
$2x - 2y = 2$

____

4. $x = y - 8$
$2x + y = -1$

____

5. $4x - y = -1$
$2y - 5x = 5$

____

6. $3x - y = 2$
$2y + 6 = 4x$

____

Solve by graphing. *(Lesson 8-1)*

7. $2y - x = 6$
$y + x = 6$

____

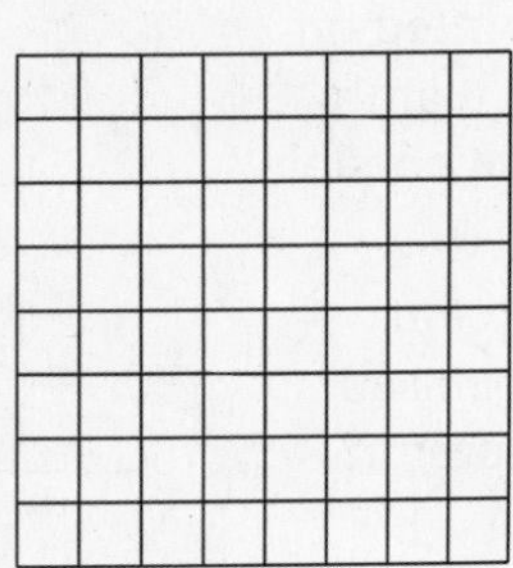

8. $y + 5 = x$
$y + 3x = -1$

____

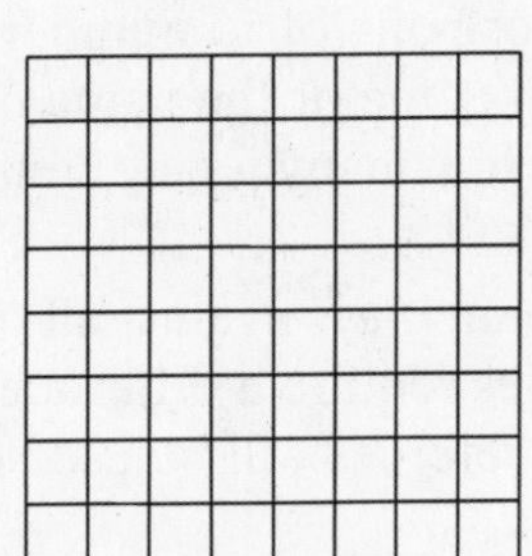

9. $y + x = -1$
$3y = 2x + 12$

____

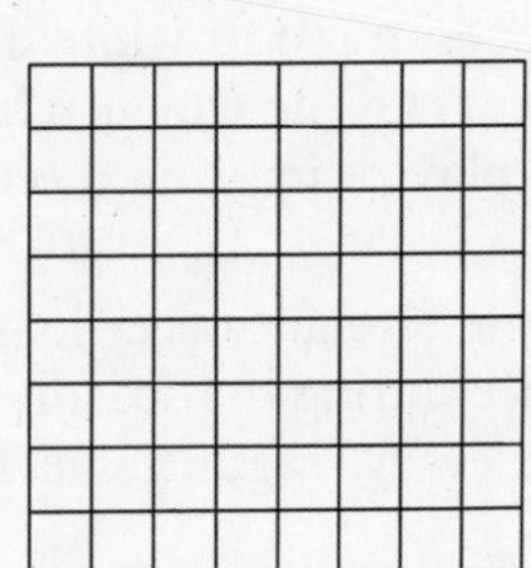

Mixed Review

Find the slope of each line by solving for *y*.

10. $2x + 4y = 9$
(7-5)

____

11. $x - 2y = 6$
(7-5)

____

12. $5y - 2x = 15$
(7-5)

____

Factor.

13. $3x^2 - 75$
(6-2)

____

14. $9y^2 - 49$
(6-2)

____

15. $0.64m^2 - 1.69$
(6-2)

____

Solve.

16. $4x - 2 = 10$
(3-3)

____

17. $3y - 8 = 19$
(3-3)

____

18. $5m + 2 = -13$
(3-3)

____

Name ____________ Class ____________ Date ____________

Daily Cumulative Review 8-4

Solve using the addition method. *(Lesson 8-3)*

1. $y - x = -2$
$2x - 3y = 1$

2. $2x + 5y = 2$
$-x - 5y = 4$

3. $2y - 6x = 2$
$x - y = 3$

4. $3y - 5x = 3$
$y - 3x = -3$

5. $2y + 3x = 3$
$x = 4 - y$

6. $5x - 4y = 6$
$x - y = 1$

Solve using the substitution method. *(Lesson 8-2)*

7. $x - y = -4$
$x - 2y = 13$

8. $2x + 5y = 1$
$x = 2 - 2y$

9. $y = x - 4$
$4y + 1 = x$

10. $x - 2y = 0$
$x = y - 4$

11. $y + 4x = 3$
$x - y = 12$

12. $y - 2x = 1$
$y = 3x - 3$

Mixed Review

Write an equation for each line that contains the given pair of points.

13. $(-2, -9), (3, 1)$ *(7-6)*

14. $(4, -7)\ (-6, 18)$ *(7-6)*

15. $(-1, -1)\ (5, -19)$ *(7-6)*

Factor.

16. $2x^2 - x - 15$ *(6-5)*

17. $3m^2 - 22m - 16$ *(6-5)*

18. $18y^2 + 39y + 18$ *(6-5)*

Multiply. Express your answer in scientific notation.

19. $(2.5 \times 10^{-3})(4.0 \times 10^{6})$ *(5-4)*

20. $(5 \times 10^{-5})(7 \times 10^{-2})$ *(5-4)*

21. $(2.4 \times 10^{6})(8.0 \times 10^{-5})$ *(5-4)*

Simplify.

22. $[(-3) + (-6)] \cdot 8$ *(2-5)*

23. $[(-3) - (-3)] + 5$ *(2-5)*

24. $(-3)^4$ *(2-5)*

Name ____________ Class ____________ Date ____________

Daily Cumulative Review 8-5

Translate to a system of equations and solve. *(Lesson 8-4)*

1. Jim has half as many marbles as Sue. Together they have 150 marbles. How many marbles does each have? ________ ________

2. A burger and three orders of fries cost \$3.86. Five burgers and two orders of fries cost \$6.43. How much does a burger cost? How much does an order of fries cost? ________ ________

3. Jeff is twice as old as Rebecca. Four years ago, Jeff's age was one more than the product of three and Rebecca's age at the time. How old are Jeff and Rebecca? ________ ________

Solve using the addition method. *(Lesson 8-3)*

4. $x + 2y = -1$
   $2x + 5y = -5$
   ____

5. $6x - y = 3$
   $y = 4x + 1$
   ____

6. $2x - 5y = 3$
   $x + 3 = y$
   ____

7. $5x - 3y = 11$
   $x + y = 7$
   ____

8. $3y - 2x = 18$
   $y - x = 8$
   ____

9. $4x - 2y = -26$
   $-x + y = 5$
   ____

Mixed Review

Solve and graph the solution.

10. $-12x < -192$ *(4-3)*
    ____

11. $4y > \frac{1}{3}$ *(4-3)*
    ____

12. $5n < 75$ *(4-3)*
    ____

Multiply.

13. $-3(2x - 5)$ *(2-7)*
    ____

14. $\frac{4}{5}(10x - 25y + 5)$ *(2-7)*
    ____

15. $5(3x + 6y - 15z)$ *(2-7)*
    ____

For each problem, tell what was done to the first equation to get the second equation.

16. $2x + 5 = 17$ *(1-7)*
    $2x = 12$
    ____

17. $n + 6 = 14$ *(1-7)*
    $n - 4 = 4$
    ____

18. $\frac{y}{5} = 16$ *(1-7)*
    $y = 80$
    ____

Name ______________________ Class ______________ Date ____________

Daily Cumulative Review 8-6

Solve. *(Lesson 8-5)*

1. Two cars leave town at the same time traveling in opposite directions. One travels 88 km/h and the other travels 72 km/h. In how many hours will they be 400 km apart?

2. It takes Jim two hours less to ride his bike from Junction City to Farmington than it takes Dave. Jim rides at 20 mi/h while Dave rides at 15 mi/h. How far is it from Junction City to Farmington?

3. A speedboat travels against a 10 km/h current for 5 hours. The return trip downstream takes 3 hours. What is the speed of the boat in still water? ____________

Translate to a system of equations and solve. *(Lesson 8-4)*

4. Alice has 136 nickels and dimes. She has 52 more nickels than dimes. How many of each coin does she have? ____________ ____________

5. Dalton's age is half of Chen's. In 10 years Chen's age will be three times what Dalton's was 5 years ago. What are their ages? ____________ ____________

Mixed Review.

Graph these linear equations using three points.

6. $y + 3x = 9$
(7-3)

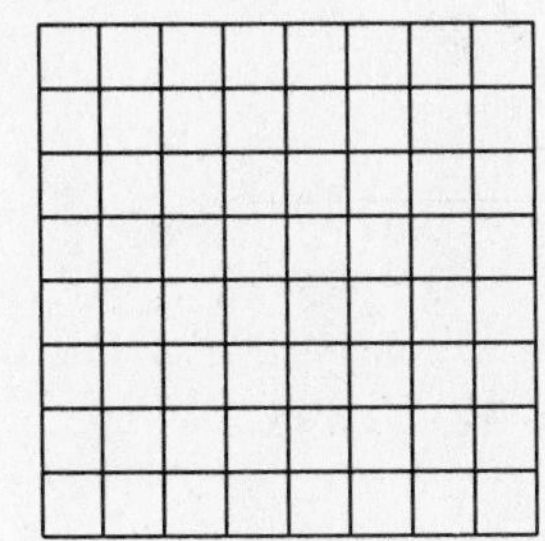

____

7. $3y - x = 3$
(7-3)

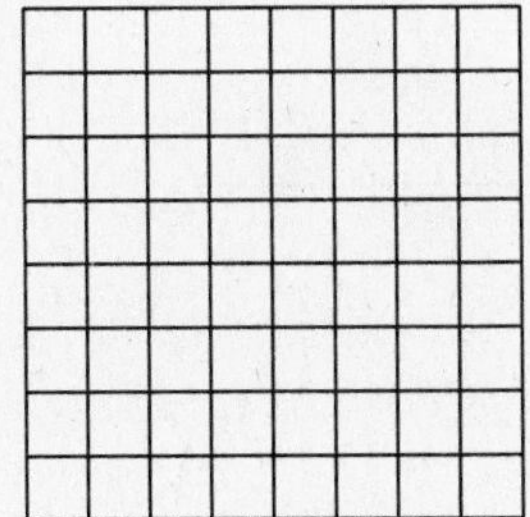

____

8. $2y - x = 4$
(7-3)

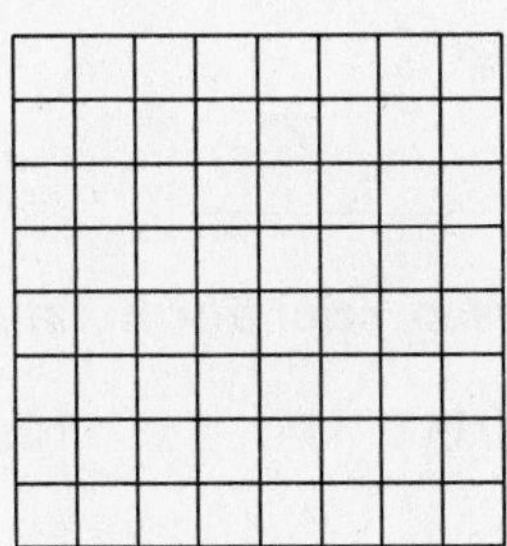

____

Factor.

9. $3x^2 + 5x$
(6-1)

____

10. $18n^5 - 10n^2$
(6-1)

____

11. $x^5 - x^3 + x^2 + x$
(6-1)

____

Solve.

12. $-5y = -40$ ____________
(3-2)

13. $\frac{-n}{5} = 16$ ____________
(3-2)

14. $\frac{2}{3}x = -34$ ____________
(3-2)

Name ______________________ Class ______________ Date __________

Daily Cumulative Review 9-1

Translate to a system of equations and solve. *(Lesson 8-6)*

1. A jar of 125 dimes and pennies contains $4.58. How many of each coin are there? ________ ________

2. The sum of the digits in a two-digit number is 12. If the digits are reversed, the new number is 36 more than the original number. Find the original number. ________ ________

3. 450 tickets were sold to a play. Tickets cost $5 for adults and $3 for students. $1600 was collected. How many of each type of ticket were sold? ________ ________

Solve. *(Lesson 8-5)*

4. Two cars leave town at the same time, traveling in the same direction. One travels at 55 mi/h, and the other at 67 mi/h. In how many hours will they be 96 mi apart? ________

5. A woman commutes to work first by train, then rides a bicycle from the station to her office. The train averages 50 mi/h, and she averages 15 mi/h on her bicycle. The total distance of her commute is 13 miles, and the combined trip takes 24 minutes. How far does she ride the train? ________

Mixed Review

Solve using the substitution method.

6. *(8-2)* $x - y = 5$, $3x + 2y = 5$ ________

7. *(8-2)* $y = x - 1$, $x - 2y = -4$ ________

8. *(8-2)* $y = 5x - 3$, $y + 7 = x$ ________

Write using scientific notation.

9. *(5-4)* 650,000 ________

10. *(5-4)* 0.000903 ________

11. *(5-4)* 15 ________

12. *(5-4)* 0.398 ________

Solve each equation for *r*.

13. *(3-7)* $d = rt$ ________

14. *(3-7)* $I = Prt$ ________

15. *(3-7)* $C = 2\pi r$ ________

Evaluate each expression for $x = 3$.

16. *(1-4)* $x^2 + 4$ ________

17. *(1-4)* $5(x + 2)$ ________

18. *(1-4)* $(2x - 4)^3$ ________

Name ______________ Class ______________ Date ______________

Daily Cumulative Review 9-2

Let $A = \{-2, -1, 0\}$, $B = \{0, 1, 2, 3, 4, 5\}$, $C = \{4, 5, 6, 7\}$, and $D = \{-1, 0, 1, 2\}$. Find each of the following. *(Lesson 9-1)*

1. $A \cap B$ ______

2. $C \cup B$ ______

3. $A \cup D$ ______

4. $A \cap D$ ______

5. $A \cup C$ ______

6. $B \cap D$ ______

7. $D \cap C$ ______

8. $A \cap C$ ______

Solve. *(Lesson 9-2)*

9. A jar of nickels and dimes contains $6.75. There are 79 coins in all. How many of each are there? ______ ______

10. A two-digit number is three less than the product of four and the sum of its digits. The tens digit is 4 less than the units digit. Find the number. ______

Mixed Review

Find the slopes of the lines containing the following points.

11. *(7-4)* $(0, 0)$ and $(2, -4)$ ______

12. *(7-4)* $(-6, 3)$ and $(12, 0)$ ______

13. *(7-4)* $(5, -9)$ and $(-6, 14)$ ______

Factor.

14. *(6-6)* $x^9 + x^5 + x^4 + 1$ ______

15. *(6-6)* $(a + b)^2 - c^2$ ______

16. *(6-6)* $25n^4 + 10n^3 + 10n^2 + 4n$ ______

Solve and graph the solutions.

17. *(4-3)* $-5n < 35$ ______

18. *(4-3)* $8 > 3n + 9n$ ______

19. *(4-3)* $3 \leq 6n$ ______

Add without using a number line.

20. *(2-3)* $-5 + (-18)$ ______

21. *(2-3)* $93 + (-200) + 6 + (-18)$ ______

22. *(2-3)* $-\frac{2}{3} + \left(-\frac{1}{6}\right)$ ______

Name ______________ Class ______________ Date ______________

Daily Cumulative Review 9-3

Graph. *(Lesson 9-2)*

1. $-2 < x$ and $x < 5$

2. $-5 \leq x$ and $x \leq 0$

3. $x < 3$ or $x > 6$

4. $x \leq -5$ or $x \geq 3$

Write using (a) roster notation and (b) set-builder notation. *(Lesson 9-1)*

5. The set N of integers less than or equal to 15.

6. The set B of positive odd integers.

7. The set M of positive multiples of 5 greater than 5.

Mixed Review

Determine whether the graphs of the equations are parallel lines.

8. *(7-8)* $2x + 6y = 12$; $3y = x + 5$

9. *(7-8)* $y = -3x + 6$; $3y = -3x + 9$

10. *(7-8)* $2y = 3x + 6$; $4y - 6x = 0$

Factor.

11. *(6-4)* $x^2 + 9x + 18$

12. *(6-4)* $y^2 - 13y + 40$

13. *(6-4)* $x^2 - xy - 2y^2$

Express as a percent. Round to the nearest tenth of a percent if necessary.

14. *(3-10)* $\frac{3}{20}$

15. *(3-10)* $\frac{6}{25}$

16. *(3-10)* $\frac{5}{8}$

17. *(3-10)* $\frac{1}{6}$

Divide.

18. *(2-6)* $\frac{2}{3} \div \left(-\frac{7}{8}\right)$

19. *(2-6)* $0 \div \left(-\frac{2}{3}\right)$

20. *(2-6)* $-9.6 \div 1.2$

Name ______________________ Class ______________ Date __________

Daily Cumulative Review 9-4

Solve. *(Lesson 9-3)*

1. $|x + 5| = 9$

2. $|x - 3| = 6$

3. $|3y - 9| = 6$

4. $-|x + 3| = -5$

5. $5|x + 2| = 15$

6. $|2x - 3| + 5 = 14$

Solve and graph. *(Lesson 9-2)*

7. $11 \leq 3x + 2 \leq 20$

8. $-16 < 2x < 20$

9. $x + 3 < 5$ or $2x + 3 > 13$

10. $x - 5 < -10$ or $2x - 3 > -3$

Mixed Review

Solve using the addition method.

11. *(8-3)* $2x + y = 12$, $x + 2y = 15$

12. *(8-3)* $x + 4y = -3$, $2x - 2y = 14$

13. *(8-3)* $9y - x = 6$, $3y + 3x = -18$

Collect like terms.

14. *(5-5)* $2x + 5x^2 - 3x$

15. *(5-5)* $5y^2 + y - 3 + 6y^2$

16. *(5-5)* $xy^2 - 2x^2y + 5x^2 + 3x^2y$

Solve.

17. *(3-3)* $6x - 9x = 15$

18. *(3-3)* $4y - 3 = 21$

19. *(3-3)* $3m + 5 = -13$

What is the meaning of each expression?

20. *(1-3)* 3^4

21. *(1-3)* $5m^2$

22. *(1-3)* y^5

23. *(1-3)* 6^1

Name ______________________ Class ______________ Date __________

Daily Cumulative Review 9-5

Solve and graph. *(Lesson 9-4)*

1. $|x| < 3$

2. $|n + 5| < 6$

3. $|4y + 3| \leq 19$

4. $|3y| < 12$

5. $|4x| \geq 20$

6. $|b - 3| > 5$

Solve. *(Lesson 9-3)*

7. $|x - 5| = 9$

8. $|3y + 4| = 19$

9. $|n + 8| = 1$

10. $3|x + 5| + 6 = 24$

11. $|2b + 5| - 7 = 12$

12. $-|y + 4| = -11$

Mixed Review

Solve by graphing.

13. *(8-1)* $y + x = 3$
$3y - 2x = -21$

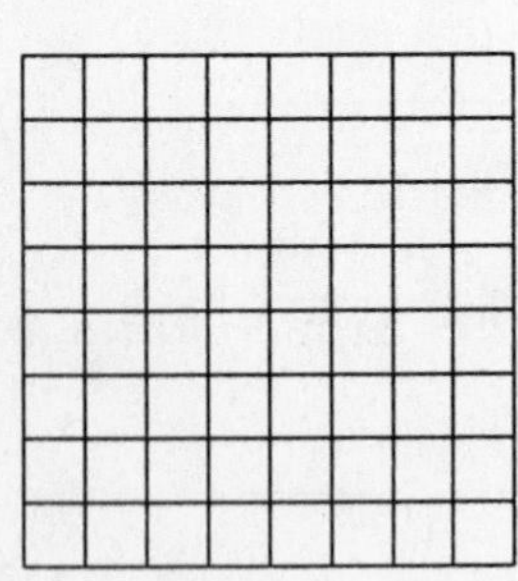

14. *(8-1)* $y - x = 5$
$y - 3x = 1$

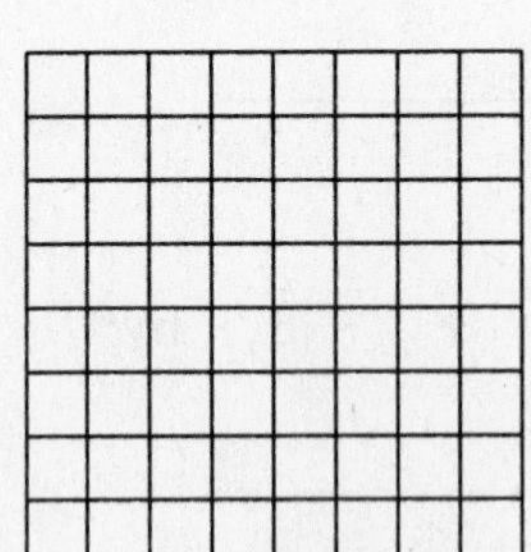

15. *(8-1)* $3y - x = 18$
$y + 2x = -1$

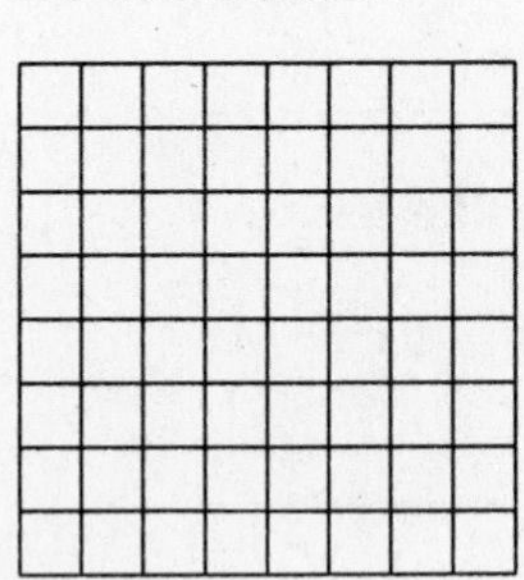

Factor.

16. *(6-2)* $25x^2 - 100$

17. *(6-2)* $2x^3 - 18x$

18. *(6-2)* $1.69x^2 - 0.64$

Add.

19. *(5-7)* $(2x^5 + 3x^4 - 2x^3) + (5x^4 + 3x^3 + x)$

20. *(5-7)* $(2x^2y^3 + 5x^2y^2) + (-6x^2y^3)$

Name ______________________ Class ______________ Date ___________

Daily Cumulative Review 9-6

Graph on a coordinate plane. *(Lesson 9-5)*

1. $y > 2x - 3$

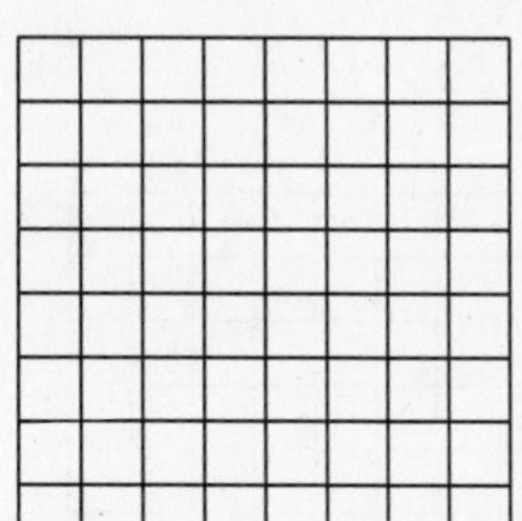

2. $x \leq 5$

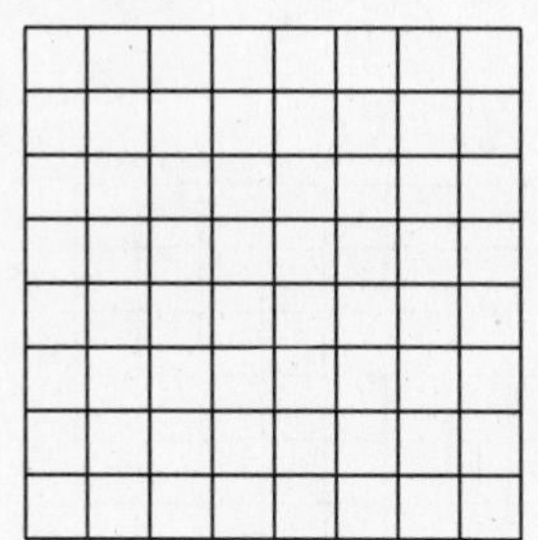

3. $x - y > -4$

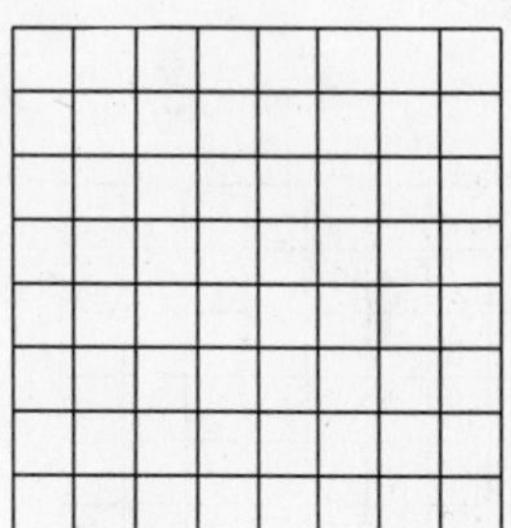

Solve and graph. *(Lesson 9-4)*

4. $|4x| \geq 24$ ____________

5. $|2x| < 16$ ____________

6. $|y - 5| > 8$ ____________

7. $|3n + 5| < 13$ ____________

8. $|2y + 7| > 9$ ____________

9. $|m + 3| < 4$ ____________

Mixed Review

Write an equation for each line that contains the given pair of points.

10. *(7-6)* $(1, -2)\ (3, 2)$ ____________

11. *(7-6)* $(-8, 6)\ (4, 3)$ ____________

12. *(7-6)* $(-2, -3)\ (4, 6)$ ____________

Simplify.

13. *(5-2)* $(x^3)^5$ ____________

14. *(5-2)* $(3y^5)^4$ ____________

15. *(5-2)* $\left(\frac{m^2}{n}\right)^8$ ____________

16. *(2-4)* $9 - (-5) + 3 - 12$ ____________

17. *(2-4)* $4 - (-5x) - 3 + 2x$ ____________

18. *(2-4)* $-42 - 19 + 3 - (-20)$ ____________

Solve.

19. *(3-5)* $3(x - 2) = 9(x + 2)$ ____________

20. *(3-5)* $5 = (3y - 6) - 19$ ____________

21. *(3-5)* $2m + 5 = 3m$ ____________

Name ____________________ Class ____________ Date ________

Daily Cumulative Review 10-1

Solve these systems by graphing. *(Lesson 9-6)*

1. $x + y > -2$
$x \leq 3$

2. $2x - 4y > 12$
$3x + 2y < 2$

3. $x - y \leq 4$
$y < 4$
$y \leq 2x$

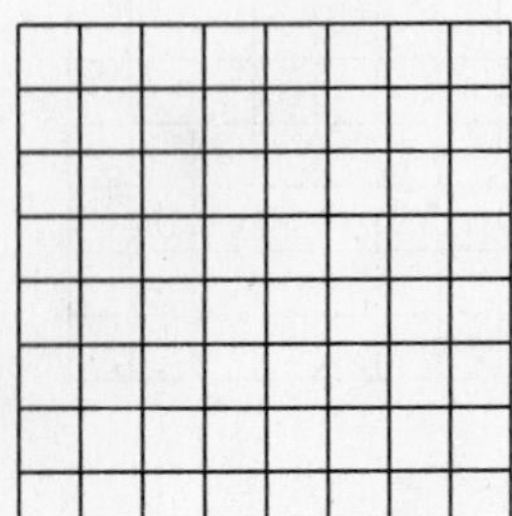

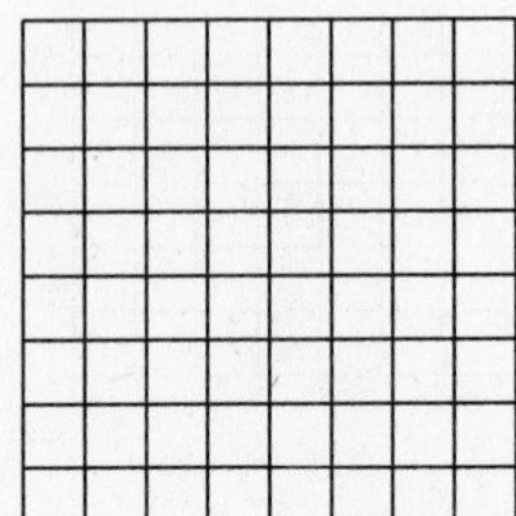

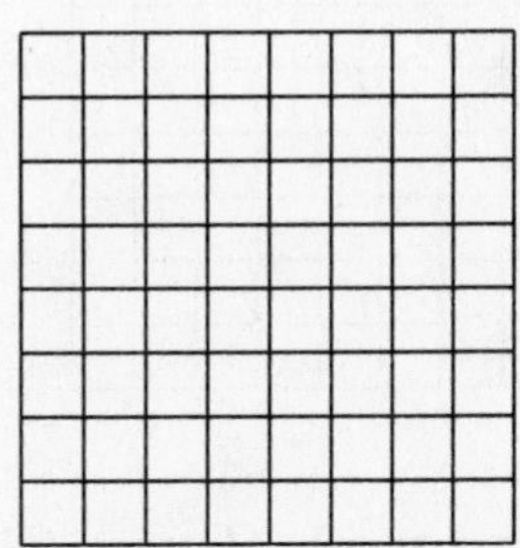

Write an inequality for each graph. *(Lesson 9-5)*

4.

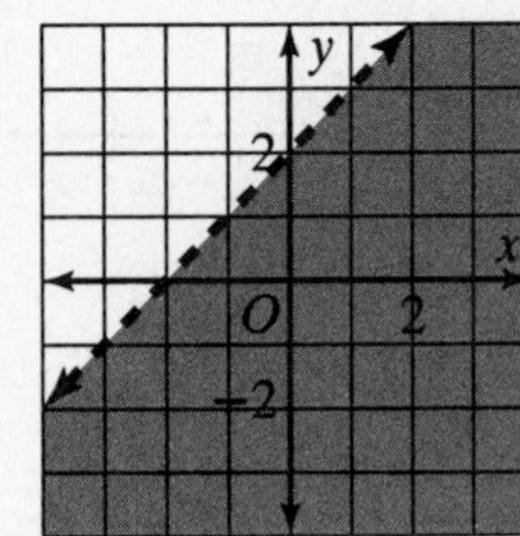

____

5.

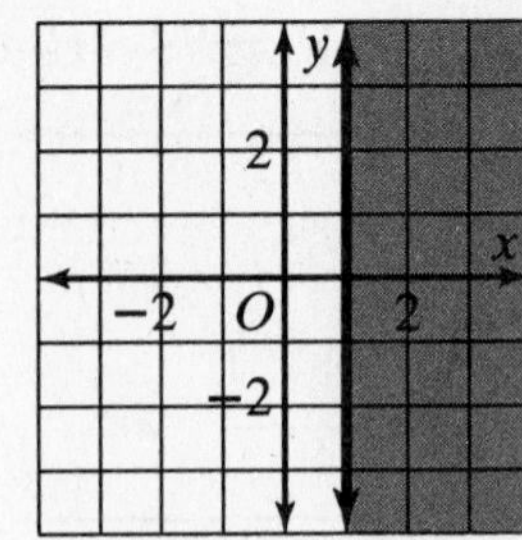

____

6.

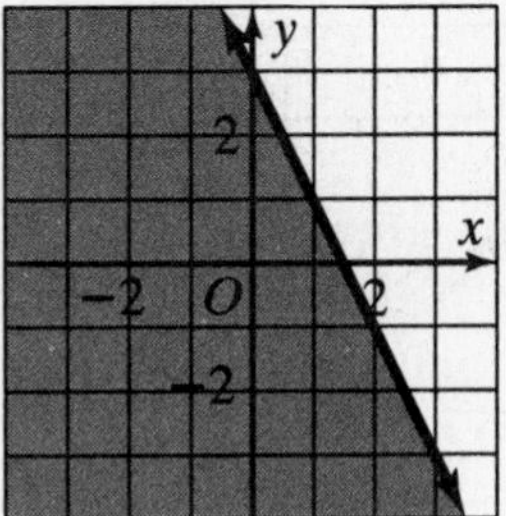

____

Mixed Review

Simplify. Express using exponents.

7. *(5-1)* $\frac{5^4}{5^2}$ ____________

8. *(5-1)* $\frac{k^7}{k^3}$ ____________

9. *(5-1)* $\frac{s^6t^2}{s^4}$ ____________

Factor.

10. *(6-1)* $a^2 - 3a$

____

11. *(6-1)* $6m^2n + 12mn^3$

____

12. *(6-1)* $x^3 - 2x^2 + 3x$

____

Solve using the substitution method.

13. *(8-2)* $x + y = 3$
$y = 2x - 3$

____

14. *(8-2)* $2s - 3t = 3$
$s = t + 2$

____

15. *(8-2)* $b - 2a = 4$
$4a - 3b = -13$

____

Name ______________________ Class ______________ Date __________

Daily Cumulative Review 10-2

Simplify. *(Lesson 10-1)*

1. $\frac{6x^4y^2}{12xy^4}$

2. $\frac{3x - 9}{3x}$

3. $\frac{z^4 - z^3}{z^7 - z^6}$

4. $\frac{a^2 + 9}{a + 3}$

5. $\frac{m^2 - 36}{m^2 + 4m - 12}$

6. $\frac{r^2 - r - 6}{r^2 + r - 12}$

Write a system of inequalities whose solution is shown by each graph. *(Lesson 9-6)*

7. 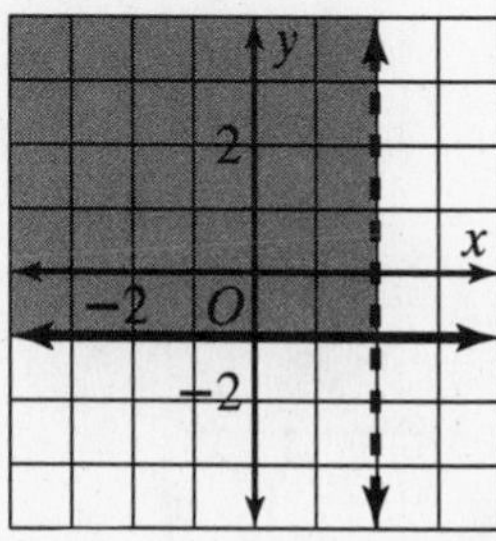

8. 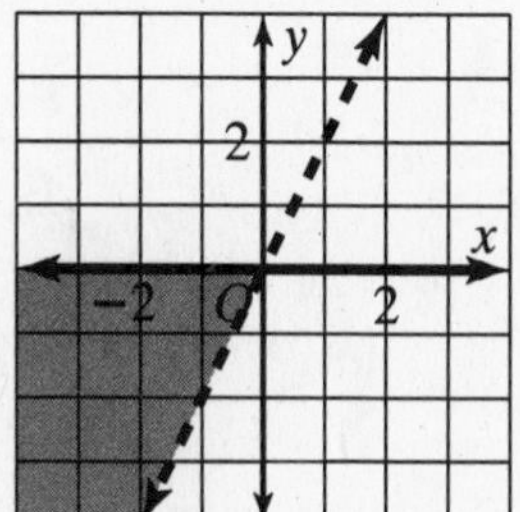

9. 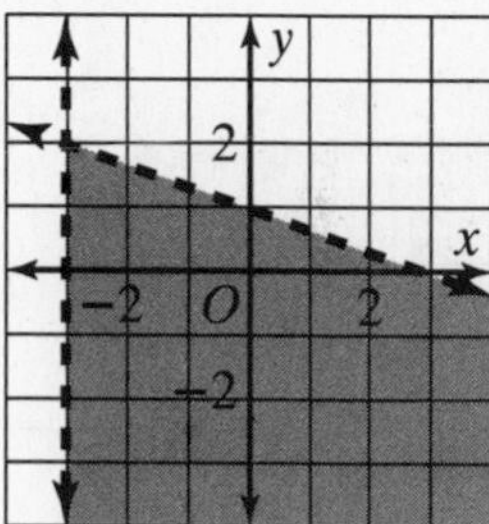

Mixed Review

Multiply.

10. $(7x^3)(-5)$ *(5-3)*

11. $(-5a^4b)(-3a^7b^8)$ *(5-3)*

12. $(4c^5)(2c^3)(-6c)$ *(5-3)*

Factor.

13. $x^2 - 8x + 15$ *(6-4)*

14. $y^2 + 15y + 26$ *(6-4)*

15. $z^2 - 2z - 35$ *(6-4)*

Write an equation for each line with the given point and slope. Express the equation in slope-intercept form.

16. $(4, 3), m = -5$ *(7-6)*

17. $(-5, 0), m = -\frac{1}{2}$ *(7-6)*

18. $(-2, -1), m = \frac{1}{7}$ *(7-6)*

Solve.

19. $5b + 3 - 8b < 9$ *(4-2)*

20. $n + \frac{1}{6} \geq \frac{1}{3}$ *(4-2)*

21. $5(q + 1) - 6q > -3$ *(4-2)*

Name ____________ Class ____________ Date ____________

Daily Cumulative Review 10-3

Multiply. Simplify the product. *(Lesson 10-2)*

1. $\frac{2x^2}{5x} \cdot \frac{10}{x^3}$

2. $\frac{7}{8a} \cdot \frac{a + 4}{14a^2}$

3. $\frac{d + 3}{4d} \cdot \frac{2d^3}{d + 3}$

4. $\frac{n - 10}{n + 8} \cdot \frac{n - 8}{n - 10}$

5. $\frac{y + 5}{y^2 + 5} \cdot \frac{y + 3}{y^2 - 25}$

6. $\frac{6x}{2x + 3} \cdot (12x + 18)$

Evaluate each expression before simplifying and after simplifying. *(Lesson 10-1)*

7. $\frac{(x + 1)^2}{x^2 - 1}$ for $x = 2$

8. $\frac{(x + 1)^2}{x^2 - 1}$ for $x = 1$

9. $\frac{7y - 21}{y - 3}$ for $y = 3$

10. $\frac{7y - 21}{y - 3}$ for $y = 5$

Mixed Review

Rewrite each division as multiplication.

11. $4 \div 7$ *(2-6)*

12. $\frac{a}{\left(\frac{1}{b}\right)}$ *(2-6)*

13. $\frac{2x - 3}{5}$ *(2-6)*

Solve. Clear the fractions first, if necessary.

14. $\frac{1}{3} + 5x = 2x - \frac{2}{3}$ *(3-6)*

15. $\frac{5}{6} - 7y = \frac{1}{2}y - \frac{1}{3}y$ *(3-6)*

16. $0.6 - 1.5z = 4 - z$ *(3-6)*

17. $1.44 + 0.72w = 0.36 - 1.2w$ *(3-6)*

Let $A = \{-4, -2, 0, 2, 4\}$, $B = \{1, 2, 3, 4\}$, and $C = \{-3, -1, 0, 1, 3\}$. Find each of the following.

18. $A \cup B$ *(9-1)*

19. $B \cap C$ *(9-1)*

20. $A \cap C$ *(9-1)*

21. $B \cap \emptyset$ *(9-1)*

22. $C \cup \emptyset$ *(9-1)*

23. $A \cup C$ *(9-1)*

Name ______________________ Class ______________ Date ________

Daily Cumulative Review 10-4

Divide and simplify. *(Lesson 10-3)*

1. $\frac{7x^5}{3} \div \frac{7x^4}{6}$ ______

2. $\frac{-6x + 2}{2} \div \frac{-9x + 3}{8}$ ______

3. $\frac{2y^2 + y - 6}{y^2 + 3y + 2} \div \frac{3y^2 - 11y - 4}{y^2 - 3y - 4}$ ______

4. $\frac{(a - 4)^4}{(a + 4)^4} \div \frac{(a - 4)^3}{(a + 4)^3}$ ______

Multiply. Simplify the product. *(Lesson 10-2)*

5. $\frac{x^2 - 7x + 12}{(x - 5)^2} \cdot \frac{x - 5}{x^2 - 16}$ ______

6. $\frac{(s - 3)^3}{(s - 2)^3} \cdot \frac{s^2 - 4s + 4}{s^2 - 6s + 9}$ ______

7. $\frac{u^2 - v^2}{2v + 3} \cdot \frac{4v^2 - 9}{u + v}$ ______

8. $\frac{b^4 - 16}{b^4 - 1} \cdot \frac{b^2 + 1}{b^2 + 4}$ ______

Mixed Review

Collect like terms.

9. $z - 4z$ *(2-8)* ______

10. $3x - 2y + 5x$ *(2-8)* ______

11. $m + m + m + 3n$ *(2-8)* ______

12. $4p + 4q + 4r + 10p$ *(2-8)* ______

13. $\frac{1}{3}a + \frac{2}{3}b - \frac{2}{3}a + \frac{1}{3}b$ *(2-8)* ______

14. $1.5c - 3.7d - 5.1c + 5d$ *(2-8)* ______

Write as an algebraic expression.

15. 3 more than z *(1-6)* ______

16. half of x *(1-6)* ______

17. 6 fewer than y *(1-6)* ______

Solve these proportions.

18. $\frac{x}{3} = \frac{36}{54}$ *(3-9)* ______

19. $\frac{3}{7} = \frac{12}{h}$ *(3-9)* ______

20. $\frac{2}{5} = \frac{y}{25}$ *(3-9)* ______

Find the reciprocal.

21. $2\frac{1}{2}$ *(2-6)* ______

22. -0.4 *(2-6)* ______

23. $\frac{2x}{7y}$ *(2-6)* ______

Name ______________________ Class ______________ Date ________

Daily Cumulative Review 10-5

Add or subtract. Simplify. *(Lesson 10-4)*

1. $\frac{4x - 2}{x + 1} + \frac{5x + 3}{x + 1}$

2. $\frac{c - 5}{c + 4} - \frac{2c - 8}{c + 4}$

3. $\frac{3x^2 - 2x + 1}{2x + 1} + \frac{x^2 + 6x}{2x + 1}$

4. $\frac{p + 7}{2p + 5} - \frac{p^2 + 3p + 4}{2p + 5}$

Divide and simplify. *(Lesson 10-3)*

5. $\frac{a^2 - 6a + 9}{a^2 + 6a + 9} \div \frac{(a - 3)^3}{(a + 3)^3}$

6. $(m + 3n) \div \frac{m^2n^2 - 9n^4}{mn^2 + 3n^3}$

7. $\frac{x^2 - 4xy}{x^4} \div (x^2 - 16y^2)$

8. $\frac{2r^2 + rs - 3s^2}{r^2 - s^2} \div (2r^2 + 5s + 3s^2)$

Mixed Review

Solve.

9. $|x + 3| = 5$ *(9-3)*

10. $|\frac{1}{2}y - 7| = 13$ *(9-3)*

11. $5|6 - z| + 4 = 19$ *(9-3)*

Complete the table for each equation. Plot the points and draw the graph.

12. $y = 1 - x^2$ *(7-2)*

x	y
–2	
–1	
0	
1	
2	

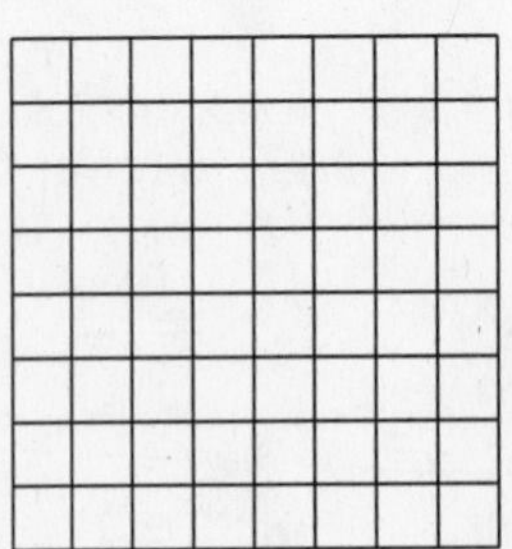

13. $y = |x| - 3$ *(7-2)*

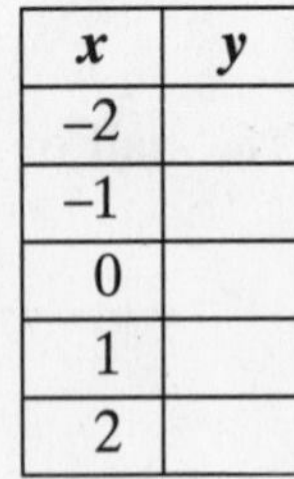

x	y
–2	
–1	
0	
1	
2	

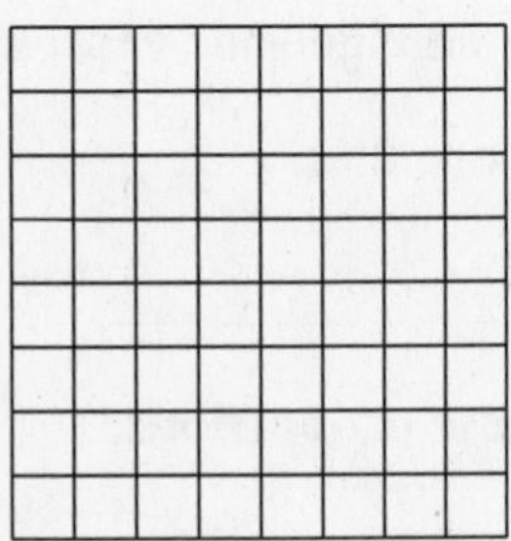

Factor by grouping.

14. $a^3 - a^2 + 3a - 3$ *(6-6)*

15. $4b^3 - 12b^2 + 5b - 15$ *(6-6)*

16. $mp + 6m - np - 6n$ *(6-6)*

Name ______________________ Class ______________ Date __________

Daily Cumulative Review 10-6

Add or subtract and simplify. *(Lesson 10-5)*

1. $\frac{5}{x} + \frac{7}{x^2}$

2. $2a + \frac{a}{a + 4}$

3. $\frac{s}{s - 1} - \frac{s + 1}{s}$

4. $\frac{2}{y + 5} - \frac{3}{y - 5}$

Add or subtract. Simplify. *(Lesson 10-4)*

5. $\frac{2a + 1}{c - 3} + \frac{5a - 2}{c - 3} + \frac{7}{c - 3}$

6. $\frac{b^2 - 6b}{4b + 7} - \frac{2b^2 + 5b}{4b + 7} - \frac{b^2 - 6}{4b + 7}$

7. $\frac{5m^2 + 6m + 9}{(2m + 1)(3m - 1)} + \frac{m^2 + 2m + 1}{(2m + 1)(3m - 1)} - \frac{4m^2 + 5m + 9}{(2m + 1)(3m - 1)}$

8. $\frac{k^2 + 4k + 4}{(k - 5)(2k - 9)} - \frac{2k^2 - 2k + 2}{(k - 5)(2k - 9)} + \frac{2k^2 - 9k - 12}{(k - 5)(2k - 9)}$

Mixed Review

Multiply.

9. *(5-11)* $(y - 2)(y^2 + 2y + 4)$

10. *(5-11)* $(m - 1)(m^3 + m^2 + m + 1)$

11. *(5-11)* $(a^2 + 2a + 1)(a^2 - 2a - 1)$

12. *(5-11)* $(x^6 - 2x^4 - 3x^2)(x^4 + 2x^2 + 3)$

Solve by graphing.

13. *(8-1)* $x + y = 2$
$x - y = -4$

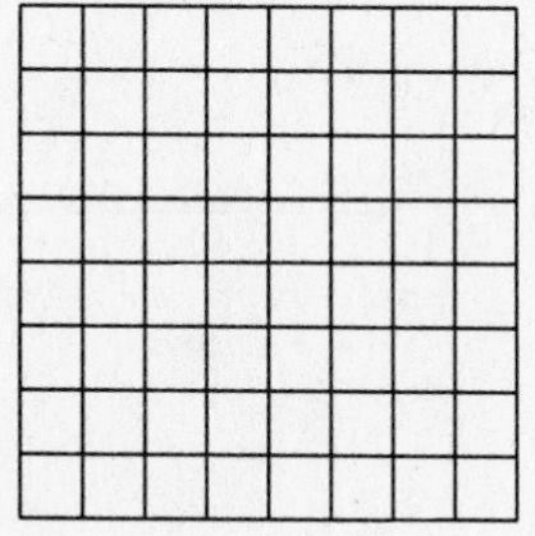

14. *(8-1)* $y = 2x$
$3x - y = 1$

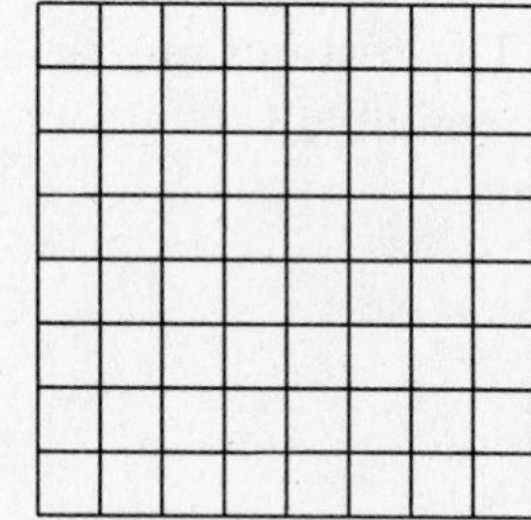

15. *(8-1)* $y = \frac{1}{2}x - 2$
$2x + y = -2$

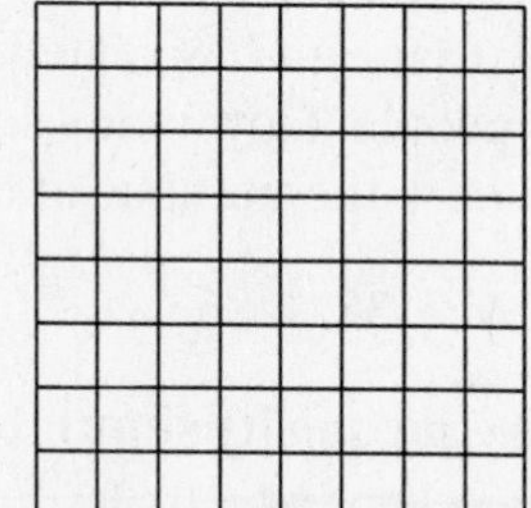

Name ______________________ Class ______________ Date __________

Daily Cumulative Review 10-7

Solve. *(Lesson 10-6)*

1. $x + \frac{5}{x} = -6$ ______

2. $\frac{7}{h} + \frac{9}{2h} = 1$ ______

3. $\frac{3}{m + 5} = \frac{2}{m - 3}$ ______

4. $\frac{y - 3}{y - 7} = \frac{4}{y - 7}$ ______

5. $\frac{a - 4}{a + 5} = \frac{a - 2}{a + 2}$ ______

6. $\frac{3b + 1}{4b - 3} = \frac{3b}{4b + 5}$ ______

Find the LCM. *(Lesson 10-5)*

7. $3(z - 2), 9(2 - z)$ ______

8. $w + 10, w - 10$ ______

9. $x^2 - 16, x^2 + x - 20$ ______

10. $3y^2 - 8y - 3, 3y^2 - 11y + 6$ ______

Mixed Review

Write as an algebraic expression.

11. 5 less than the product of 3 and a number ______
(3-4)

12. $\frac{1}{5}$ the difference of a number and 10 ______
(3-4)

13. 7 more than the quotient of 9 and a number ______
(3-4)

Which equation(s) can be used to solve each problem?

14. Two dozen roses cost $120. How much is each rose?
(2-9) Let r = the cost of each rose. ______

A. $120 \div 24 = r$ **B.** $120 - r = 24$ **C.** $24r = 120$

15. A restaurant has seated 35 patrons. The restaurant's seating capacity is
(2-9) 86 people. How many seats are still available?
Let a = the number of available seats. ______

A. $a = 35 + 86$ **B.** $35 + a = 86$ **C.** $a = 86 - 35$

Write the inequality shown by the graph.

16. 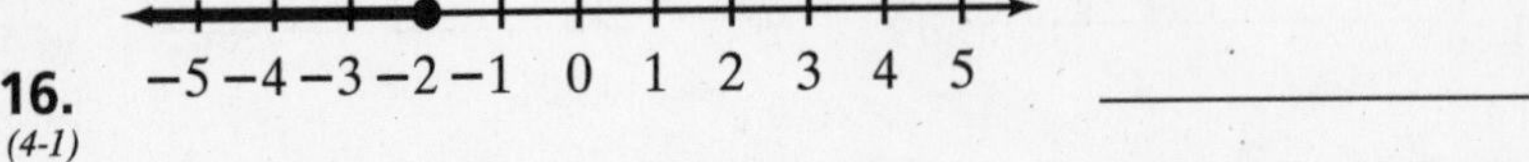

(4-1) ______

Name ________________ Class ________________ Date ________

Daily Cumulative Review 10-8

Solve. *(Lesson 10-7)*

1. If worker A can complete a certain job in 2 hours and worker B can complete the same job in 3 hours, how long will it take them to complete the job if they work together? ________

2. One car travels 20 mi/h faster than another. In the time it takes for one to travel 100 mi the other travels 140 mi. Find their speeds. ________ ________

3. The reciprocal of 6 plus the reciprocal of what number is the reciprocal of 10? ________

Solve. *(Lesson 10-6)*

4. $\frac{1}{x-1} - \frac{1}{x+1} = \frac{2x}{x^2-1}$ ________

5. $\frac{2x}{x^2+x-2} + \frac{3x}{x^2-3x+2} = \frac{x}{x^2-4}$ ________

6. $1 - \frac{b^2+9}{b+3} = \frac{b-7}{b+3}$ ________

Mixed Review

Solve using the strategy *Make a Table.*

7. A small company doubles its annual profit every year for a period of 5 years.
(5-12) The first year its profit was \$50,000. If the company continues in this manner, in which year will their annual profit first be over \$1,000,000? ________

Write an expression for each of the following.

8. A pitcher has 3 times as much water as orange juice concentrate in it.
(3-11) Let c = the number of ounces of orange juice concentrate. Write an expression for the total amount of liquid in the pitcher. ________

9. Brand *A* Mixed Nuts is one half peanuts and Brand *B* Mixed Nuts is
(3-11) one third peanuts. Let a = the number of cups of Brand *A*. Write an expression for the total amount of peanuts in a 5 cup mixture of Brand *A* and Brand *B*. ________

The formula $I = prt$ gives a rule for determining the amount of simple interest (I) paid on a principal amount (p) at a rate (r) for a term of t years. Find the amount of simple interest (I) for the given values of p, r, and t.

10. p = \$5000, r = 15%, t = 5 years
(1-9)

____

11. p = \$1000, r = 5%, t = 20 years
(1-9)

____

Name ____________________ Class ____________________ Date ____________

Daily Cumulative Review 10-9

Solution A is 70% acid and solution B is 40% acid. These solutions will be mixed to produce 1 gal of solution that is 50% acid. Use this information for Exercises 1 and 2. *(Lesson 10-8)*

1. Let x be the amount of solution A (in gallons). Complete the columns to show expressions for the amount of solution, percent of acid, and amount of acid in each solution.

	Amount of solution	Percent acid	Amount of acid
Solution A			
Solution B			
Final solution			

2. How much of each solution should be used to make 1 gal of a solution that is 50% acid?

__________ __________

Solve. *(Lesson 10-7)*

3. If team A can complete a job in 3 h and team A together with team B can complete the job in 1 h, how long will it take team B to complete the job, working alone? __________

4. If a tub takes 5 min to fill and 9 min to drain, how long will it take to fill if the drain is open? __________

Mixed Review

Factor.

5. $4s^2 - 36$ *(6-7)* __________

6. $t^3 + 12t^2 + 36t$ *(6-7)* __________

7. $u^3 - u^2 - 16u + 16$ *(6-7)* __________

Solve.

8. $A = \frac{a + b}{2}$, for a *(3-7)* __________

9. $y = mx + b$, for m *(3-7)* __________

10. $a^2 + b^2 = c^2$, for b^2 *(3-7)* __________

Determine whether the graphs of the equations are parallel lines.

11. *(7-8)* $3x - 2y = 6$
$12x - 8y = 24$ __________

12. *(7-8)* $x = \frac{1}{3}y - 7$
$3x - y = 5$ __________

Name ____________________ Class ____________ Date ________

Daily Cumulative Review 10-10

Divide. *(Lesson 10-9)*

1. $\frac{6t^2 - 3t + 4}{2}$ ____________

2. $\frac{3t^3 + 15t^2 + 8t}{3t}$ ____________

3. $\frac{4a^3b^2 - 7a^2b^3 - 12ab^4}{2ab^2}$ ____________

4. $(x^2 - 5x + 6) \div (x - 2)$ ____________

5. $(v^3 - v + 1) \div (v + 1)$ ____________

6. $\frac{6s^3 - 3s^2 + 2s - 1}{2s - 1}$ ____________

Solve. *(Lesson 10-8)*

7. A chemist wishes to make 2 L of a 70% alcohol solution from a 50% alcohol solution and an 80% alcohol solution. How much of each solution should be used? ________ ________

8. A store wishes to make a mixture of peanuts and cashews that will sell for $6.40 per pound. If the peanuts sell for $4.90 per pound and the cashews sell for $9.40 per pound how much of each should be used to make a 3-pound mixture? ________ ________

Mixed Review

Solve.

9. *(3-6)* $\frac{9}{5} - \frac{m}{5} + \frac{3}{5} = 1 - \frac{2}{3}m$ ____________

10. *(3-6)* $\frac{1}{4}x - \frac{1}{3} = -\frac{2}{3}$ ____________

11. *(3-6)* $2.5 - 0.9x = 1.5 - 0.4x$ ____________

Solve by drawing a diagram.

12. *(1-8)* Luci is rolling out pastry dough to make croissants. The dough is in a 12 in. by 18 in. rectangle, and she is going to cut out triangles shaped as shown at the right. How many triangles of this shape can she cut out of the dough? ____________

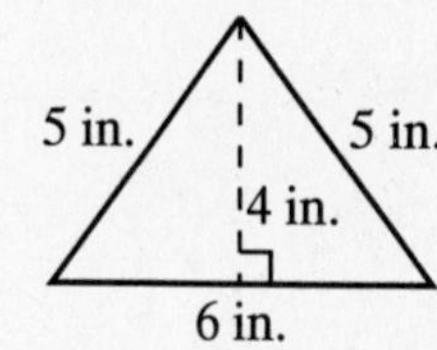

Add or subtract.

13. *(5-7)* $(4x^3 - 5x^2 + x - 3) + (-x^3 - 7x^2 + 10)$ ____________

14. *(5-8)* $(6y^4 - 3y^3 + y^2) - (y^3 - 2y^2 + y - 13)$ ____________

Name ______________ Class ______________ Date ______________

Daily Cumulative Review 10-11

Simplify. *(Lesson 10-10)*

1. $\dfrac{\frac{1}{2}+\frac{1}{3}}{\frac{1}{4}}$ ______

2. $\dfrac{1+\frac{1}{x}}{\frac{1}{x^2}}$ ______

3. $\dfrac{\frac{3}{5}-1}{1+\frac{1}{4}}$ ______

4. $\dfrac{\frac{1}{b}+1}{b-\frac{1}{b}}$ ______

5. $\dfrac{a+\frac{1}{b}}{b-\frac{1}{a}}$ ______

6. $\dfrac{\left(\frac{v}{u-v}\right)}{\left(\frac{u+v}{u^2-v^2}\right)}$ ______

Divide. *(Lesson 10-9)*

7. $(2x^3 + 4x^2 - 5x - 1) \div (x^2 + x - 2)$ ______

8. $(a^4 + 2a^2 - 5) \div (a^2 - 4)$ ______

9. $(r^4 - s^4) \div (r + s)$ ______

Mixed Review

Solve using the strategy *Use Logical Reasoning*.

10. *(4-6)* Jose, Karenna, Tami, Denison, and Ely participated in a walkathon. Tami finished first. Denison finished before Ely and Karenna but after Jose. Ely finished last. In what order did they finish?

______

Multiply.

11. *(5-9)* $7x(-x + 8)$ ______

12. *(5-9)* $(5x - 3)(x + 6)$ ______

13. *(5-9)* $(3x + 4y)(3x - 4y)$ ______

Show that each integer can be written as the ratio of two integers.

14. *(2-2)* 21 ______

15. *(2-2)* 1.3 ______

16. *(2-2)* -0.33 ______

17. *(2-2)* $4\frac{1}{3}$ ______

18. *(2-2)* -6 ______

19. *(2-2)* $-1\frac{2}{5}$ ______

Tell whether each pair of expressions is equivalent.

20. *(1-2)* $ab + cd$ and $ba + dc$ ______

21. *(1-2)* $ab + cd$ and $cd + ab$ ______

22. *(1-2)* $ab + c$ and $ac + b$ ______

23. *(1-2)* ab and $a + b$ ______

Name ______________________ Class ______________ Date __________

Daily Cumulative Review 10-12

Complete the proof of the following theorem by supplying the reasons. *(Lesson 10-11)*

Theorem: For any rational number a, and non-zero rational numbers b, c, and d,

$$\frac{a}{b} \div \frac{c}{d} = \frac{ad}{bc}$$

Proof

a. $\frac{a}{b} \div \frac{c}{d} = \frac{a}{b} \cdot \frac{d}{c}$	**1.** ______________
b. $\frac{a}{b} = a \cdot \frac{1}{b}$ and $\frac{d}{c} = d \cdot \frac{1}{c}$	**2.** ______________
c. $\frac{a}{b} \cdot \frac{d}{c} = \left(a \cdot \frac{1}{b}\right)\left(d \cdot \frac{1}{c}\right)$	**3.** ______________
d. $= (a \cdot d)\left(\frac{1}{b} \cdot \frac{1}{c}\right)$	**4.** ______________
e. $= ad\left(\frac{1}{bc}\right)$	**5.** ______________
f. $= \frac{ad}{bc}$	**6.** ______________
g. $\frac{a}{b} \div \frac{c}{d} = \frac{ad}{bc}$	**7.** ______________

Simplify. *(Lesson 10-10)*

8. $\dfrac{\left(\frac{1}{a+b} + \frac{1}{a^2 - b^2}\right)}{\left(\frac{a}{a+b} - \frac{b}{a-b}\right)}$ ______________

9. $\dfrac{\left(\frac{s}{t-1} + \frac{t}{s-1}\right)}{\left(\frac{st}{st - s - t + 1}\right)}$ ______________

10. $\dfrac{\left(\frac{x+1}{x^2} - \frac{1}{x+1}\right)}{\left(\frac{x}{x-1}\right)}$ ______________

Mixed Review

Solve using the *Try, Test, Revise* strategy.

11. *(1-10)* One number is 3 times another number. Their sum is 16. What are the two numbers? ______________ ______________

12. *(1-10)* The length of a rectangle is 5 cm greater than the width. The perimeter of the rectangle is 30 cm. What are the length and width of the rectangle? ______________ ______________

Evaluate each polynomial for the given value.

13. *(5-6)* $x^2 + 3x$ for $x = 4$ ______________

14. *(5-6)* $5x^4 - 3x + 7$ for $x = -2$ ______________

Find the slopes of the lines containing these points.

15. *(7-4)* $(-3, 5)$ and $(5, 21)$ ______________

16. *(7-4)* $(4, 7)$ and $(0, 13)$ ______________

Name ______________________ Class ______________ Date ____________

Daily Cumulative Review 11-1

Solve. *(Lesson 10-12)*

1. Jill brought a basket of cherries to the office to share with her co-workers. Pete took $\frac{1}{8}$ of the cherries. Bruce took the same number of cherries as Pete. Later, Merle took $\frac{1}{6}$ of the remaining cherries. At the end of the day, Leanne took $\frac{1}{2}$ of the cherries that were left, leaving 30 cherries for Jill to take home. How many cherries did she bring to work? ____________

2. For a certain number, one quarter of it, one sixth of it, and two thirds of it are added together, and the result is 78. What is the number? ____________

Complete the proof of the following theorem by supplying the reasons. *(Lesson 10-11)*

Theorem: For any number a and any non-zero numbers b and c, if $\frac{a}{b} = \frac{1}{c}$, then $ac = b$.

Proof

a. $\frac{a}{b}(bc) = \frac{1}{c}(bc)$	**3.** ____________
b. $\left(a \cdot \frac{1}{b}\right)(bc) = \frac{1}{c}(bc)$	**4.** ____________
c. $\left(a \cdot \frac{1}{b}\right)(bc) = \frac{1}{c}(cb)$	**5.** ____________
d. $a\left(\frac{1}{b} \cdot b\right)c = \left(\frac{1}{c} \cdot c\right)b$	**6.** ____________
e. $a \cdot 1 \cdot c = 1 \cdot b$	**7.** ____________
f. $ac = b$	**8.** ____________

Mixed Review

Simplify.

9. *(10-1)* $\dfrac{12x^2y^3}{-4xy^2}$ ____________

10. *(10-1)* $\dfrac{n^2 - 36}{n^2 + 12n + 36}$ ____________

11. *(10-1)* $\dfrac{b^2 - b - 30}{b^2 + b - 20}$ ____________

Solve and graph.

12. *(9-2)* $-5 \le x + 3 < 7$ ____________

13. *(9-2)* $-7 < 2x - 3 < 11$ ____________

14. *(9-2)* $-6 \le 3x \le 18$ ____________

Write using standard notation.

15. *(5-4)* 4.8×10^{-3} ____________

16. *(5-4)* 7.005×10^{6} ____________

Name ______________________ Class ______________ Date ____________

Daily Cumulative Review 11-2

Identify each square root as rational or irrational. *(Lesson 11-1)*

1. $\sqrt{3}$ ____ **2.** $-\sqrt{81}$ ____ **3.** $\sqrt{24}$ ____ **4.** $\sqrt{1}$ ____

5. $-\sqrt{50}$ ____ **6.** $\sqrt{169}$ ____ **7.** $\sqrt{125}$ ____ **8.** $\sqrt{300}$ ____

Solve. *(Lesson 10-12)*

9. Twelve plus two thirds of a given number, when divided in half, equals the square root of 64. What is the number? ____

10. Jim had twice as many baseball cards as Mike, who had 10 fewer than Justin, who had 6 more than Jason. Jason had 40 cards. How many cards did the four boys have together? ____

Mixed Review

Solve.

11. *(9-4)* $|2x + 3| \leq 11$ ____ **12.** *(9-4)* $|3x - 2| < 8$ ____ **13.** *(9-4)* $|4x + 2| > 0$ ____

Solve using the addition method.

14. *(8-3)* $x + 2y = 1$, $2x + 5y = 4$ ____

15. *(8-3)* $x - y = -3$, $3x - 2y = 0$ ____

16. *(8-3)* $3x + y = 1$, $5x + 2y = -1$ ____

Multiply.

17. *(5-10)* $(2x^2 + 3)(2x^2 - 3)$ ____ **18.** *(5-10)* $(3x - 2y)^2$ ____ **19.** *(5-10)* $\left(3x + \frac{1}{2}\right)\left(3x - \frac{1}{2}\right)$ ____

Solve.

20. *(3-3)* $4x + 5 = -31$ ____ **21.** *(3-3)* $2x + 6x = -56$ ____ **22.** *(3-3)* $7(n - 5) = 28$ ____

Calculate.

23. *(1-4)* $(10 - 3)^2$ ____ **24.** *(1-4)* $12 - 3^2$ ____ **25.** *(1-4)* $2 \cdot 3^3$ ____

Name ______________ Class ______________ Date ______________

Daily Cumulative Review 11-3

Simplify. *(Lesson 11-2)*

1. $\sqrt{25x^2}$ ______________

2. $\sqrt{b^2 + 6b + 9}$ ______________

3. $\sqrt{(-8)^2}$ ______________

4. $\sqrt{\frac{196}{n^8}}$ ______________

5. $\sqrt{(5x)^3(5x)^3}$ ______________

6. $\sqrt{y^2 - 26y + 169}$ ______________

Simplify. *(Lesson 11-1)*

7. $\sqrt{484}$ ______________

8. $-\sqrt{64}$ ______________

9. $-\sqrt{1}$ ______________

10. $-\sqrt{289}$ ______________

11. $\sqrt{40^2 + 9^2}$ ______________

12. $\sqrt{\sqrt{81}}$ ______________

13. $\left(\sqrt{9 + 16}\right)^2$ ______________

14. $\left(\sqrt{9} + \sqrt{16}\right)^2$ ______________

Mixed Review

Multiply. Simplify the product.

15. *(10-2)* $\frac{y - 2}{y + 3} \cdot \frac{y + 4}{y - 2}$ ______________

16. *(10-2)* $\frac{2}{x} \cdot \frac{x^3}{2x + 4}$ ______________

17. *(10-2)* $\frac{3y^2}{y} \cdot \frac{3}{12y}$ ______________

Graph each line using the *y*-intercept and slope.

18. *(7-5)* $y = \frac{3}{2}x - 3$

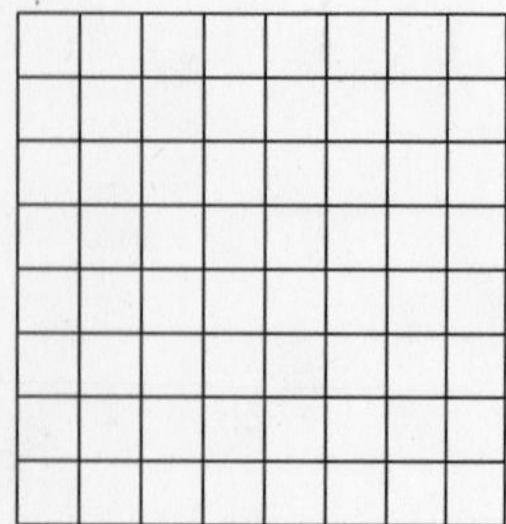

19. *(7-5)* $y + 4 = \frac{1}{2}x$

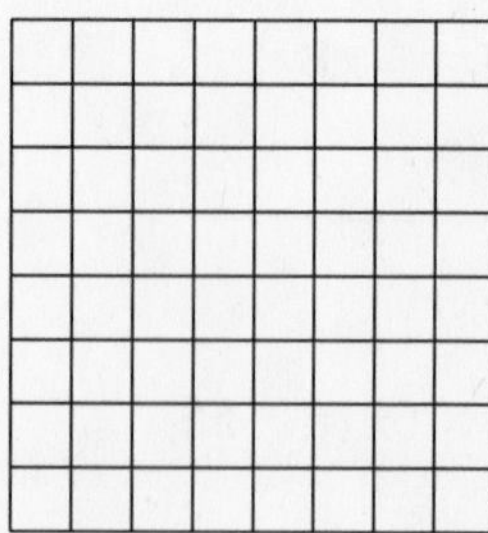

20. *(7-5)* $y + 2x = 5$

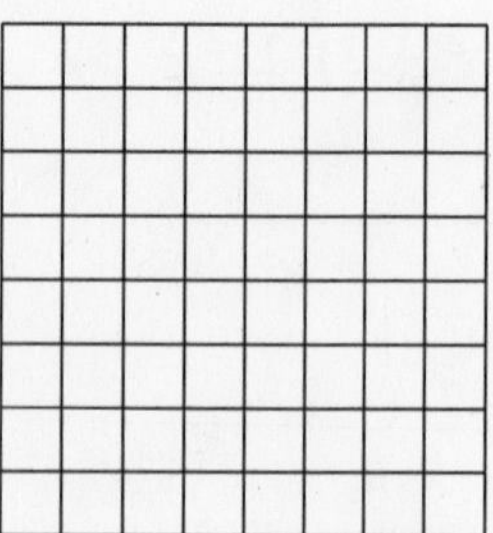

Solve.

21. *(6-8)* $6x^2 = 9x$ ______________

22. *(6-8)* $y^2 - 3y = 18$ ______________

23. *(4-3)* $63x \leq 7$ ______________

24. *(4-3)* $-15 > 2x - 7x$ ______________

Name ______________________ Class ______________ Date __________

Daily Cumulative Review 11-4

Simplify. Assume that all variables are nonnegative. *(Lesson 11-3)*

1. $\sqrt{63}$ ________
2. $\sqrt{12t^3}$ ________
3. $\sqrt{27s^2}$ ________
4. $\sqrt{21}$ ________
5. $\sqrt{40}$ ________
6. $\sqrt{9b^5}$ ________
7. $\sqrt{3x^2 + 18x + 27}$ ________
8. $\sqrt{4x^2 + 16xy + 16y^2}$ ________
9. $\sqrt{200(x + 3)^7}$ ________

Simplify. *(Lesson 11-2)*

10. $\sqrt{25x^4}$ ________
11. $\sqrt{(2a^2)(2a^2)}$ ________
12. $\sqrt{(2a^2)^2(2a^2)^2}$ ________
13. $\sqrt{4(y^2 + 1)^6}$ ________
14. $\sqrt{\frac{9s^2}{16t^8}}$ ________
15. $\sqrt{\frac{1}{u^{10}}}$ ________
16. $\sqrt{\frac{x^6}{4}}$ ________
17. $\sqrt{\frac{x^8}{4}}$ ________
18. $\sqrt{\frac{d^{10}}{c^{10}}}$ ________

Mixed Review

Evaluate for $x = -3$, $y = -7$, and $z = 5$.

19. $yz - x$ *(2-5)* ________
20. $2x - 3y + 10z$ *(2-5)* ________
21. $-4(x - 2y) + 6z$ *(2-5)* ________

Solve.

22. $4m - 3 = 13(m - 3)$ *(3-5)* ________
23. $\frac{2n - 3}{3} = 2n + 3$ *(3-5)* ________
24. $4(3p + 1) = -2(1 - 3p)$ *(3-5)* ________

Factor.

25. $x^2 - 6x + 9$ *(6-3)* ________
26. $9y^2 + 24xy + 16x^2$ *(6-3)* ________
27. $z^4 - 16$ *(6-3)* ________

In what quadrant is each point located?

28. $(-5, 6)$ *(7-1)* ________
29. $(2, -3)$ *(7-1)* ________
30. $(4, 1)$ *(7-1)* ________
31. $(-1, 8)$ *(7-1)* ________

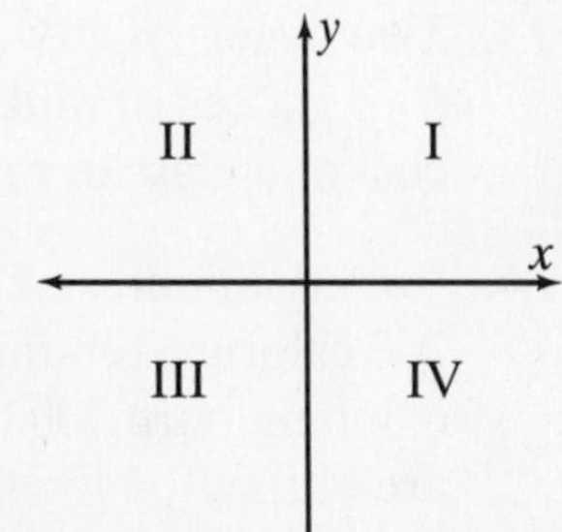

Name ______________________ Class ______________ Date __________

Daily Cumulative Review 11-5

Multiply and simplify. *(Lesson 11-4)*

1. $\sqrt{8} \cdot \sqrt{2}$ ________

2. $\sqrt{8} \cdot \sqrt{4}$ ________

3. $\sqrt{2xy} \cdot \sqrt{6x^3y^2}$ ________

4. $\sqrt{2ab^3} \cdot \sqrt{10a^2b^2c}$ ________

5. $\sqrt{st^5} \cdot \sqrt{7t} \cdot \sqrt{14s}$ ________

6. $\sqrt{x^2} \cdot \sqrt{x}$ ________

Evaluate and simplify for $x = 3$ and $y = \sqrt{3}$. *(Lesson 11-3)*

7. $\sqrt{6 + x^2}$ ________

8. $\sqrt{6 + y^2}$ ________

9. $\sqrt{x + y^2}$ ________

10. $\sqrt{x - y^2}$ ________

11. $\sqrt{x^3 - y^2}$ ________

12. $\sqrt{x^4 - y^6}$ ________

Mixed Review

Write with a single exponent.

13. *(1-3)* $\frac{3^5}{3^2}$ ________

14. *(1-3)* $\frac{7^8}{7^6}$ ________

15. *(1-3)* $\frac{2^{10}}{2^3}$ ________

16. *(1-3)* $\frac{5^7}{5^6}$ ________

Divide.

17. *(2-6)* $18 \div (-3)$ ________

18. *(2-6)* $\frac{-300}{-25}$ ________

19. *(2-6)* $-51 \div (17)$ ________

Multiply. Simplify the product.

20. *(10-2)* $\frac{-3}{r} \cdot \frac{r^4}{r - 3}$ ________

21. *(10-2)* $\frac{7s}{3} \cdot \frac{s + 5}{21s^2}$ ________

22. *(10-2)* $\frac{t - 6}{t + 3} \cdot \frac{t + 3}{t + 6}$ ________

Translate to a system of equations and solve.

23. *(8-4)* Two bagels and two glasses of milk cost $2.90. Three bagels and four glasses of milk cost $4.80. Find the cost of a bagel and the cost of a glass of milk. ________ ________

24. *(8-4)* Twenty minutes of jogging and ten minutes of stair climbing burn 250 calories. Ten minutes of jogging and twenty minutes of stair climbing burn 200 calories. Find how many calories per minute are burned by jogging and how many calories per minute are burned by stair climbing. ________ ________

Name ______________________ Class ______________ Date __________

Daily Cumulative Review 11-6

Simplify. *(Lesson 11-5)*

1. $\sqrt{\frac{25}{81}}$ __________
2. $\sqrt{\frac{1}{49}}$ __________
3. $-\sqrt{\frac{25}{9}}$ __________
4. $\sqrt{\frac{50}{98}}$ __________
5. $\frac{\sqrt{20}}{\sqrt{5}}$ __________
6. $\frac{\sqrt{5}}{\sqrt{3}}$ __________
7. $\sqrt{\frac{1}{2}}$ __________
8. $\frac{5}{\sqrt{x}}$ __________
9. $\frac{\sqrt{6x^2}}{\sqrt{xy^2z}}$ __________

Multiply and simplify. *(Lesson 11-4)*

10. $\sqrt{x}(\sqrt{x} + \sqrt{x^3})$ __________
11. $\sqrt{0.01s^{2n}} \cdot \sqrt{s}$ __________
12. $\sqrt{4x^2 + 8x + 4} \cdot \sqrt{(x + 1)^3}$ __________
13. $\sqrt{u}(\sqrt{2u^3} - 2)$ __________

Mixed Review

Add or subtract.

14. $(5x^4 - 3x^3 + 7x^2 - 1) + (4x^3 - 2x^2 + x - 10)$ __________ *(5-7)*
15. $(-8x^5 + 3x^4 - 2x + 1) - (4x^4 + x^3 - 3x - 5)$ __________ *(5-8)*
16. $(9x^2 - 4x^2y + 3y) + (-5x + 7x^2y - 8y)$ __________ *(5-7)*
17. $(15x^2y^2 - 16xy^2 + 5x) - (3y + 8xy^2 + 10x)$ __________ *(5-8)*

Solve.

18. $\frac{1}{3} + \frac{1}{5} = \frac{1}{r}$ *(10-6)* __________
19. $\frac{s}{9} - \frac{9}{s} = 0$ *(10-6)* __________
20. $\frac{t+3}{t-7} = \frac{10}{t-7}$ *(10-6)* __________

Solve.

21. *(8-5)* A train leaves a station, traveling north at 40 mi/h. One half hour later, a second train leaves the station, traveling north on a parallel track at 50 mi/h. When will it overtake the first train? __________

22. *(8-5)* An airplane flew 1750 mi in 3.5 h with a tail wind. The return trip took 4 h against the same wind. Find the wind speed and the speed of the plane in still air. __________ __________

Name ______________________ Class ______________ Date ____________

Daily Cumulative Review 11-7

Add or subtract. *(Lesson 11-6)*

1. $5\sqrt{10} - 10\sqrt{10}$ ________
2. $\sqrt{200} - \sqrt{50}$ ________
3. $\sqrt{32} + \sqrt{8}$ ________
4. $\sqrt{8} - \sqrt{2}$ ________
5. $2\sqrt{2x} - \sqrt{8x}$ ________
6. $3\sqrt{3} - \sqrt{3}$ ________

Rationalize the denominator. *(Lesson 11-5)*

7. $\frac{5\sqrt{6}}{\sqrt{3}}$ ________
8. $\frac{1}{\sqrt{x^5}}$ ________
9. $\frac{\frac{2}{3}}{\sqrt{\frac{2}{3}}}$ ________
10. $\frac{\sqrt{\frac{1}{3}}}{\sqrt{\frac{2}{3}}}$ ________
11. $\frac{3\sqrt{6}}{4\sqrt{2}}$ ________
12. $\frac{1}{2\sqrt{2}}$ ________

Mixed Review

Solve.

13. $A = \frac{3a + c}{4}$, for c *(3-7)* ________
14. $\frac{a}{b} = \frac{c}{d}$, for $\frac{d}{b}$ *(3-7)* ________
15. $z = x + xy$, for x *(3-7)* ________

Arrange each polynomial in descending order.

16. $13y^3 - 11y^4 + y^6 - 10y^8 + 3 - y$ *(5-6)* ________
17. $-7z^5 + z + 8z^7 + 15 - z^6$ *(5-6)* ________

Solve these systems graphically.

18. $x = -2$
    $y = 3$ *(8-1)*

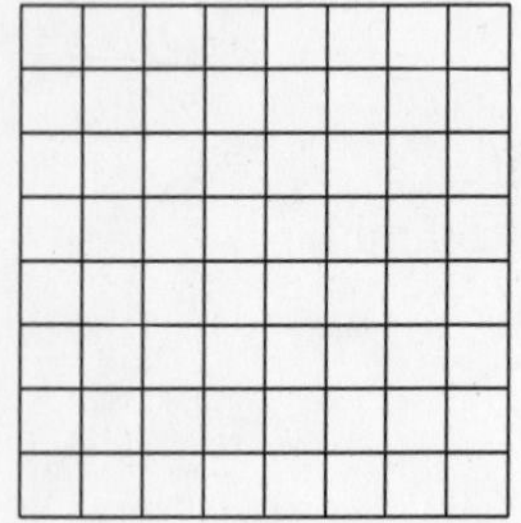

____

19. $x - 3y = 6$
    $x + y = 2$ *(8-1)*

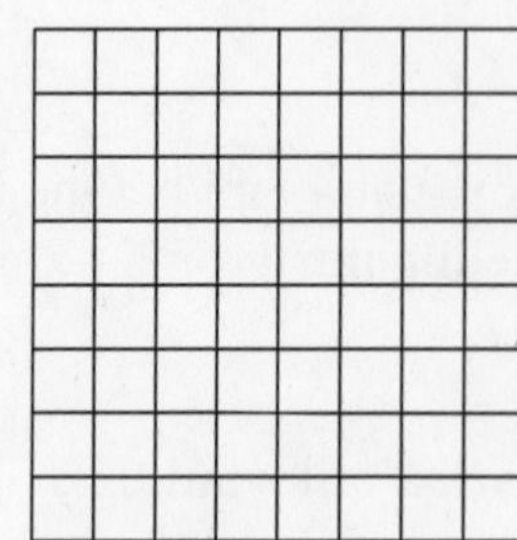

____

20. $y = \frac{1}{2}x - 3$
    $y = -x$ *(8-1)*

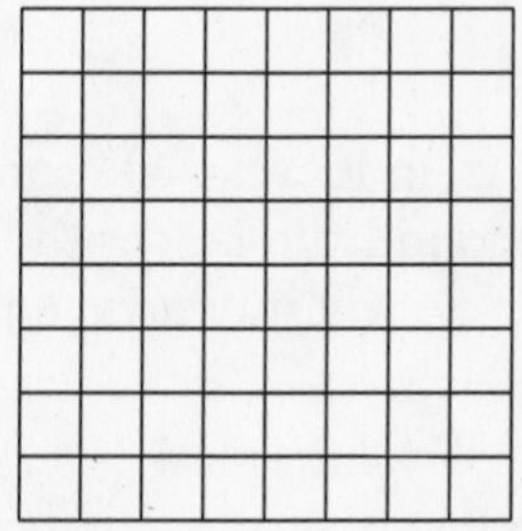

____

Name ______________________ Class ______________ Date ____________

Daily Cumulative Review 11-8

Find the length of the third side of each right triangle. *(Lesson 11-7)*

1. ________

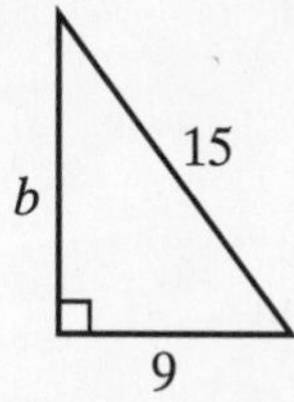

2. ________

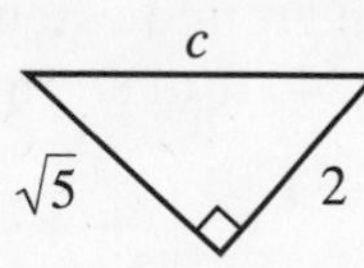

3. ________

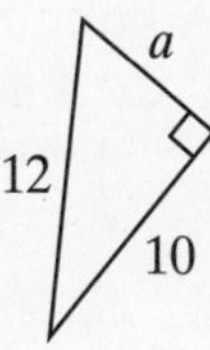

Add or subtract. *(Lesson 11-6)*

4. $3\sqrt{20} - 2\sqrt{5}$ ________

5. $\sqrt{4x + 4} - \sqrt{(x + 1)^3}$ ________

6. $\sqrt{12a^2b^3} - 2\sqrt{27b^3} + \sqrt{3b}$ ________

7. $\sqrt{2 + x^2} + \sqrt{18x^4 + 9x^6}$ ________

Mixed Review

Solve by drawing a diagram.

8. *(1-8)* The organizer of an outdoor arts-and-crafts show was asked to mark off square sections for individual booths. The show is to be held on a 300 ft by 180 ft field. The booths are to be 12 ft by 12 ft, with 3 ft between each pair of booths in a single row, and 16 feet between rows of booths. At most, how many booths could there be? ________

Evaluate.

9. *(2-1)* $|-6| + |5|$ ________

10. *(2-1)* $|-3| \cdot |-12| + |6|$ ________

11. *(2-1)* $|-8| \cdot |0| + |-5|$ ________

Solve these systems by graphing.

12. *(9-6)* $y > -x$
$y < x + 1$

13. *(9-6)* $2x + 6y \geq 12$
$x + y < 4$

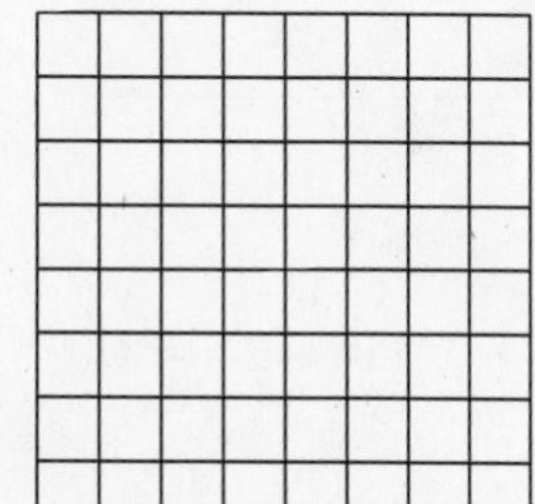

14. *(9-6)* $y \geq x$
$y < 3$
$x > -2$

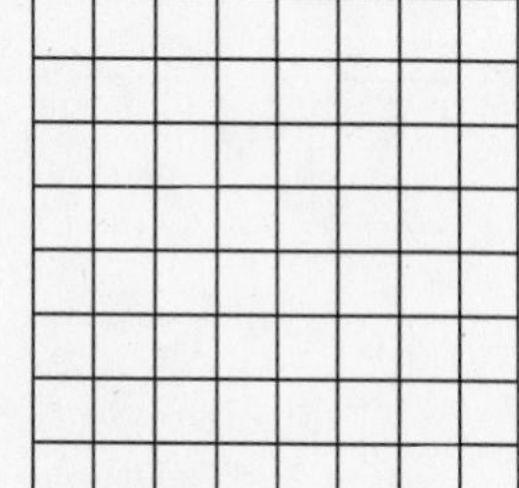

Name ______________________ Class ______________ Date __________

Daily Cumulative Review 11-9

Solve. Round answers to the nearest tenth. *(Lesson 11-8)*

1. A kite that is tethered to the ground extends horizontally 950 ft. If the kite is attached with 1240 ft of string, how high is the kite? (Assume the string is taut.)

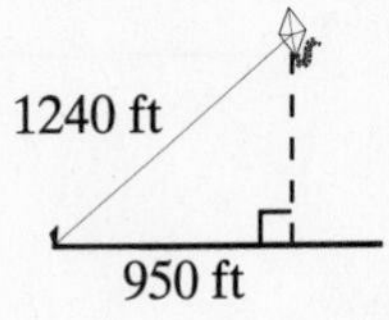

____

2. How much wire is needed for each of the guy wires for the antenna shown below?

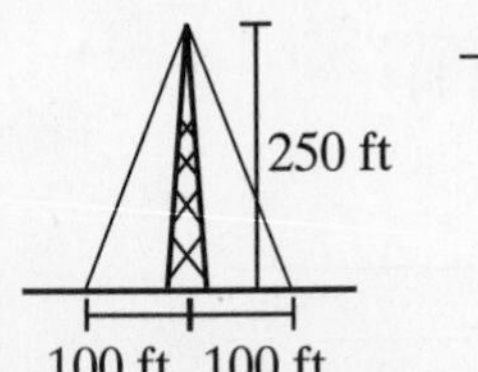

____

Find the length of the side not given for a right triangle with hypotenuse *c* and legs *a* and *b*. *(Lesson 11-7)*

3. $a = 15, b = 36, c =$ ____

4. $a =$ ____ $, b = 8, c = 10$

5. $a = 2, b =$ ____ $, c = 4$

6. $a = 2, b = 2, c =$ ____

7. $a =$ ____ $, b = 5, c = 10$

8. $a = 3, b =$ ____ $, c = 4$

9. $a = 8, b = 15, c =$ ____

10. $a =$ ____ $, b = 24, c = 25$

Mixed Review

Write an equivalent expression using a commutative property.

11. $y + 5$ *(1-2)* __________

12. xy *(1-2)* __________

13. $xy + 5$ *(1-2)* __________

14. $ab + c$ *(1-2)* __________

Multiply.

15. $(-x^3)(2x^2)$ *(5-3)* __________

16. $(-n^3)(-3n^3)$ *(5-3)* __________

17. $(6y^4)(7y^2)$ *(5-3)* __________

Solve.

18. $(x + 20)(x + 17)$ *(6-8)* __________

19. $x^2 - 11x + 24 = 0$ *(6-8)* __________

20. $5x^2 - 3x = 2$ *(6-8)* __________

Name ______________________ Class ______________ Date __________

Daily Cumulative Review 12-1

Solve. *(Lesson 11-9)*

1. $\sqrt{x} = 15$ ________
2. $\sqrt{2x - 3} = 7$ ________
3. $5 - 2\sqrt{2x} = -7$ ________
4. $-\sqrt{3x} = 8$ ________
5. $\sqrt{2x + 3} = \sqrt{3x - 4}$ ________
6. $\sqrt{4x^2 + 9} = 5$ ________

Solve. Round answers to nearest tenth. *(Lesson 11-8)*

7. A bird is sitting on top of a telephone pole 12 m high. She sees a worm on the ground 10 m from the pole. How far is the bird from the worm? ________

8. What is the diagonal length of a soccer field that is 100 m long and 60 m wide? ________

Mixed Review

Divide and simplify.

9. *(10-3)* $\frac{9x^3}{4} \div \frac{3x}{2}$ ________
10. *(10-3)* $\frac{x^2 - 4}{x + 2} \div \frac{x - 2}{x + 9}$ ________
11. *(10-3)* $\frac{x^2 - x - 6}{x + 5} \div x - 3$ ________

Solve.

12. *(9-3)* $|y + 1| = 3$ ________
13. *(9-3)* $|2x + 7| = 13$ ________
14. *(9-3)* $8 + |3m + 14| = 7$ ________

Find the slopes of the lines containing these points.

15. *(7-4)* $(0, 0)\ (-3, 6)$ ________
16. *(7-4)* $(1, -3)\ (11, 2)$ ________
17. *(7-4)* $(5, 16)\ (-17, -17)$ ________

Simplify.

18. *(5-2)* $\left(-\frac{x}{2y}\right)^4$ ________
19. *(5-2)* $\left(\frac{a}{b^4c}\right)^3$ ________
20. *(5-2)* $\left(\frac{2z^2}{x}\right)^5$ ________
21. *(1-5)* $3x + 5y + 8x$ ________
22. *(1-5)* $p^2 + z + 3p^2 + 4z$ ________
23. *(1-5)* $3x^2 + xy + 4xy$ ________

Name ______________________ Class ______________ Date __________

Daily Cumulative Review 12-2

Find the range of each function for the given domain. *(Lesson 12-1)*

1. $f(x) = 2x - 7$ when the domain is the set of whole numbers less than 5. ________

2. $f(x) = -x^2 + 3$ when the domain is the set of integers between -3 and 4. ________

3. $f(x) = \frac{x^2}{2}$ when the domain is the set of integers between -5 and 5. ________

4. $f(x) = |x| + x$ when the domain is the set of integers between -3 and 5. ________

Solve. *(Lesson 11-9)*

5. $\sqrt{4x - 5} = 9$ ________

6. $\sqrt{x - 4} = \sqrt{\frac{x}{2}}$ ________

7. $\sqrt{3x^2 + 9} = 6$ ________

8. $\sqrt{3m + 8} = \sqrt{3m - 2}$ ________

9. $3 + \sqrt{y + 2} = 9$ ________

10. $\sqrt{x} = 1.3$ ________

Mixed Review

Divide.

11. $\frac{x^2 - 3x^3 + x^5}{x}$ *(10-9)* ________

12. $\frac{12n^3 + 15n^2 - 9n}{3n}$ *(10-9)* ________

13. $\frac{15x^3y^2 - 25x^2y^5 + 10x^4y^3}{5x^2y^2}$ *(10-9)* ________

Solve and graph.

14. $-5 \le x + 3 < 3$ *(9-2)* ________

15. $-14 < 2x < 4$ *(9-2)* ________

16. $-3 < 2x + 3 < 7$ *(9-2)* ________

Write using scientific notation.

17. 93,000,000 *(5-4)* ________

18. 0.381 *(5-4)* ________

19. 27.6 *(5-4)* ________

20. 0.0030001 *(5-4)* ________

Solve.

21. $|-x| = |-5|$ *(3-8)* ________

22. $3|y| = 18$ *(3-8)* ________

23. $-2|n| + 3 = -5$ *(3-8)* ________

Name ______________________ Class ______________ Date ________

Daily Cumulative Review 12-3

Graph each function for the domain {−6, −4, −2, 0, 2, 4}. *(Lesson 12-2)*

1. $f(x) = x + 3$

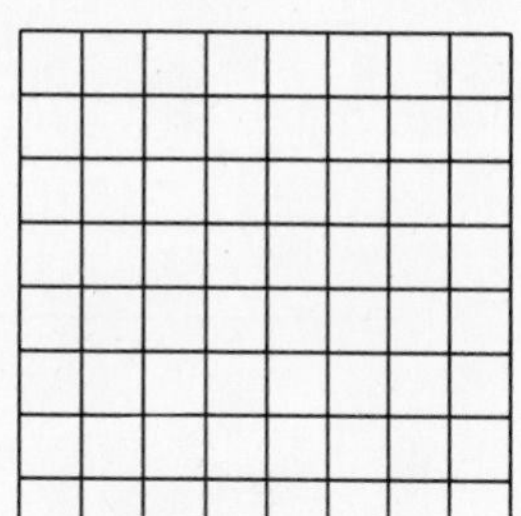

2. $f(x) = \frac{x}{2}$

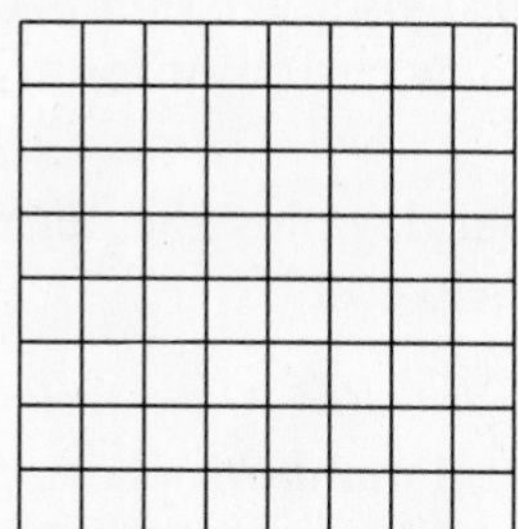

3. $f(x) = -2 - x$

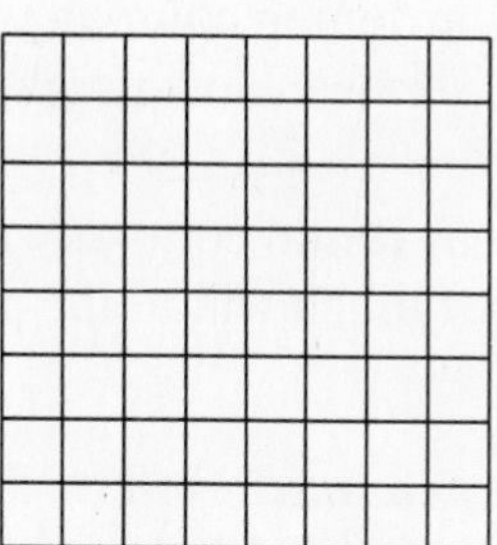

Find the indicated ranges. *(Lesson 12-1)*

4. The function $F(C) = \frac{9}{5}C + 32$ gives the Fahrenheit temperature in degrees as a function of the Celsius temperature C. Find the Fahrenheit temperature at 20°C, 5°C, and 0°C. ______ ______ ______

5. The function $K(m) = 1.6m$ gives speed in km/h as a function of speed in mi/h. Find the speed in km/h of three cars traveling at 45, 55, and 65 mi/h, respectively. ______ ______ ______

Mixed Review

Simplify.

6. *(11-5)* $\sqrt{\frac{2}{11}}$ ______

7. *(11-5)* $\sqrt{\frac{3c}{m^3}}$ ______

8. *(11-5)* $\sqrt{\frac{a}{b}}$ ______

9. *(10-1)* $\frac{3m - 12}{6}$ ______

10. *(10-1)* $\frac{y^5 - y^4}{y^3 - y^2}$ ______

11. *(10-1)* $\frac{x^2 - 9}{(x + 3)^2}$ ______

Solve using the addition method.

12. *(8-3)* $y + 2x = 1$
$2y + x = 8$ ______

13. *(8-3)* $2x - y = 3$
$3x - 2y = 0$ ______

14. *(8-3)* $3x + y = -2$
$5x + 2y = -6$ ______

Factor.

15. *(6-5)* $6x^2 - 3x - 45$ ______

16. *(6-5)* $4x^2 + 44x + 96$ ______

17. *(6-5)* $30 + 7n - 2n^2$ ______

Name ______________________ Class ______________ Date ________

Daily Cumulative Review 12-4

Write a linear function describing each situation. Use the function to solve the problem. *(Lesson 12-3)*

1. A gardening company charges a $50 sign-up fee plus $20 per week for service. How much will it cost a new customer for a year of service? ______

2. A car rental company charges $35 per day plus 25¢ per mile. How much will a one-day, 400-mile trip cost? ______

Graph each function. The domain is all real numbers. *(Lesson 12-2)*

3. $f(x) = 3x - 2$

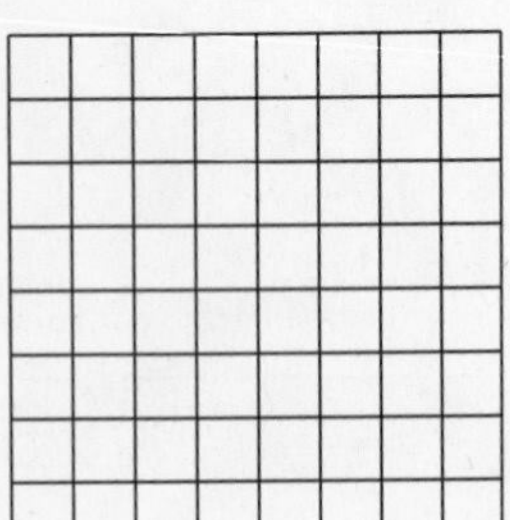

4. $g(x) = |x| - 2$

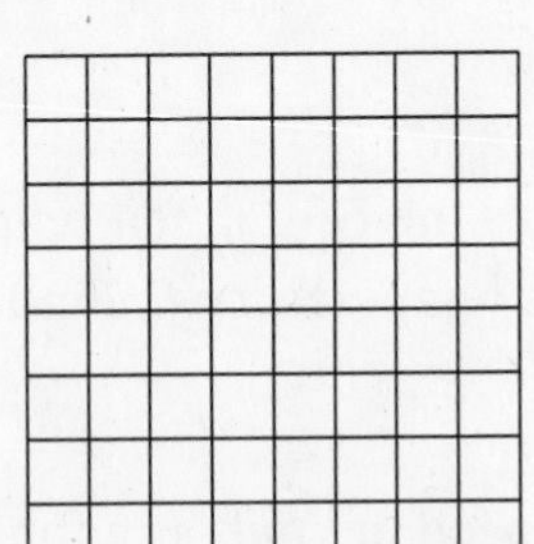

5. $h(x) = 3 - x$

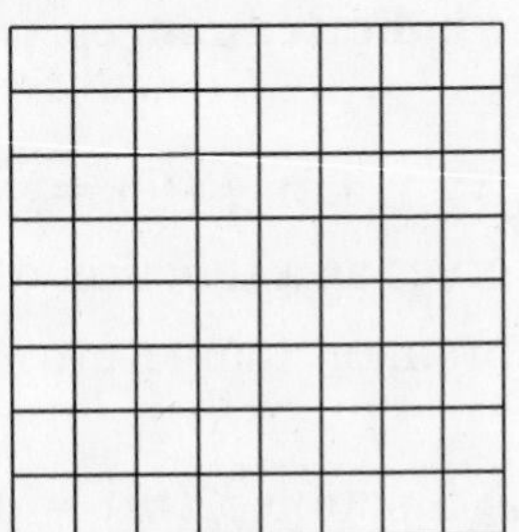

Mixed Review

Determine the values for the variable that will make each expression a real number.

6. $\sqrt{4x}$ *(11-2)* ______

7. $\sqrt{n - 5}$ *(11-2)* ______

8. $\sqrt{2y - 5}$ *(11-2)* ______

9. $\sqrt{x^2 + 4}$ *(11-2)* ______

Solve and graph.

10. $|x| < 5$ *(9-4)* ______

11. $|5x| \leq 15$ *(9-4)* ______

12. $|x + 3| > 2$ *(9-4)* ______

Factor.

13. $81 - y^2$ *(6-2)* ______

14. $27x^2 - 12$ *(6-2)* ______

15. $x^5 - 9x^3$ *(6-2)* ______

Write as a decimal.

16. 10% ______ *(3-10)*

17. 95% ______ *(3-10)*

18. 150% ______ *(3-10)*

19. 0.5% ______ *(3-10)*

Name ______________________ Class ______________ Date ____________

Daily Cumulative Review 12-5

Graph each function. *(Lesson 12-4)*

1. $y = -x^2 + 4$

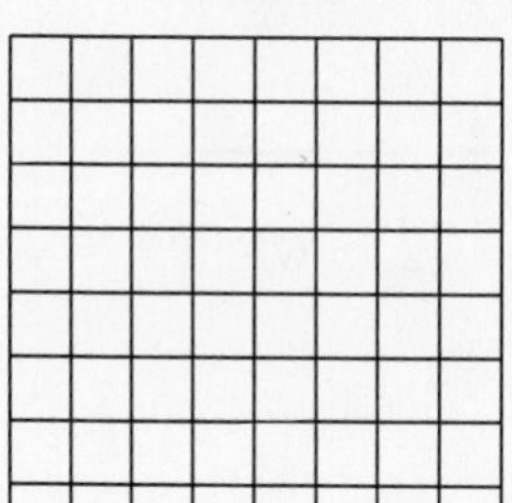

2. $y = x^2 - 2x$

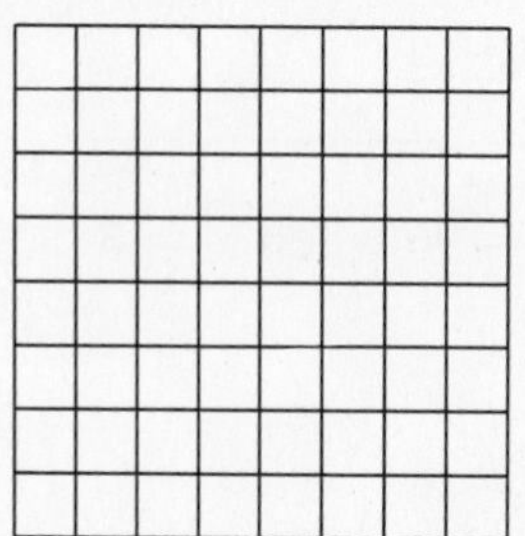

3. $y = x^2 - 5$

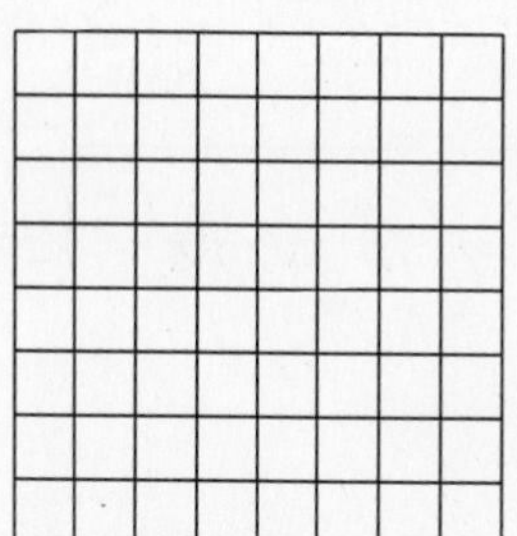

Write a linear function describing each situation. Use the function to solve the problem. *(Lesson 12-3)*

4. Long distance calls cost 25¢ plus 7¢ per minute. Find the cost of a 23-minute call. ______ ______

5. Renting a rototiller costs \$4.50 per hour plus \$2.50 for a can of gas. What will be the cost of a 5-hour job? ______ ______

Mixed Review

Simplify.

6. $\sqrt{225}$ *(11-1)* ______

7. $-\sqrt{441}$ *(11-1)* ______

8. $-\sqrt{289}$ *(11-1)* ______

9. $\sqrt{81}$ *(11-1)* ______

Find the LCM.

10. $x + 3,\ x - 5$ *(10-5)* ______

11. $3n^2m,\ nm^2$ *(10-5)* ______

12. $x^2 + 6x + 9,\ x^2 - 9$ *(10-5)* ______

Determine whether the graphs of the equations are perpendicular lines.

13. *(7-8)* $2x + 4y = 9$; $y = 2x + 8$ ______

14. *(7-8)* $y = \frac{3}{4}x + 5$; $3y - 4x = 22$ ______

15. *(7-8)* $x + y = 15$; $x - y = 15$ ______

Identify the degree of each term and the degree of the polynomial.

16. $3x^3 + 2x - 1$ *(5-5)* ______

17. $6a^2b + 5ab^2 + 3b$ *(5-5)* ______

18. $x^4 + 2x^3 - x + 5$ *(5-5)* ______

Name ______________________ Class ______________ Date ____________

Daily Cumulative Review 12-6

Find an equation of variation where y varies directly as x, and the following are true. *(Lesson 12-5)*

1. $y = 40$ when $x = 16$ ____________

2. $y = 39$ when $x = 65$ ____________

3. $y = 141$ when $x = 47$ ____________

4. $y = 1.25$ when $x = 1.5$ ____________

5. $y = 96$ when $x = 8$ ____________

6. $y = 22.75$ when $x = 7$ ____________

Graph each function. *(Lesson 12-4)*

7. $y = x^2 - 6x + 9$

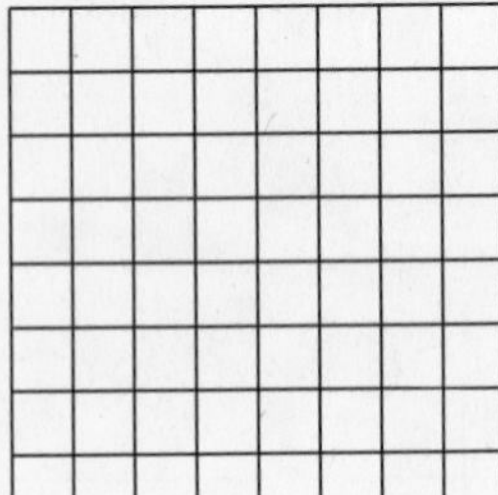

8. $y = -x^2 + 2$

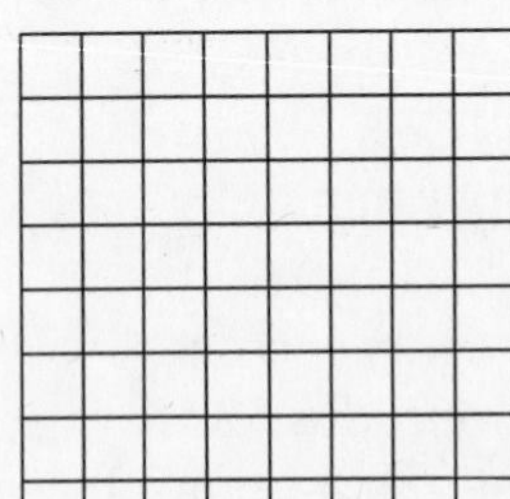

9. $y = x^2 + 4x + 4$

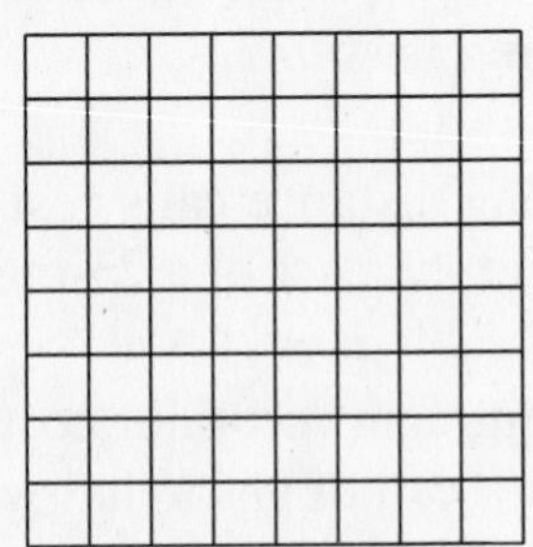

Mixed Review

Simplify.

10. $\sqrt{18}$ *(11-3)* ____________

11. $\sqrt{12x^2}$ *(11-3)* ____________

12. $\sqrt{500}$ *(11-3)* ____________

13. $\sqrt{2x^2 + 8x + 8}$ *(11-3)* ____________

Solve.

14. A jar of 75 dimes and nickels contains \$6.00. How many of each coin are in the jar? *(8-6)* ____________ ____________

15. $(x + 3)(2x - 5) = 0$ *(6-8)* ____________

16. $x^2 - x - 20 = 0$ *(6-8)* ____________

17. $x^2 - 5x - 14 = 0$ *(6-8)* ____________

18. $2x - 3 \leq 21$ *(4-4)* ____________

19. $12 - 7y > 47$ *(4-4)* ____________

20. $25 + 2n < 17 + 6n$ *(4-4)* ____________

Factor.

21. $-3x + 15$ *(2-7)* ____________

22. $xy - xz + xa$ *(2-7)* ____________

23. $ny + 3n$ *(2-7)* ____________

Name ______________________ Class ______________ Date __________

Daily Cumulative Review 12-7

Find an equation of variation where *y* varies inversely as *x*, and the following are true. *(Lesson 12-6)*

1. $y = 150$ when $x = 0.2$ ____________

2. $y = 1.5$ when $x = 3$ ____________

3. $y = \frac{1}{5}$ when $x = 5$ ____________

4. $y = 30$ when $x = 150$ ____________

5. $y = 0.6$ when $x = 40$ ____________

6. $y = 0.1$ when $x = 0.5$ ____________

Solve. *(Lesson 12-5)*

7. The cost to fill a tank with gas varies directly as the size of the tank. It costs $37.50 to fill a 25-gallon tank. What is the cost of filling a 21-gallon tank? ____________

8. The distance between two cities is 45 mi. They are shown to be 3 in. apart on the map. What is the actual distance between two cities which are shown to be 11 in. apart on the map? ____________

Mixed Review

Add or subtract. Simplify.

9. *(10-4)* $\frac{10x}{7} - \frac{3x}{7}$ ____________

10. *(10-4)* $\frac{3y}{y + 3} + \frac{9}{y + 3}$ ____________

11. *(10-4)* $\frac{-n}{n + 2} + \frac{6n + 5}{n + 2}$ ____________

Write an equation in slope-intercept form for each line with the given point and slope.

12. *(7-6)* $(-3, 6), m = -1$ ____________

13. *(7-6)* $(10, 0), m = \frac{4}{5}$ ____________

14. *(7-6)* $\left(\frac{1}{2}, \frac{1}{2}\right), m = -4$ ____________

Solve and graph the solution.

15. *(4-3)* $-6y \leq 42$ ____________

16. *(4-3)* $10x < 150$ ____________

17. *(4-3)* $-16y \geq 80$ ____________

Rename each additive inverse without parentheses.

18. *(2-8)* $-(10x + 5)$ ____________

19. *(2-8)* $-(3a - 5b - 8c)$ ____________

20. *(2-8)* $-(5x - 3y + 18)$ ____________

Name ______________________ Class ______________ Date __________

Daily Cumulative Review 13-1

Find an equation of joint variation. Then solve for the missing value. *(Lesson 12-7)*

1. a varies jointly as b and c. One set of values is $a = 8, b = 4,$ and $c = 3$. Find a when $b = 9$ and $c = 9$. ________ ________

2. m varies jointly as $n, p,$ and q. One set of values is $m = 35, n = 2,$ $p = 5,$ and $q = 5$. Find m when $n = 4, p = 10,$ and $q = 6$. ________ ________

3. r varies jointly as $s, t,$ and v. One set of values is $r = 67.5, s = 0.5,$ $t = 6,$ and $v = 9$. Find r when $s = 4, t = 0.1,$ and $v = 25$. ________ ________

Find an equation of variation where *y* varies inversely as *x*. One pair of values is given. *(Lesson 12-6)*

4. $y = 0.6$ when $x = 10$

____

5. $y = 8$ when $x = 0.125$

____

6. $y = 2$ when $x = 25$

____

7. $y = 1.5$ when $x = 3$

____

Mixed Review

Find the length of the third side of each right triangle.

8. *(11-7)*

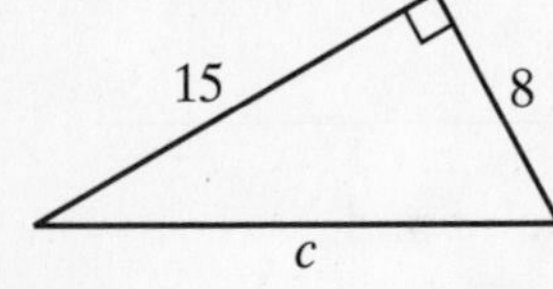

____

9. *(11-7)*

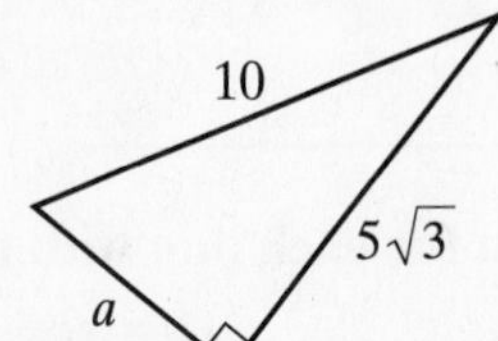

____

10. *(11-7)*

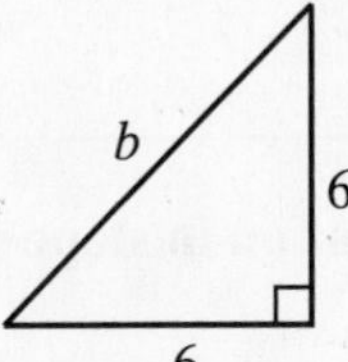

____

Solve.

11. *(10-6)* $\frac{x + 1}{x - 5} = 4$

____

12. *(10-6)* $\frac{5}{x + 1} = \frac{1}{x - 1}$

____

13. *(10-6)* $\frac{x + 5}{x - 3} = \frac{8}{x - 3}$

____

14. *(8-4)* Alice is 21 years older than her son. Seven years ago, she was four times as old as he. What are their ages now? ________ ________

Factor.

15. *(6-7)* $6n^2 + 36n + 30$

____

16. *(6-7)* $x^2 + 64$

____

17. *(6-7)* $3x^4 + 6x^3 + 3x^2$

____

Name ______________________ Class ______________ Date ________

Daily Cumulative Review 13-2

Solve. *(Lesson 13-1)*

1. $x^2 + 4x = 0$ ________
2. $x^2 - 5x - 14 = 0$ ________
3. $x(x + 3) = 10$ ________
4. $2x^2 - 7x - 15 = 0$ ________
5. $3x^2 + 14x = -15$ ________
6. $9x^2 - 27x = 0$ ________

Find an equation of combined variation. Then solve for the missing value.
(Lesson 12-7)

7. x varies directly as y and inversely as z. One set of values is $x = 5$, $y = 40$, and $z = 4$. Find x when $y = 14$ and $z = 3$. ________ ________

8. m varies directly as n and inversely as p. One set of values is $m = 2$, $n = 8$, and $p = 5$. Find m when $n = 3$ and $p = 1.5$. ________ ________

Mixed Review

Multiply and simplify.

9. $\sqrt{24} \cdot \sqrt{2}$ *(11-4)* ________
10. $\sqrt{3x^2y^3} \cdot \sqrt{12xy}$ *(11-4)* ________
11. $\sqrt{18} \cdot \sqrt{a^5} \cdot \sqrt{b^{15}}$ *(11-4)* ________

Solve these systems by graphing.

12. *(9-6)* $x < 5$
    $y > -x + 3$

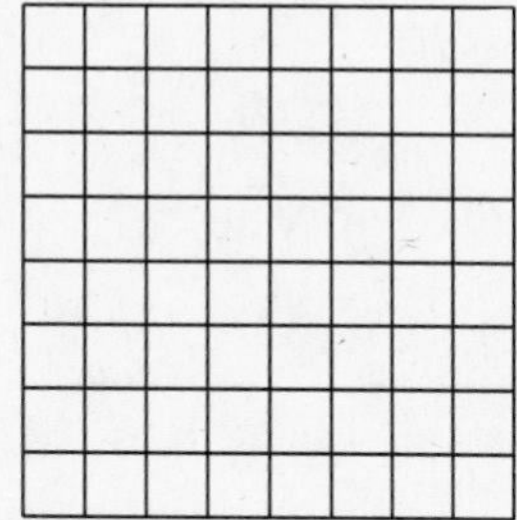

13. *(9-6)* $y - 2x > 0$
    $y < x + 2$

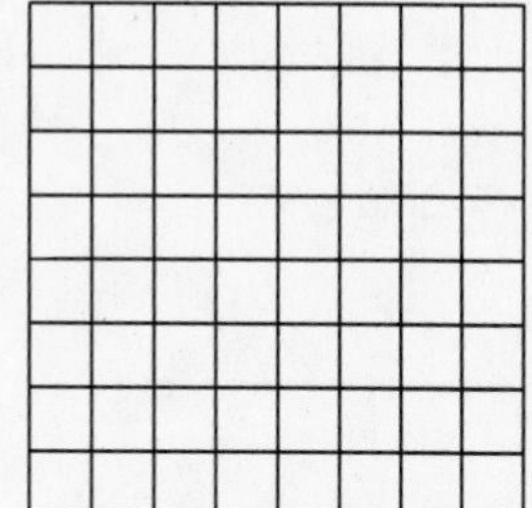

14. *(9-6)* $y - x \geq 4$
    $3y + 2x \leq -3$

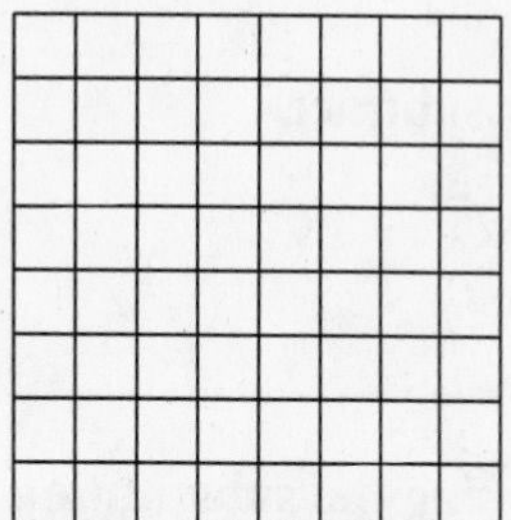

Write using scientific notation.

15. 0.009002 *(5-4)* ________
16. 6,020,000,000 *(5-4)* ________
17. 3,298 *(5-4)* ________

Name ______________________ Class ______________ Date ____________

Daily Cumulative Review 13-3

Solve. *(Lesson 13-2)*

1. $2x^2 = 50$ ____________

2. $(x + 5)^2 = 36$ ____________

3. $x^2 + 8x + 16 = 11$ ____________

4. $(x - 9)^2 = 15$ ____________

5. $3(2x + 1)^2 = 27$ ____________

6. $4x^2 - 9 = 0$ ____________

Solve. *(Lesson 13-1)*

7. $25x^2 + 10x = 0$ ____________

8. $x(x + 2) = 15$ ____________

9. $3x^2 - 14x + 15 = 0$ ____________

10. $8x^2 + 18x + 9 = 0$ ____________

11. $9x^2 + 36x = 0$ ____________

12. $1 = \frac{1}{6}x^2$ ____________

Mixed Review

Graph each function. The domain is all real numbers.

13. *(12-2)* $f(x) = \frac{1}{2}|x|$

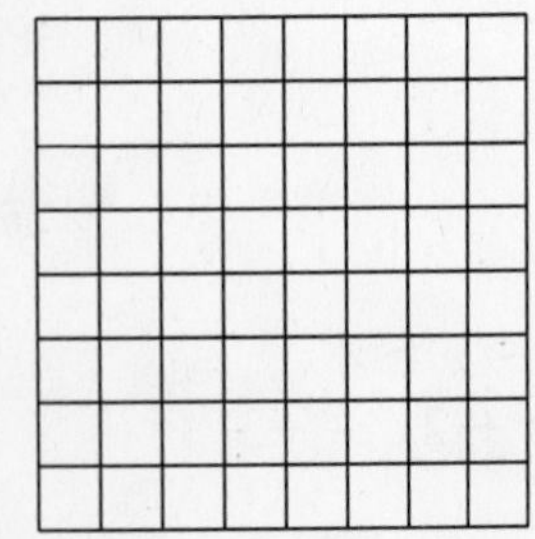

14. *(12-2)* $g(x) = 3x - 4$

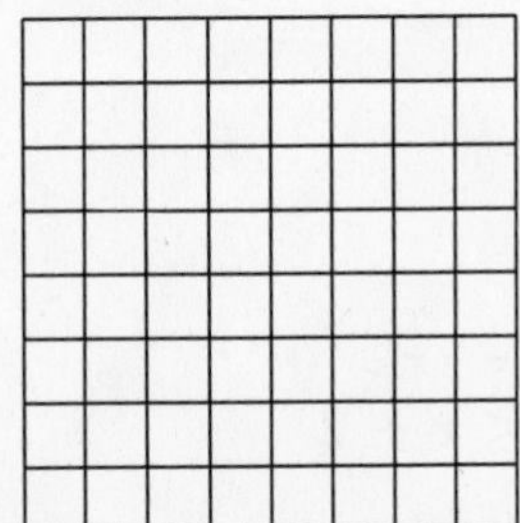

15. *(12-2)* $h(x) = -2|x|$

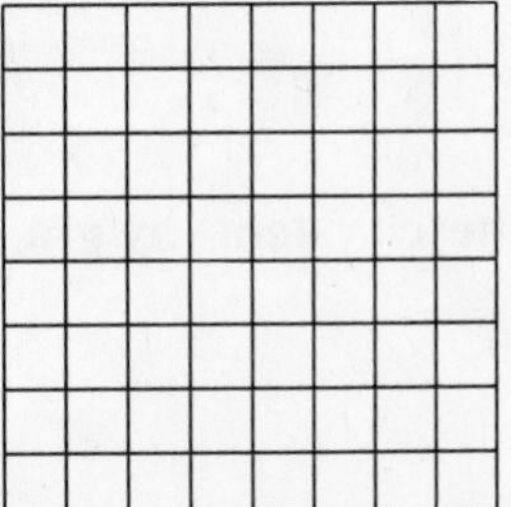

Add or subtract.

16. *(11-6)* $2\sqrt{x} - 5\sqrt{x}$ ____________

17. *(11-6)* $5\sqrt{2} + 3\sqrt{18}$ ____________

18. *(11-6)* $2\sqrt{72} - 5\sqrt{50}$ ____________

Solve using the substitution method.

19. *(8-2)* $x - y = -5$
$2y - 3x = 4$ ____________

20. *(8-2)* $x = y + 5$
$5x - 2y = 1$ ____________

21. *(8-2)* $2x - y = 22$
$5x + 2y = 1$ ____________

Name ______________ Class ______________ Date ______________

Daily Cumulative Review 13-4

Solve by completing the square. *(Lesson 13-3)*

1. $x^2 + 8x + 15 = 0$ ______________

2. $x^2 - 3x - 40 = 0$ ______________

3. $x^2 - 6x + 2 = 0$ ______________

4. $x^2 + 10x + 10 = 0$ ______________

5. $2x^2 - 7x - 5 = 0$ ______________

6. $2x^2 + 5x - 1 = 0$ ______________

Solve. *(Lesson 13-2)*

7. $4x^2 = 32$ ______________

8. $(x - 3)^2 = 15$ ______________

9. $(x + 5)^2 = 81$ ______________

10. $x^2 + 18x + 81 = 17$ ______________

11. $x^2 - 6x + 9 = 16$ ______________

12. $16x^2 - 9 = 0$ ______________

Mixed Review

Simplify.

13. $\sqrt{\frac{8}{3}}$ *(11-5)* ______________

14. $\sqrt{\frac{3}{12}}$ *(11-5)* ______________

15. $\sqrt{\frac{4n}{m}}$ *(11-5)* ______________

16. $\sqrt{\frac{5}{9}}$ *(11-5)* ______________

Solve.

17. $|x + 9| = 3$ *(9-3)* ______________

18. $|\frac{1}{4}x + 5| = 7$ *(9-3)* ______________

19. $3|x - 4| + 6 = 12$ *(9-3)* ______________

Find the slope of each line by solving for *y*.

20. $5x + 2y = 15$ *(7-5)* ______________

21. $8x - 2y = 9$ *(7-5)* ______________

22. $3x + 7y = 12$ *(7-5)* ______________

Multiply.

23. $(-3x^3)(5x^5)$ *(5-3)* ______________

24. $(-4x^2y^5)(-8x^3y^9)$ *(5-3)* ______________

25. $(n^5)(3n^2)(-2n^4)$ *(5-3)* ______________

Name ______________________ Class ______________ Date __________

Daily Cumulative Review 13-5

Solve using the quadratic formula. *(Lesson 13-4)*

1. $x^2 - 3x - 40 = 0$ ______

2. $x^2 + x - 11 = 0$ ______

3. $4x^2 - 4x - 15 = 0$ ______

4. $3x^2 + 5x - 2 = 0$ ______

5. $3x^2 + 2x + 5 = 0$ ______

6. $3x^2 - 8x - 14 = 0$ ______

Complete the square. *(Lesson 13-3)*

7. $x^2 - 7x$ ______

8. $x^2 - 10x$ ______

9. $y^2 + 18y$ ______

Mixed Review

Graph each function.

10. $f(x) = x^2 - 4$ *(12-4)*

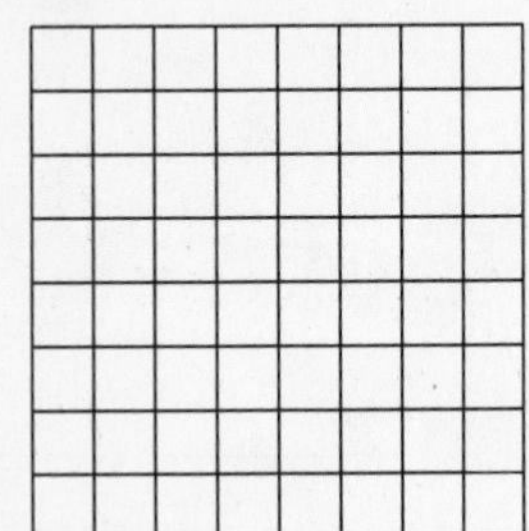

11. $y = x^2 + x$ *(12-4)*

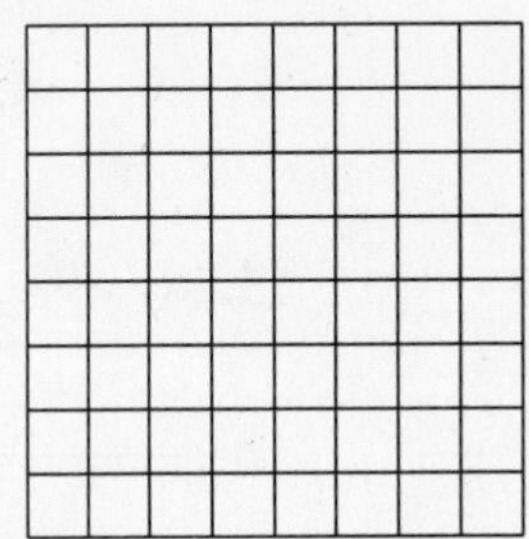

12. $y = -2x^2 + 3$ *(12-4)*

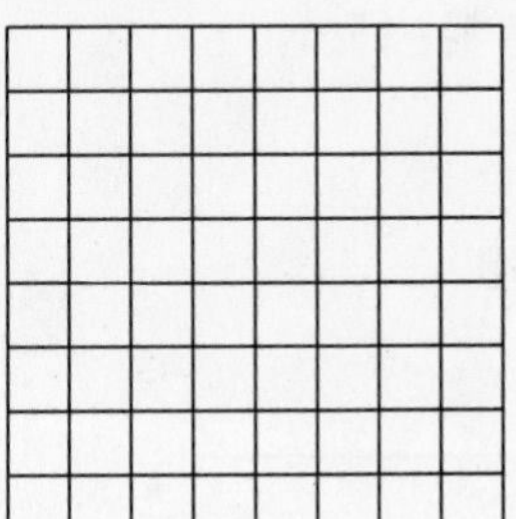

Identify each square root as rational or irrational.

13. $\sqrt{8}$ *(11-1)* ______

14. $\sqrt{16}$ *(11-1)* ______

15. $\sqrt{25}$ *(11-1)* ______

16. $\sqrt{98}$ *(11-1)* ______

Solve and graph.

17. $-5 < x + 4 < 5$ *(9-2)* ______

18. $-9 \leq 2x + 3 \leq 9$ *(9-2)* ______

19. $|x + 4| < 7$ *(9-2)* ______

Find the slopes of the lines containing these points.

20. $(0, 0)\ (-6, -9)$ *(7-4)* ______

21. $(7, 4)\ (9, 0)$ *(7-4)* ______

22. $(-7, 6)\ (4, -2)$ *(7-4)* ______

Name ______________________ Class ______________ Date __________

Daily Cumulative Review 13-6

Solve each rational equation. *(Lesson 13-5)*

1. $x + 4 = \frac{5}{x + 4}$

2. $\frac{9}{x - 4} = x + 4$

3. $\frac{3}{y - 1} + \frac{3}{y + 1} = 1$

4. $\frac{1}{x - 1} + \frac{1}{x - 3} = 0$

5. $\frac{16}{x - 2} + \frac{16}{x + 2} = 6$

6. $\frac{y + 3}{y} = \frac{1}{y + 3}$

Solve using the quadratic formula. Approximate solutions to the nearest tenth. *(Lesson 13-4)*

7. $3x^2 = 22$

8. $5x^2 - 2x - 8 = 0$

9. $x^2 - x - 21 = 0$

10. $5x^2 - 3x - 11 = 0$

11. $x^2 + 5x - 9 = 0$

12. $2x^2 + 3x + 1 = 0$

Mixed Review

Determine the values for the variable that will make each expression a real number.

13. *(11-2)* $\sqrt{2x}$

14. *(11-2)* $\sqrt{x - 5}$

15. *(11-2)* $\sqrt{3x + 5}$

16. *(11-2)* $\sqrt{2x^2 + 3}$

Simplify.

17. *(10-1)* $\frac{x + 5}{x^2 - 25}$

18. *(10-1)* $\frac{a^9 - a^8}{a^7 - a^6}$

19. *(10-1)* $\frac{y^2 + 4y + 4}{y^2 - y - 6}$

Solve by graphing.

20. *(8-1)* $3y + 2x = 18$
$y - x = 1$

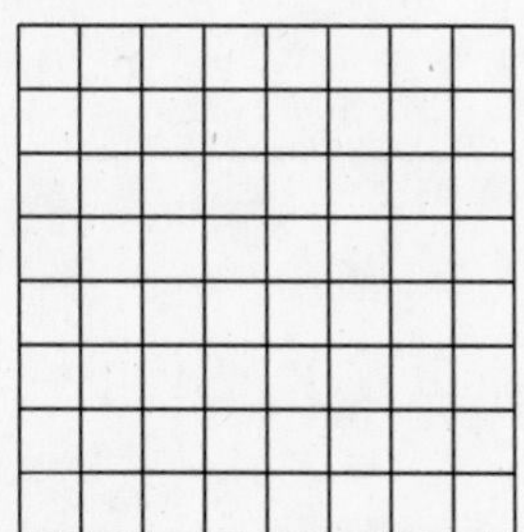

21. *(8-1)* $2y + x = 3$
$5y - 2x = 30$

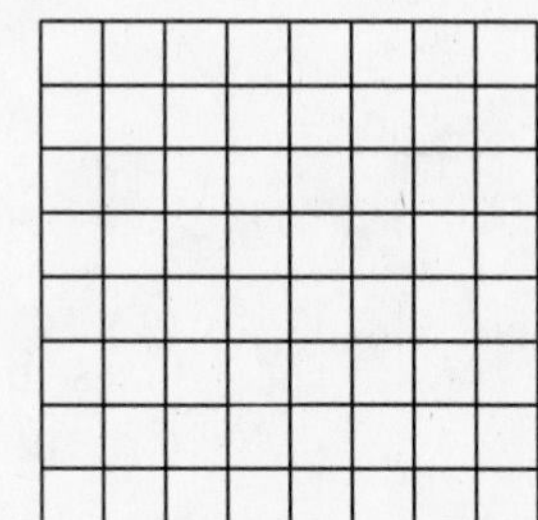

22. *(8-1)* $y + 2x = 0$
$2y - x = -10$

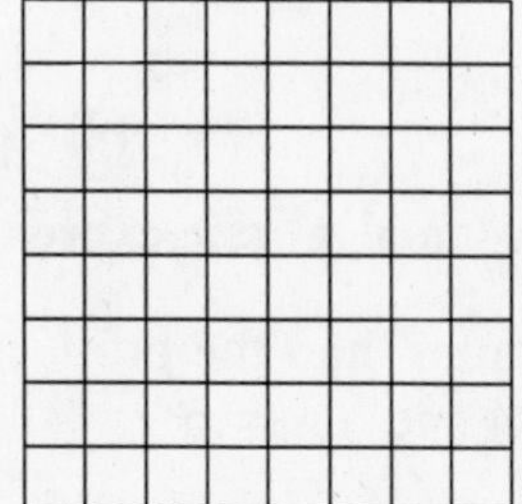

Name ______________________ Class ______________ Date __________

Daily Cumulative Review 13-7

Solve each radical equation. *(Lesson 13-6)*

1. $\sqrt{4y} = 10$

2. $\sqrt{x - 3} = 7$

3. $\sqrt{\frac{x}{4}} = 3$

4. $\sqrt{3x} + 5 = 9$

5. $\sqrt{\frac{x + 3}{3}} = 7$

6. $x - 4 = \sqrt{x + 8}$

Solve each rational equation.

7. $x - 4 = \frac{2}{x - 4}$

8. $\frac{1}{x - 3} - \frac{3}{x^2 - 9} = 0$

9. $\frac{6}{x^2} + \frac{1}{x} = 1$

10. $\frac{x^2}{x - 5} = \frac{7}{x - 5}$

11. $\frac{3}{x - 3} - \frac{1}{x} = \frac{1}{2}$

12. $x + 5 = \frac{9}{x + 5}$

Mixed Review

Find an equation of variation where *y* varies directly as *x*, and the following are true.

13. *(12-5)* $y = 15$ when $x = 3$

14. *(12-5)* $y = 0.9$ when $x = 0.4$

15. *(12-5)* $y = 375$ when $x = 75$

Divide.

16. *(10-9)* $\frac{12x^4 + 2x^3 + x^2 - 18}{6}$

17. *(10-9)* $(x^2 - 3x - 28) \div (x + 4)$

Factor.

18. *(6-4)* $x^2 - 8xy + 7y^2$

19. *(6-4)* $x^2 - 5x - 104$

20. *(6-4)* $n^2 + 3np - 70p^2$

Write as an algebraic expression.

21. *(3-4)* 7 more than the product of 4 and a number

22. *(3-4)* 8 less than the quotient of a number and 3

Daily Cumulative Review Answers

Daily Review 1-1

1. variable expression; c
2. numerical expression
3. numerical expression
4. variable expression; x
5. variable expression; h
6. variable expression; b
7. 13 **8.** 11 **9.** 20 **10.** 25 **11.** 11 **12.** 9
13. commutative property of addition
14. associative property of addition
15. distributive property
16. associative property of multiplication
17. no; yes; no; no; no **18.** yes; yes; yes; yes; yes
19. no; no; yes; no; no **20.** yes; yes; no; yes; no

Daily Review 1-2

1. 25 **2.** 3 **3.** 56 **4.** 4 **5.** 7 **6.** 11 **7.** 12
8. 120 **9.** 5 **10.** 27 **11.** 32 **12.** 21.93
13. 42 **14.** $\frac{2}{3}$ **15.** $1\frac{1}{2}$ **16.** 12 **17.** 0.353
18. $\frac{1}{27}$ **19.** 0.8 **20.** 7.69 **21.** $\frac{3}{8}$ **22.** $1\frac{3}{4}$
23. 2.64 **24.** $\frac{2}{9}$ **25.** 39.25 **26.** $1\frac{3}{8}$ **27.** $\frac{11}{14}$

Daily Review 1-3

1. $\frac{5}{12}$ **2.** 14 **3.** $\frac{11}{14}$ **4.** $8y$ **5.** $\frac{3}{n}$ **6.** $\frac{7z}{12h}$ **7.** 19
8. 17 **9.** 11 **10.** 5 **11.** 11 **12.** 9 **13.** 643
14. 4.51 **15.** $1\frac{5}{12}$ **16.** $4\frac{2}{5}$ **17.** 14.01 **18.** $\frac{13}{42}$
19. 26 **20** 3.92 **21.** 42 **22.** 4 **23.** 8 **24.** $\frac{5}{6}$
25. 4 **26.** $\frac{1}{6}$ **27.** $\frac{1}{3}$

Daily Review 1-4

1. 16 **2.** 75 **3.** 36 **4.** 1 **5.** 0 **6.** 76 **7.** yx
8. $h + 5$ **9.** $ed + f$ or $f + de$ **10.** 6 **11.** 5
12. 14 **13.** 4 **14.** 21 **15.** 2
16. coefficients: 5, 7; like terms: $5a$ and $7a$; constant: 6
17. coefficients: 7, 4, 3, 2; like terms: $7x$ and $2x$, $4y$ and $3y$; constants: none
18. coefficients: 5, 3, 15, 7; like terms: $5m$ and $15m$, $3n$ and $7n$; constants: 5, 8
19. coefficients: 3, 4, 1, 5, 1; like terms: $3b$ and b, $4c$ and $5c$; constants: none

Daily Review 1-5

1. 5 **2.** 49 **3.** 50 **4.** 100 **5.** 81 **6.** 15
7. 8^4 **8.** b^4 **9.** $7h^3$ **10.** $\frac{1}{9}$ **11.** 5 **12.** $\frac{8j}{11q}$
13. 14 **14.** 6 **15.** 29 **16.** $12 - 8 = 4$
17. $2(3) + 5 = 11$ **18.** $7 + 9 = 16$
19. $6 + 3(10) = 36$

Daily Review 1-6

1. $20x$ **2.** $9m + 5n$ **3.** $11y^2 + 9y$ **4.** $\frac{5}{8}y$
5. $4z^2 + 13z + 1$ **6.** $\frac{5}{2}a + 2b$ **7.** 33 **8.** 50
9. 64 **10.** 39 **11.** 51 **12.** 41 **13.** $x + 7$
14. qp **15.** $xz + y$ or $y + zx$ **16.** 64 **17.** 98
18. 36 **19.** 0 **20.** 19 **21.** 17 **22.** no **23.** no
24. yes

Daily Review 1-7

1. $15h$ **2.** $x + 12$ **3.** $b - 5$ **4.** $\frac{c}{7}$ **5.** $y + 9$
6. $\frac{16}{d}$ **7.** $3(4p + 7)$ **8.** $6(3m + 5)$
9. $8(p + 3q + 9)$ **10.** $9(1 + 6r + 7t)$
11. $10(y + 21z)$ **12.** $7(2 - 7r + s)$ **13.** 5^7
14. q^4 **15.** $6n^5$ **16.** 16^2 **17.** 8^4 **18.** 9^2
19. 9 **20.** 11 **21.** 21 **22.** 49 **23.** 19
24. 13 **25.** 48 **26.** 144 **27.** 36

Daily Review 1-8

1. {29} **2.** {7} **3.** {5} **4.** {7} **5.** $d - 9$ **6.** $2d$
7. $(5 + p) + q$ **8.** $3(mn)$ **9.** $9 + (h + j)$
10. $17b$ **11.** $6j + 3h$ **12.** $\frac{4}{5}z$ **13.** $7 \cdot 7 \cdot 7 \cdot 7$
14. $j \cdot j \cdot j \cdot j \cdot j$ **15.** $2m \cdot m \cdot m$
16. $4h \cdot h \cdot h \cdot h \cdot h \cdot h$

Daily Review 1-9

1. \$10 **2.** 2 lim, 4 lim and 6 lim **3.** {15}
4. {35} **5.** {6} **6.** {14} **7.** {36} **8.** {18}
9. {7} **10.** {24} **11.** {35} **12.** 74 **13.** 100
14. 32 **15.** 10^3 **16.** 6^7 **17.** 9^5
18. $7(3 + 4h)$ **19.** $5(8x + 3y + 9)$
20. $4(8a + 5b + 2)$

Daily Review 1-10

1. \$144 **2.** 240 ft **3.** 1270 ft **4.** $3m + 21$
5. $32 + 8b$ **6.** $10h + 18$ **7.** $5n + 30$
8. $18x + 63$ **9.** $12a + 44$ **10.** $x - 9$
11. $2b$ **12.** $y + 10$
13. $r + (t + s)$; $t + (s + r)$; $(s + t) + r$
14. $7(c \cdot b)$; $(7b)c$; $b \cdot (7 \cdot c)$
15. $4 + (y + 9x)$; $9x + (4 + y)$; $(y + 4) + 9x$

Daily Review 2-1

1. 8 **2.** 7 **3.** 2 **4.** 3 **5.** 2 **6.** 6 **7.** 26.25 ft
8. 240 ft **9.** 146.25 ft **10.** 40 ft **11.** 276.25 ft
12. 6.25 ft **13.** $\frac{11}{4}$ **14.** $\frac{13}{8}$ **15.** $\frac{35}{10}$

16. $\frac{61}{5}$ **17.** $\frac{43}{7}$ **18.** $\frac{1071}{100}$ **19.** $\frac{1}{8}, \frac{3}{16}, \frac{1}{4}, \frac{3}{8}, \frac{1}{2}$
20. $\frac{3}{10}, \frac{3}{5}, \frac{7}{10}, \frac{4}{5}, \frac{8}{5}$ **21.** 8^6 **22.** h^5 **23.** $7m^3$
24. 10^4 **25.** $2x^2$ **26.** $3y^4$ **27.** 51 **28.** 14
29. 34 **30.** 5 **31.** 81 **32.** 48 **33.** 36 **34.** 25
35. 38

Daily Review 2-2

1. 15 **2.** 36 **3.** 24 **4.** 14 **5.** 22 **6.** 0
7. 60°, 60°, 120°, 120° **8.** 21, 22, 23 **9.** 11, 14
10. 32 **11.** 400 **12.** 144 **13.** 37 **14.** 0
15. 45 **16.** 28 **17.** 42 **18.** 2 **19.** 4.26
20. 7.66 **21.** 12.18 **22.** 2 **23.** $\frac{3}{8}$ **24.** $\frac{1}{2}$
25. $1\frac{1}{4}$ **26.** $\frac{7}{10}$ **27.** $4\frac{1}{4}$

Daily Review 2-3

1.

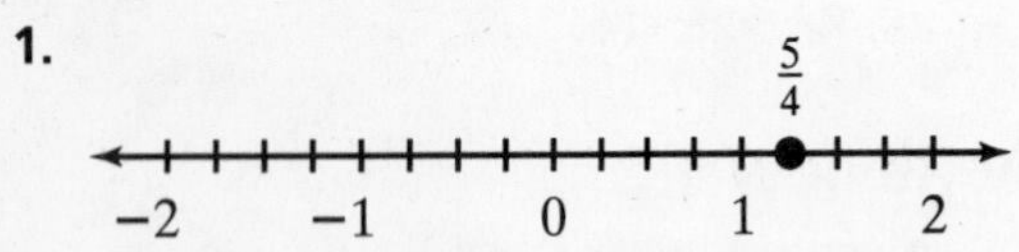

2.

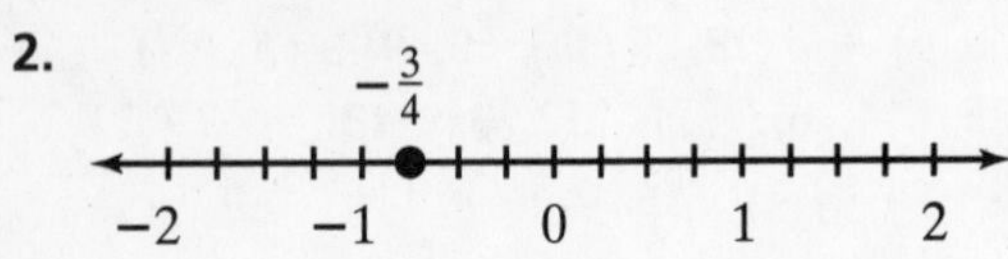

3.

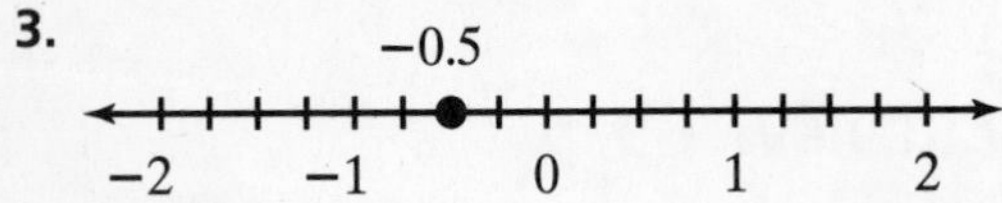

4.

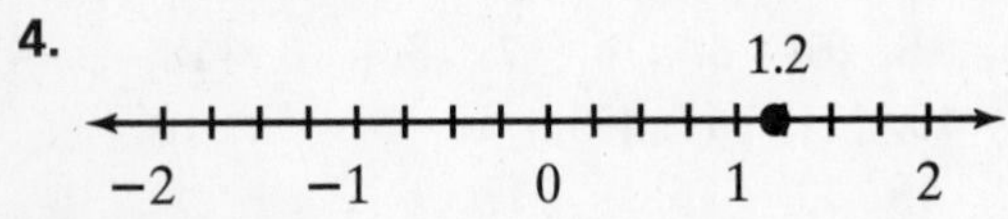

5.

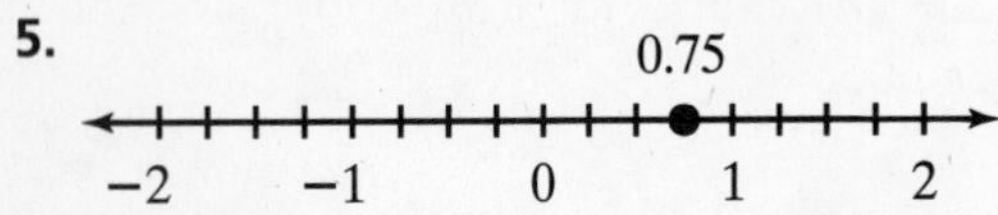

6.

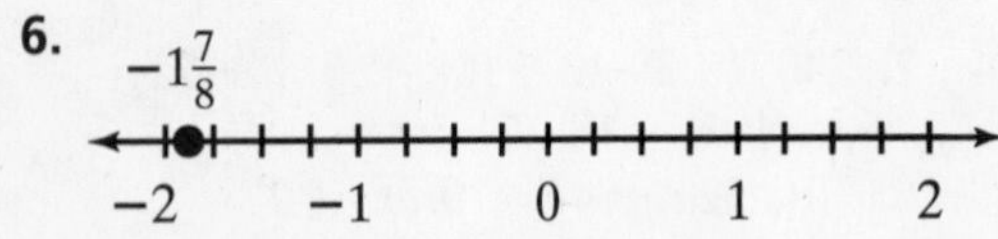

7. –17, –12, –8, –3, 15 **8.** –35, –31, –28, –16, –5, 27
9. $\frac{b}{2}$ **10.** $2h + 7$ **11.** $m + 3n$ **12.** 49 **13.** 20
14. 14 **15.** 9^4 **16.** p^7 **17.** $15n^5$ **18.** {3}
19. {2} **20.** {12} **21.** {5}

Daily Review 2-4

1. 4 **2.** –4.8 **3.** 0 **4.** $-\frac{2}{3}$ **5.** $-\frac{1}{10}$ **6.** $-1\frac{1}{21}$
7. < **8.** > **9.** > **10.** < **11.** < **12.** >
13. > **14.** < **15.** < **16.** 24 **17.** 9 **18.** 7
19. 16 **20.** 24 **21.** 6 **22.** $\frac{3}{7}$ **23.** $\frac{7}{13}$ **24.** $3b$
25. $\frac{3x}{4z}$ **26.** $\frac{3p}{r}$ **27.** $\frac{2m}{3n}$ **28.** 315 **29.** $\frac{2}{7}$ **30.** $\frac{1}{24}$
31. 1.92 **32.** 0.21 **33.** 0.091 **34.** 0.04223
35. $\frac{4}{27}$ **36.** $\frac{1}{9}$ **37.** 0.21

Daily Review 2-5

1. –11 **2.** 0 **3.** – 64 **4.** 5 **5.** $\frac{4}{7}$ **6.** –15.2
7. –54 **8.** 39 **9.** $\frac{5}{3}$ **10.** −0.517 **11.** −451
12. 3.7 **13.** 0 **14.** 8 **15.** $-\frac{2}{9}$ **16.** $9y + 54$
17. $15m + 24$ **18.** $16p + 28q + 40$
19. $18 + 2j$ **20.** $88z + 80$
21. $42v + 35w + 35$ **22.** 28 **23.** $1\frac{1}{2}$ **24.** 9
25. 8 **26.** 8 **27.** 2 **28.** 40 **29.** 190 **30.** 3
31. 38 **32.** 23 **33.** 9 **34.** 36

Daily Review 2-6

1. –63 **2.** 32 **3.** –0.36 **4.** $\frac{1}{3}$ **5.** –21 **6.** $\frac{1}{2}$
7. 19 **8.** –27 **9.** 3 **10.** $9x + 19$ **11.** $14x$
12. $13y^2 + 4y$ **13.** $\frac{5}{4}h$ **14.** $14a + 12b$
15. $12b + 15$ **16.** $21m + 19n$ **17.** $2(9x + 8)$
18. $7(a + 3b + 9)$ **19.** $5(6p + 7q + 9)$
20. {5} **21.** {10} **22.** {1} **23.** {3} **24.** {6}
25. {5} **26.** 48 m **27.** 88 ft **28.** 374 mm

Daily Review 2-7

1. –12 **2.** 7 **3.** 0 **4.** 1.3 **5.** –2 **6.** $\frac{2}{3}$ **7.** –3
8. –20 **9.** 16 **10.** 256 **11.** −32 **12.** −1
13. 45 **14.** 100 **15.** 2 **16.** 45 **17.** 30 **18.** 4
19. 15 **20.** 13 **21.** 36 **22.** 48 **23.** 1.56
24. $-\frac{3}{2}$ **25.** $5j$ **26.** $n + 7$ **27.** $\frac{1}{2}bh$
28. $3h - 2$ **29.** $p + q$ **30.** $a - 4c$

Daily Review 2-8

1. $5y - 30$ **2.** $-4x + 12y + 32$
3. $3a - 6b - 30$ **4.** $12x - y - 7$ **5.** $-\frac{1}{3}a + \frac{2}{9}$
6. $-5.1 + 12x + 10.5y$ **7.** $-\frac{1}{12}$ **8.** $\frac{5}{16}$ **9.** $-\frac{10}{7}$
10. $\frac{b}{a}$ **11.** $\frac{m}{l}$ **12.** $\frac{5y}{2x}$ **13.** $\frac{-4u}{3w}$ **14.** $2b$
15. $-9z$ **16.** 140 cars **17.** 5 **18.** 8 **19.** 7
20. 2 **21.** < **22.** < **23.** > **24.** < **25.** <
26. < **27.** > **28.** > **29.** < **30.** > **31.** <
32. <

Daily Cumulative Review Answers (continued)

Daily Review 2-9

1. $7m - 7$ **2.** $3x + 2$ **3.** $7a - 3b$
4. $-4m - 6n$ **5.** $9(h - 7j)$ **6.** $4(12 - m)$
7. $\frac{1}{3}(m - 2n - 5)$ **8.** $a(x - y)$ **9.** $x(7 - a)$
10. $b(x - y + 3z)$ **11.** $9 + y$ **12.** qp
13. $n + 7m$ or $m \cdot 7 + n$ **14.** $x + (y + 17)$
15. $14(mn)$ **16.** $(5x^2 + x) + 9$ **17.** –29
18. 15 **19.** 17 **20.** $-\frac{2}{5}$ **21.** –2.03 **22.** 7.4
23. $6x + 30$ **24.** $5 + 5y$ **25.** $2a + 2b + 14$

Daily Review 2-10

1–2. Answers may vary. Samples: **1.** Let p = the number of points scored by the Panthers. $p + 14 = 23$ **2.** Let t = the cost of one T-shirt. $5t = 9$ **3.** $-3x - 19$ **4.** $-5a + 6b$
5. $2x + 7y - 8z$ **6.** $-4a + 5b - 11$
7. $7x + 8y$ **8.** $-13x - 2y - 15$ **9.** $x = 10$
10. $y = 20$ **11.** $y = 7$ **12.** $x = 28$
13. $x = 5$ **14.** $d = 18$ **15.** 72 ft^2 **16.** 225 cm^2
17. 472.5 $in.^2$ **18.** 27 **19.** 13 **20.** 11 **21.** 7
22. 8 **23.** 17

Daily Review 3-1

1. Additive inverses **2.** Distributive property of multiplication over subtraction **3.** Commutative property of multiplication **4.** Associative property of addition **5–7.** Answers may vary. Samples: **5.** Let c = the price of each CD. $4c = 33.20$ **6.** Let t = the time it takes the sound of thunder to reach you. $1087t = 16{,}000$ **7.** Let m = the number of baskets missed. $m + 39 = 50$ **8.** –42 **9.** 20 **10.** –0.18
11. $\frac{2}{7}$ **12.** $-\frac{4}{15}$ **13.** 0.88 **14.** $-\frac{1}{25}$ **15.** $\frac{4}{11}$
16. $-\frac{10}{9}$ **17.** 45 **18.** 144 **19.** 24 **20.** 16
21. 49 **22.** 3 **23.** 8^2 **24.** 10^3 **25.** 5^4

Daily Review 3-2

1. –5 **2.** 11 **3.** –9 **4.** –2.3 **5.** 2.4 **6.** $-\frac{1}{6}$
7. Multiplicative inverses **8.** Multiplicative identity **9.** Distributive property of multiplication over addition **10.** Commutative property of multiplication **11.** $11a$ **12.** $29x$
13. $12y + 9$ **14.** $7x^2 + 6x$ **15.** $10m + 6n$
16. $14a + 2b + 11$ **17.** $5a + 30$ **18.** $14y + 49$
19. $4x + 36$ **20.** $-4b + 24$ **21.** $6x - 3y + 15$
22. $3m - \frac{5}{3}n + 6$ **23.** $20x - 10y + 40$
24. $-3x + 27$ **25.** $4a + 2b - \frac{7}{2}$ **26.** 4^6
27. $3y^4$ **28.** $8n^5$

Daily Review 3-3

1. –6 **2.** 9 **3.** –24 **4.** –38 **5.** 18 **6.** –7
7. –6 **8.** –11 **9.** 3.1 **10.** –6 **11.** $\frac{19}{12}$
12. 11.6 **13.** $a + 7$ **14.** $5h$ **15.** $n - 4$
16. $3(x + 12)$ **17.** $7(y + 8)$
18. $4(x + 2y + 6)$ **19.** $4(x - 9)$
20. $b(x - 12)$ **21.** $\frac{1}{3}(2y - z + 4)$ **22.** 57
23. –3.59 **24.** $\frac{2}{7}$ **25.** 1.3 mL **26.** 1.2 mL
27. 2.1 mL

Daily Review 3-4

1. 6 **2.** 4 **3.** 6 **4.** 6 **5.** –0.7 **6.** 4 **7.** 4
8. –21 **9.** 30 **10.** 3 **11.** –6 **12.** $\frac{3}{14}$
13. $-\frac{8}{15}$ **14.** –36 **15.** 9 **16.** 32 **17.** –1
18. –12 **19.** $(3 + x) + y$ **20.** $m(n \cdot 8)$
21. $(7x + x) + z$ **22.** $-5m - 3$ **23.** $-4x + 9$
24. $3a + 7b - 11$ **25.** $\frac{1}{3}$ **26.** $\frac{1}{5b}$ **27.** $\frac{14}{19r}$
28. 18 **29.** 12 **30.** 10 **31.** 3 **32.** 10 **33.** 13

Daily Review 3-5

1. $5n - 17$ **2.** $\frac{n}{3} + 9$ **3.** $2(n - 7)$
4. $3(n - 5)$ **5.** $\frac{1}{2}n + 8$ **6.** $\frac{1}{3}(n + 5)$ **7.** –6
8. 13 **9.** –9 **10.** 15 **11.** 12 **12.** 2 **13.** 36
14. –10 **15.** $-\frac{5}{21}$ **16.** –0.24 **17.** $-\frac{1}{20}$
18. 7.35 **19.** –8 **20.** 17 **21.** $\frac{3}{2}$ **22.** 125
23. 0 **24.** $-\frac{3}{2}$ **25.** $x - 5$ **26.** $-6n + 12$
27. $5a + 4$ **28.** $-7m - 17$ **29.** $6y + 7$
30. $4b + 6$ **31.** –16, –14, –11, 5, 12
32. –35, –24, –21, –10, –2

Daily Review 3-6

1. 11 **2.** –6 **3.** –3 **4.** 4 **5.** $-\frac{8}{5}$ **6.** 4
7. $3n + 6$ **8.** $\frac{1}{2}n - 5$ **9.** $3(n + 8)$ **10.** 24
11. 14 **12.** 45 **13.** 21 **14.** 4 **15.** 16 **16.** 16
17. 225 **18.** 29 **19.** 84 $in.^2$ **20.** 121.5 cm^2
21. 775 ft^2 **22.** 16 **23.** –5 **24.** –14 **25.** 6
26. 10 **27.** $\frac{3}{2}$

Daily Review 3-7

1. $\frac{7}{11}$ **2.** –1 **3.** $-\frac{1}{3}$ **4.** 3 **5.** $\frac{1}{4}$ **6.** 2 **7.** 7
8. –5 **9.** 1 **10.** 5 **11.** –2 **12.** –4 **13.** 9
14. 12 **15.** 27 **16.** 15 **17.** –1 **18.** 4 **19.** 4

Daily Cumulative Review Answers (continued)

20. 3 **21.** 11 **22.** 5 **23.** $\{\frac{1}{2}\}$ **24.** {14}
25. {3} **26.** {3} **27.** {4} **28.** {14}

Daily Review 3-8

1. $r = \frac{I}{Pt}$ **2.** $d = 4A - a - b - c$ **3.** $w = \frac{A}{l}$
4. $A = \frac{f}{\sigma}$ **5.** $r^3 = \frac{3V}{4\pi}$
6. $y_2 = mx_2 - mx_1 + y_1$ **7.** $-\frac{7}{5}$ **8.** −3 **9.** 24
10. 7 **11.** −11 **12.** 10 **13.** −10 **14.** −42
15. 3 **16.** Answers may vary. Sample: Let r = the hourly earnings. $40r = 330$ **17.** 63 **18.** $-\frac{4}{3}$
19. 2.8 **20.** $-5x + 20$ **21.** $-12n + 18m + 48$
22. $-4y + 4.8$ **23.** $-7y + 63$
24. $-2m + 4n + 8$ **25.** $-12x + 3.6$

Daily Review 3-9

1. 37, −37 **2.** 11, −11 **3.** 9, −9 **4.** $\frac{7}{3}, -\frac{7}{3}$
5. 2, −2 **6.** 3, −3 **7.** $h = \frac{V}{lw}$ **8.** $x = \frac{y - b}{m}$
9. $h = \frac{s - 2\pi r^2}{2\pi r}$ **10.** m **11.** $\frac{2}{3}$ **12.** $\frac{12b}{23}$
13. $7z$ **14.** $\frac{1}{6m}$ **15.** $3d$ **16.** −7 **17.** −54
18. −15 **19.** 1.25 **20.** 36 **21.** 32
22–27. Answers may vary. Samples: **22.** $\frac{-5}{1}$
23. $\frac{36}{10}$ or $\frac{18}{5}$ **24.** $\frac{-17}{8}$ **25.** $\frac{17}{-100}$ **26.** $\frac{13}{3}$
27. $\frac{-55}{10}$ or $\frac{11}{-2}$

Daily Review 3-10

1. 5 teachers **2.** 50 L **3.** 25, −25 **4.** 10, −10
5. 4, −4 **6.** $4n - 15$ **7.** $\frac{n}{5} + 6$ **8.** $\frac{1}{2}(n + 12)$
9. 4 **10.** −11 **11.** 5 **12.** −5 **13.** −4 **14.** 3
15. 125 **16.** 300 **17.** 36 **18.** 30 **19.** 57
20. 16 **21.** 14 **22.** 18 **23.** $\frac{5}{2}$

Daily Review 3-11

1. 60% **2.** \$3.51 **3.** \$1650; \$21,650 **4.** \$3000
5. 5 **6.** 15 **7.** 35 **8.** 24 **9.** $\frac{45}{7}$ **10.** 70
11. 200 posts **12.** −15 **13.** 4 **14.** 10 **15.** $-\frac{7}{8}$
16. −11 **17.** −7.7 **18.** 13 **19.** −15 **20.** 3.9
21. 4 **22.** −19 **23.** −12 **24.** $9 + x$ **25.** qp
26. $9 + 7m$ or $m \cdot 7 + 9$

Daily Review 3-12

1. 35, 37, 39 **2.** \$1200 **3.** 13 ft; 6 ft
4. 62.5% **5.** 7.2 **6.** 50 **7.** 35%

8.

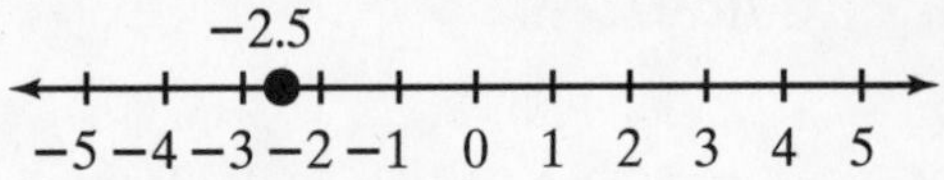

9.

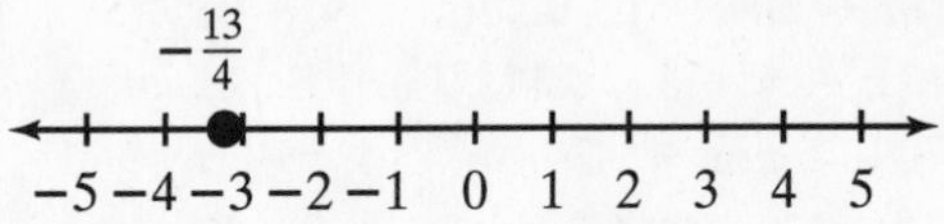

10.

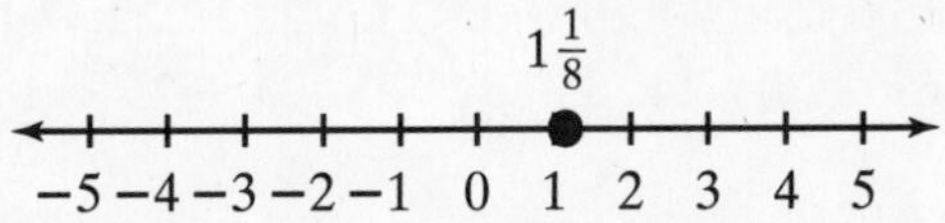

11. > **12.** < **13.** > **14.** < **15.** > **16.** >
17. < **18.** > **19.** < **20.** < **21.** < **22.** >
23. Transitive property **24.** Associative property of addition **25.** Commutative property of addition **26.** Distributive property of multiplication over addition

Daily Review 4-1

1. 20 days; Sunday **2.** 24 matches **3.** \$10.71
4. \$15.75 **5.** −16 **6.** −58 **7.** $-\frac{1}{2}$ **8.** $-\frac{1}{12}$
9. −0.56 **10.** −2.97 **11.** −22 **12.** 21 **13.** $-\frac{8}{9}$
14. $-\frac{7}{8}$ **15.** −8.1 **16.** 2.64 **17.** −15 **18.** 17
19. −3.2 **20.** 1.8 **21.** $-\frac{1}{2}$ **22.** $\frac{13}{10}$ **23.** $16x$
24. $\frac{7}{8}b + \frac{2}{3}$ **25.** $8m^2 + 5m$

Daily Review 4-2

1. $x > -2$ **2.** $x \leq -1$ **3.** $x < 3$
4. 35 m by 35 m **5.** 125, 126, 127 **6.** −49
7. 72 **8.** 1.5 **9.** −16.1 **10.** −70 **11.** 57.6
12. $-\frac{1}{3}$ **13.** $\frac{1}{2}$ **14.** $\frac{1}{4}$ **15.** 3 **16.** −75
17. undefined **18.** −19 **19.** $\frac{7}{6}$ **20.** $-\frac{10}{21}$
21. 60 **22.** −12 **23.** $\frac{2}{3}$ **24.** 6.3 **25.** 20%
26. 184

Daily Review 4-3

1. $x > -4$ **2.** $y \leq 5$ **3.** $n \geq 7$ **4.** $r > -8$
5. $z < 8$ **6.** $a \leq -10$ **7.** no **8.** yes **9.** no
10. no **11.** $9x - 99$ **12.** $-4y + 32$
13. $6x + 15y - 24$ **14.** $6m - \frac{9}{2}n + \frac{1}{12}$
15. $-4.5c + 6d$ **16.** $2a - 4b + \frac{2}{5}$ **17.** −5
18. 80 **19.** −13 **20.** 21 **21.** −4 **22.** $\frac{1}{9}$
23. 7 **24.** −3 **25.** −6 **26.** −16 **27.** 7
28. −10 **29.** −4 **30.** 2 **31.** $\frac{5}{9}$

Daily Cumulative Review Answers (continued)

Daily Review 4-4

1. $x < -6$ **2.** $x \geq -\frac{10}{3}$ **3.** $y > -11$ **4.** $y < \frac{7}{2}$
5. $x \leq -0.6$ **6.** $y \geq -1.25$
7. $y > -3$;

−5 −4 −3 −2 −1 0 1 2 3 4 5

8. $x \leq 1$;

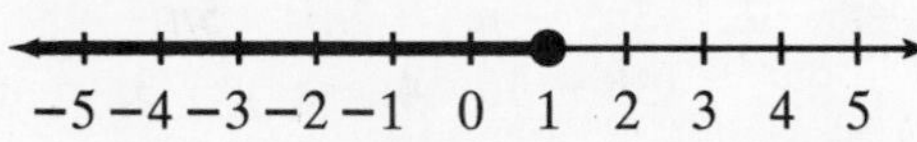

9. $x < 2$;

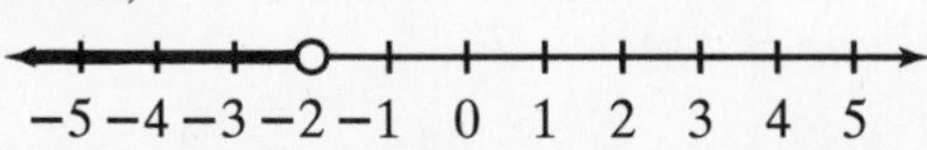

10. $n + 9$ **11.** $5x$ **12.** $m - 18$ **13.** $19n + 8$
14. $\frac{1}{2}(n - 17)$ **15.** $\frac{n}{4} + 11$ **16.** $(8x + x) + y$
17. $(9 \cdot 7)x$ **18.** $(4 \cdot 3)(x + y)$ **19.** $>$ **20.** $<$
21. $>$ **22.** $>$ **23.** $>$ **24.** $<$ **25.** $>$
26. $<$ **27.** $>$

Daily Review 4-5

1. $x > 9$ **2.** $y < -3$ **3.** $x \geq -2$ **4.** $y \leq 1$
5. $y < 7$ **6.** $x > -\frac{1}{6}$
7. $x < -2$;

−5 −4 −3 −2 −1 0 1 2 3 4 5

8. $x > -3$;

−5 −4 −3 −2 −1 0 1 2 3 4 5

9. $x \leq 3$;

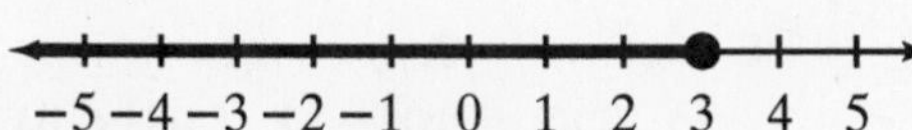

10. $8(1 + 5a)$ **11.** $7(2x + y)$
12. $3(2m + 3n + 5)$ **13.** $5(y - 7)$
14. $-6(m + 8)$ **15.** $a(x - 17)$
16. $\frac{1}{5}(3n - 2m + 4)$ **17.** $d(x - y + 3)$
18. $-3(5h + 6j)$ **19.** 18 combinations **20.** 4
21. 8 **22.** −5 **23.** 45, −45 **24.** 12, −12
25. $\frac{14}{3}, -\frac{14}{3}$

Daily Review 4-6

1. $15 < n$ **2.** $\frac{1}{2}x \geq 16$ **3.** $2m + 8 > -m$
4. $x < -6$ **5.** $x > -5$ **6.** $y \leq -5$ **7.** 8^3
8. y^7 **9.** $6m^4$ **10.** −16 **11.** −1 **12.** −132
13. 24 **14.** 144 **15.** 2 **16.** 196 **17.** 28
18. 64 **19.** 49 in.^{2} **20.** 225 m^2 **21.** 6.25 cm^2

Daily Review 5-1

1. ball B in cup A, C in B, D in C, and A in D
2. 162; 882 **3.** 7 m **4.** \$7142.86; \$7857.14
5. 16 **6.** 27 **7.** 81 **8.** 400 **9.** 100 **10.** 14
11. −29 **12.** 8 **13.** $-\frac{1}{14}$ **14.** −44 **15.** −435
16. 3.5

Daily Review 5-2

1. m^{13} **2.** $a^{10}b^{11}$ **3.** $x^6y^8z^4$ **4.** h^3 **5.** x^3y^4
6. $\frac{m}{n^5}$ **7.** president: Nina, vice president: Leonardo, secretary: Kara, treasurer: Marcus
8. Luc, by 1 min **9.** −72 **10.** 72 **11.** 3.5
12. −13.12 **13.** $-\frac{5}{36}$ **14.** $\frac{3}{2}$ **15.** −2
16. 0 **17.** 61 **18.** 1.9 **19.** $\frac{3}{4}$ **20.** $-\frac{10}{21}$
21. 4 **22.** 14 **23.** 12 **24.** 206, −206
25. 18, −18 **26.** 45, −45

Daily Review 5-3

1. 3^8 **2.** y^{21} **3.** $36x^{10}$ **4.** $\frac{n^{15}}{32}$ **5.** $\frac{a^{18}}{b^6}$
6. $\frac{9x^{18}y^{10}}{z^8}$ **7.** $\frac{1}{81}$ **8.** 1 **9.** $\frac{1}{32}$ **10.** 1 **11.** 1
12. $\frac{1}{81}$ **13.** $y < -12$ **14.** $n > -14$ **15.** $x < \frac{1}{20}$
16. $m > 25$ **17.** $h \leq -23$ **18.** $y \leq -12$
19. $x < 5$ **20.** $y \geq 1$ **21.** $n \leq 10$ **22.** $y > -5$
23. $x < -3$ **24.** $y > -15$ **25.** no **26.** no
27. no **28.** yes **29.** $>$ **30.** $>$ **31.** $<$
32. $>$ **33.** $<$ **34.** $>$ **35.** $<$ **36.** $<$ **37.** $<$

Daily Review 5-4

1. $56x^5$ **2.** $-x^9$ **3.** $18y^9$ **4.** a^8 **5.** $\frac{2}{3n}$ **6.** $\frac{2a^8}{5b^2}$
7. $125m^{18}$ **8.** $\frac{16x^{12}}{y^{28}}$ **9.** $\frac{a^4b^8}{25c^{18}}$ **10.** $5x, 3y$
11. $8a, -4b, 7$ **12.** $5m, -\frac{2}{3}n, -8p, q$ **13.** $21a$
14. $11x^2 + 5x$ **15.** $10m + 8n + 4$ **16.** $-7y$
17. $-11x$ **18.** $5y - 3x$ **19.** $2.7m - 3.2n$
20. $-\frac{1}{3}a + \frac{2}{3}b$ **21.** $1.1x - 5.6y$ **22.** 7 **23.** −3
24. −24 **25.** 6 **26.** 7 **27.** −7 **28.** −2
29. −6 **30.** 5

Daily Review 5-5

1. 4.6×10^4 **2.** 8.07×10^{-4} **3.** 4.9×10^{-8}

Daily Cumulative Review Answers (continued)

4. a^5b^{10} **5.** $-\frac{y^5}{2x^5}$ **6.** $21m^7n^5$ **7.** 11 **8.** 55
9. 9 **10.** 42 **11.** 8 **12.** 22 **13.** 49 **14.** 121
15. 24 **16.** 206.25 ft **17.** 130.2 ft **18.** 56.25 ft
19. 56.25 **20.** 50% **21.** 248 **22.** 65%
23. 84 **24.** 49.8

Daily Review 5-6

1. 1, 0; 1 **2.** 3, 2, 0; 3 **3.** 3, 2, 1; 3 **4.** 5, 4, 3, 1; 5
5. 6.72×10^2 **6.** 4×10^2 **7.** 1.6×10^8 **8.** 13
9. -100 **10.** $-\frac{5}{9}$ **11.** -4.9 **12.** $\frac{1}{8}$ **13.** 0
14. -7 **15.** -27 **16.** -6 **17.** -15.7
18. -1.85 **19.** $-\frac{5}{8}$ **20.** $2y + 6$ **21.** $8a - 4$
22. $7x - 15$ **23.** $2x - 23$ **24.** -5 **25.** $\frac{15}{8}$
26. -3

Daily Review 5-7

1. $3x^5 + 3x^2 + x$ **2.** $3m^3 + 5m + 9$
3. $3y^3 - y^2 + 3y - 5$ **4.** $10x^3 + y^2 - xy$
5. $2n^2 + 6n + 5$ **6.** $2b^3 - 1\frac{1}{4}$
7. $3x^2, 8x, -3; 3, 8, -3$
8. $x^5y^3, -3xy^2, 8x^2y, -3; 1, -3, 8, -3$
9. $n^5, -3n^2; 1, -3$ **10.** $-8b^5, 3b, -9; -8, 3, -9$
11. $x^5, -x^4, -x^3, -x^2, 1; 1, -1, -1, -1, 1$
12. $-5m^5, m, -5; -5, 1, -5$ **13.** $y > -6$
14. $3x < 10$ **15.** $\frac{3}{x^3}$ **16.** $\frac{1}{27x^3}$ **17.** $\frac{a}{b^2}$ **18.** $\frac{3}{n}$
19. $x > 3$;

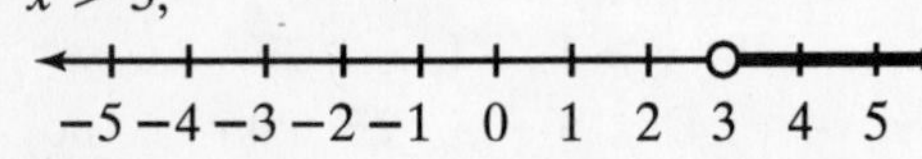

20. $n < 11$;

−4 −2 0 2 4 6 8 10 12 14 16

21. $y > \frac{1}{4}$;

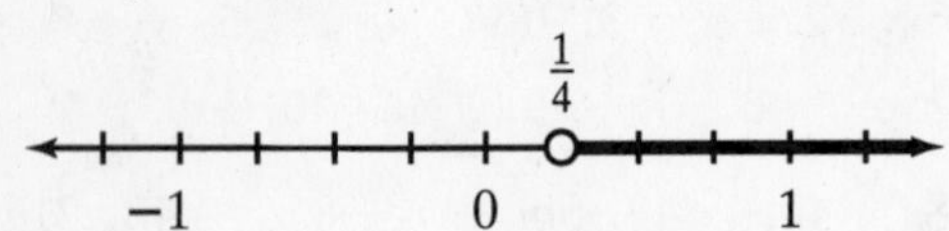

Daily Review 5-8

1. $3x - 2$ **2.** $3x^4 + x^3 + x - 7$
3. $2x^5 + 2x^4 - x^3 + x + 5$
4. $6x^3 + x^2 + 3x + 13$
5. $7x^5 + 3x^4 - 3x^3 - 5x^2 + x + 6$
6. $7x^2 - x + 11$ **7.** 40 **8.** -13 **9.** 48 **10.** 0
11. -52 **12.** 80 **13.** $5(x + 2)$
14. $3(a - 3b + 5)$ **15.** $4(2x - 5y)$

16–19. Answers may vary. Samples: **16.** $\frac{-25}{10}$ or $\frac{-5}{2}$
17. $\frac{667}{100}$ **18.** $\frac{-8}{1}$ **19.** $\frac{4}{100}$ or $\frac{1}{25}$ **20.** $-\frac{1}{4}$
21. 2 **22.** $\frac{1}{2}$ **23.** $n = \frac{PV}{RT}$ **24.** $V = \frac{nRT}{P}$
25. $b = \frac{2A}{h}$

Daily Review 5-9

1. $2x^2 - x$ **2.** $-3n^4 - n^3 - 2n^2 - 5n - 9$
3. $-b^3 + 8b^2 + 13b - 15$ **4.** $-x^2y - 3xy^2$
5. $3x^2 + 3x - 7$ **6.** $2x^2 + 8x + 4$
7. $b^2c + bc^2 + c^2 + 2bc$ **8.** $3x^2 + 5$
9. $5n^5 - n^4 - 3n^3 + 4n^2 + n + 3$
10. $y^2 + x^2 - xy + 5x$ **11.** $\frac{x^{10}y^{20}}{z^{10}}$ **12.** $\frac{n^4}{m^8p^{12}}$
13. $192x^7$ **14.** $\frac{1}{x^{10}}$
15. $y \leq -4$;

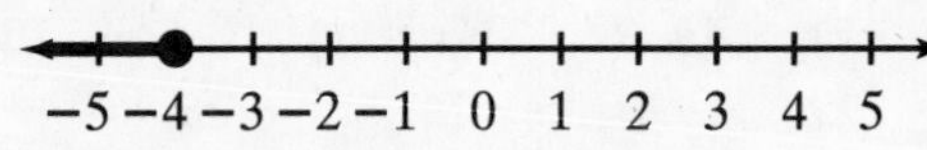

16. $x > 7$;

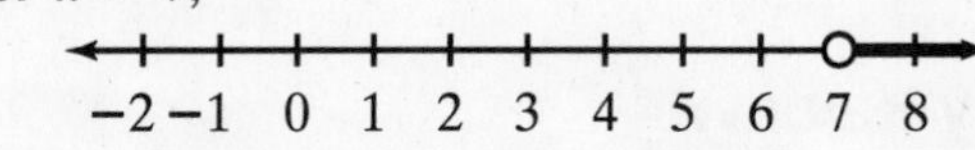

17. $x > 2$;

−5 −4 −3 −2 −1 0 1 2 3 4 5

18. 0.1 **19.** 0.05 **20.** 1.08 **21.** 0.009

Daily Review 5-10

1. $12y^2 - 32y$ **2.** $3x^3 - 15x^2$
3. $n^5 - 4n^4 + 3n^3 + 8n^2$ **4.** $x^2 + 2x - 15$
5. $y^3 + 3y^2 - 9y - 27$ **6.** $3m^2 + 19m - 40$
7. $6n + 19$ **8.** $6x^2 - 3$ **9.** $6y^2 + 5y + 7$
10. $-2x + 7$ **11.** 2.85×10^2 **12.** 5.98×10^{-4}
13. 6×10^6 **14.** 2.75×10^{-1} **15.** x **16.** $\frac{y^3}{3}$
17. $2y^2$ **18.** $\frac{1}{10a^2}$ **19.** $-2, -8$ **20.** $4, -4$
21. $30, -30$ **22.** $-3x + 9$ **23.** $-2y + 3$
24. $-n + 2$

Daily Review 5-11

1. $4x^2 + 12x + 9$ **2.** $y^2 - 25$ **3.** $b^2 - 4b + 4$
4. $9n^2 - 25$ **5.** $m^2 + 16m + 64$
6. $9x^2 - 24x + 16$ **7.** $2x^2 - 11x - 21$
8. $2y^2 - 21y + 40$ **9.** $3m^2 - 15m$
10. $y^3 - 2y^2 + 3y - 6$ **11.** $-10x^3 - 40x^2$

Daily Cumulative Review Answers (continued)

12. $2n^2 + 18n + 40$ **13.** $\frac{3}{2x}$ **14.** $\frac{m}{n}$ **15.** $\frac{5}{2}$
16. $\frac{1}{10}$ **17.** $n > -\frac{7}{5}$ **18.** $x \le 20$ **19.** $y \ge -4$
20. $3x^2, -5x, 8; 3, -5, 8$
21. $y^2, -y, -20; 1, -1, -20$
22. $3a^2b, 9ab^2, 6b^2, -5; 3, 9, 6, -5$ **23.** $\frac{7}{3}$ **24.** 10
25. 28 **26.** $\frac{7}{2}$

Daily Review 5-12

1. $y^3 - 1$ **2.** $2n^3 + 8n^2 + 12n + 8$ **3.** $x^4 - 16$
4. $3b^4 + 24b^3 + 48b^2$ **5.** $9 - 6n^2 + n^4$
6. $z^4 - 2z^3 + 3z^2 - 2z + 1$ **7.** $b^2 + 4b + 4$
8. $25x^2 + 30x + 9$ **9.** $4n^2 - 25$
10. $4y^2 - 28y + 49$ **11.** $m^2 - \frac{1}{4}$ **12.** $z^4 - 0.36$
13. $x^2 - y^2$ **14.** a^2 or $a^2 - b^2 + b^2$
15. 8 added to both sides **16.** both sides multiplied by 3 **17.** 10 subtracted from both sides **18.** 1 **19.** 5 **20.** 20

Daily Review 6-1

1. \$1560 **2.** 19 balls **3.** $\frac{9}{4} - 3x^2 + x^4$
4. $2y^3 + 3y^2 + 4$ **5.** $-5n^3 + 10n^2 + 30n$
6. $y^5 + 2y^4 - y^2$ **7.** $49 - 9x^4$ **8.** $z^4 - 1$
9. $9y^2$ **10.** $-\frac{n^3}{m^3}$ **11.** $32x^{10}z^{15}$ **12.** $\frac{16a^4}{b^4}$
13. -45 **14.** -43 **15.** 12 **16.** -3 **17.** $-1\frac{1}{4}$
18. 8 **19.** $x - 3$ **20.** $m + n$ **21.** $\frac{y}{2}$
22. $c + b$ **23.** $\frac{x}{4}$ **24.** $6z$

Daily Review 6-2

1. $x^2(3 - 5x^2)$ **2.** $3y(y - 2)$
3. $x^2y^2(2x - 7y^3)$ **4.** $n^2(n^3 - n + 1)$
5. $m^4(7m - 2)$ **6.** $3x(x + 1)$ **7.** 9 weeks
8. 1534 marbles **9.** $x^3 + x^2 + x + 1$
10. $-15y^3 + 5y^5$ **11.** $3n^2 + 11n + 10$
12. $-15a + 18b - 21c$ **13.** $2x - 3y + 5$
14. $10x + 5y$ **15.** $-4x - 5$ **16.** $-4y + 16$
17. $-x - 7$ **18–21.** Answers may vary. Samples:
18. $\frac{-8}{1}$ **19.** $\frac{7}{2}$ **20.** $\frac{24}{10}$ or $\frac{12}{5}$ **21.** $-\frac{1111}{1000}$ **22.** $\frac{1}{2}$
23. $\frac{1}{5}$ **24.** 5

Daily Review 6-3

1. $3(y^2 + 2)(y^2 - 2)$ **2.** $(4 + x)(4 - x)$
3. $3(0.8x^2 + 1)(0.8x^2 - 1)$ **4.** $(6 + y)(6 - y)$
5. $(3y + 2x)(3y - 2x)$
6. $(13 + 5x^3)(13 - 5x^3)$ **7.** $3x(x - 3)$
8. $2m^2(1 - 3m^2)$ **9.** $y^3(y^2 - 1 + y + y^3)$
10. $2xy(x + 2y + 4)$ **11.** $a^2b(1 + 3b)$
12. $x^2(5x + 1)$ **13.** $2x^3 + 4x^2 + 3x - 3$
14. $p^3 - p^2 + 8p + 5$
15. $-3y^3 + 2y^2 + 5y + 8$
16. n^2 **17.** x^3y **18.** 1 **19.** $\frac{1}{x^2}$
20. $x > -3$;

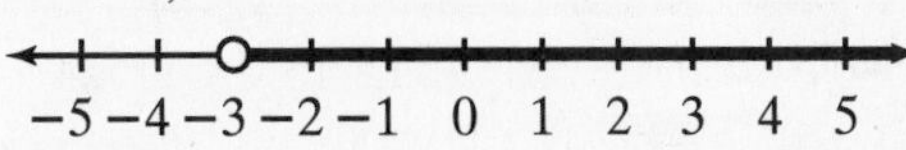

21. $x \ge \frac{1}{2}$;

−2 −1 0 1 2

22. $y > 7$;

−2 −1 0 1 2 3 4 5 6 7 8

23. 4 **24.** 4 **25.** 70 **26.** 60

Daily Review 6-4

1. $2(x + 3)^2$ **2.** $(x - 13)^2$ **3.** $(0.5x + 10)^2$
4. $(x + 5)^2$ **5.** $5(x - 2)^2$ **6.** $(7x - 4)^2$
7. $(x + 9)(x - 9)$ **8.** $(1.5y + 0.8)(1.5y - 0.8)$
9. $2(3p + 2)(3p - 2)$ **10.** $(n^5 + 1)(n^5 - 1)$
11. $y(y + 5)(y - 5)$ **12.** $5\left(x + \frac{1}{5}\right)\left(x - \frac{1}{5}\right)$
13. $-2x + 5$
14. $3y^5 + y^4 + 2y^3 + 8y^2 - 5$ **15.** $x < -2$
16. $y \le -2$ **17.** $m < 21$ **18.** 50% **19.** 37.5%
20. 95% **21.** 24% **22.** $3n + 2$ **23.** $\frac{n}{3} - 5$
24. 0 **25.** 6 **26.** -13

Daily Review 6-5

1. $(x + 2)(x + 6)$ **2.** $(y - 6)(y + 5)$
3. $(m - 1)(m - 2)$ **4.** $(x + 11)(x - 5)$
5. $(m + 5)(m + 15)$ **6.** $(x - 4)(x - 14)$
7. $(x + 2)^2(x - 2)^2$ **8.** $(y + 9)^2$ **9.** $5\left(y - \frac{1}{2}\right)^2$
10. $(2n + 3)^2$ **11.** $(c^3 + 3b)^2$ **12.** $2(x - 8)^2$
13. -9 **14.** -4 **15.** 11 **16.** -25
17. $-3y + 15$ **18.** $2y - 3x + 1$
19. $-15x + 40y - 10$ **20.** 26 **21.** $\frac{3}{4}$ **22.** 9
23. 5 **24.** -4 **25.** 50 **26.** $27n^{15}$ **27.** $\frac{9}{x^6}$
28. $\frac{x^8y^4}{z^{12}}$ **29.** y^{16}

Daily Review 6-6

1. $(x + 3)(2x - 1)$ **2.** $(2n + 5)(2n - 3)$
3. $(y - 8)(5y + 4)$ **4.** $(7m - 8)(m - 5)$
5. $(x - 4)(3x - 9)$ **6.** $(2y + 5)(3y - 4)$
7. $(x + 5)(x - 4)$ **8.** $(y - 6)(y - 3)$

Daily Cumulative Review Answers (continued)

9. $(a + 3b)(a + 7b)$ **10.** $(n - 5)(n + 2)$
11. $(x + 13)(x + 2)$ **12.** $(28y + z)(2y + z)$
13. $3x^3 + 4x^2 + 5$
14. $-x^5 + x^4 - 7x^3 - x^2 + x + 13$
15. $7.5 < n$ **16.** $x + 3 < -2$
17. $x \leq 18$

−6 −3 0 3 6 9 12 15 18 21 24

18. $y > 1$;

−5 −4 −3 −2 −1 0 1 2 3 4 5

19. $y < 12$;

−6 −3 0 3 6 9 12 15 18 21 24

20. 7, −7 **21.** 35, −35 **22.** 3, −3

Daily Review 6-7

1. $(2x + 5)(x^2 - 3)$ **2.** $(5x^2 + 4)(x - 2)$
3. $(n - m)(a + b)$ **4.** $(y + 3)(a - b)$
5. $(y^2 - 5)(3y^3 + 4)$ **6.** $(z^2 + 3)(6z - 5)$
7. $(2x + 5)(x - 8)$ **8.** $(3y - 7)(2y + 3)$
9. $(5 - 2b)(5 - 5b)$ **10.** $3(x + 2)(2x + 7)$
11. $(10x + 7)(3x - 2)$ **12.** $y(2y + 9)(y - 8)$
13. $2x(x - 8)$ **14.** $3ab(a + 3)$ **15.** $7(2x^2 + 1)$
16. $x^2 - 9$ **17.** $4x^2 - 25$ **18.** $n^4 - y^2$
19. 500,000 **20.** 0.00256 **21.** 500.03 **22.** 2.5
23. 0.16 **24.** 0.005 **25.** 0.036 **26.** $R = \frac{PV}{nT}$
27. $b = \frac{2A}{h}$ **28.** $\pi = \frac{3V}{4r^3}$

Daily Review 6-8

1. $3(x + 5)(x - 5)$ **2.** $y(y + 8)^2$
3. $(z^4 + 16)(z^2 + 4)(z + 2)(z - 2)$
4. $2(x + 3)(x - 5)$ **5.** $15(n + 1)^2$
6. $y^3(2y + 1)(y - 6)$ **7.** $(3y^2 - 2)(y - 5)$
8. $(2b + 7)(4b^2 + 5)$ **9.** $(a + b)(a - 5)$
10. $(x + y)(z - 5)$ **11.** $(y^5 + 3)(y^4 + 2)$
12. $(2x + 7)(x^2 - 5)$ **13.** $-6n^2 + 6n$
14. $2x^3 - 6x^2 + 5x - 15$ **15.** $x^2 - 49$
16. $5x^2 - 3x$ **17.** $mn^2 - 2m^2n$ **18.** $-3y^3 + 5$
19. $y \leq 60$ **20.** $x < 8$ **21.** $z < -2$ **22.** 7
23. 4 **24.** 10 **25.** 15 **26.** −15 **27.** $\frac{15}{4}$

Daily Review 6-9

1. 8, −3 **2.** 0, −5 **3.** 7, −7 **4.** 5, −4
5. −2, −1 **6.** $\frac{1}{10}, -\frac{1}{9}$ **7.** $5(x + 2)(x - 2)$
8. $3(x + 5)^2$ **9.** $y(3y + 4)^2$
10. $(y^4 + 1)(y^2 + 1)(y + 1)(y - 1)$
11. $(n + 2)^2(n - 2)^2$
12. $3(y^2 + 4)(y + 2)(y - 2)$ **13.** $x^3 - 2x + 4$
14. $3y^{11} - 4y^9 + 4y^7 + 8y^5 - 3y^3$
15. $(10x + 7)(10x - 7)$
16. $(1.5y + 0.8)(1.5y - 0.8)$
17. $(n^3 + 9)(n^3 - 9)$ **18.** F **19.** T **20.** T
21. T **22.** 2 **23.** 5 **24.** −5 **25.** $-\frac{1}{4}$
26. −41 **27.** 7.6

Daily Review 7-1

1. 5 s and about 7.24 s
2. 20 and 22; −22 and −20
3. 9, −15 **4.** $0, \frac{3}{4}$ **5.** −4, 6 **6.** $-4, \frac{3}{2}$
7. −3 **8.** −4 **9.** −3 **10.** 4 **11.** 1
12. 2 **13.** {3} **14.** {7} **15.** {1} **16.** {8}
17. {7} **18.** {10} **19.** 6 **20.** 3 **21.** −8
22. 1 **23.** −3 **24.** −10

Daily Review 7-2

1–9.

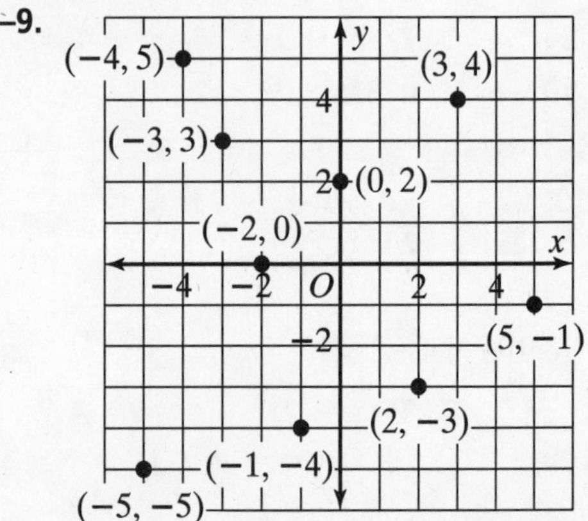

10. 45 m by 55 m **11.** 8 in.; 13 in. **12.** >
13. < **14.** < **15.** > **16.** > **17.** < **18.** >
19. > **20.** < **21.** 6 **22.** 2 **23.** −1 **24.** −2
25. −7 **26.** −6 **27.** −4 **28.** 12 **29.** −6
30. 15 **31.** 8 **32.** −6 **33.** 4 **34.** −12
35. −17

Daily Cumulative Review Answers (continued)

Daily Review 7-3

1.

x	0	−1	1	2	−2
y	0	3	−3	−6	6

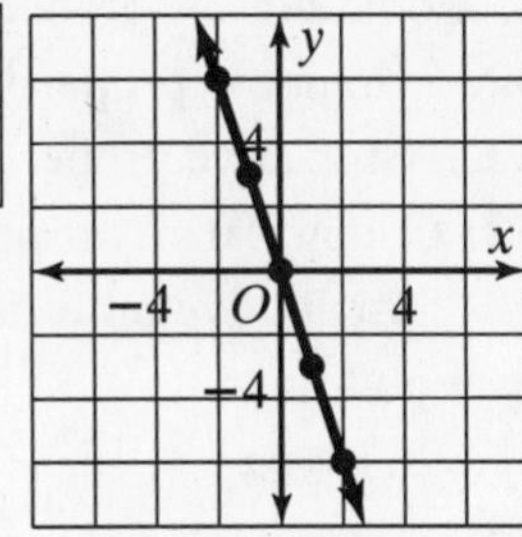

2.

x	0	1	−1	2	3
y	−1	1	−3	3	5

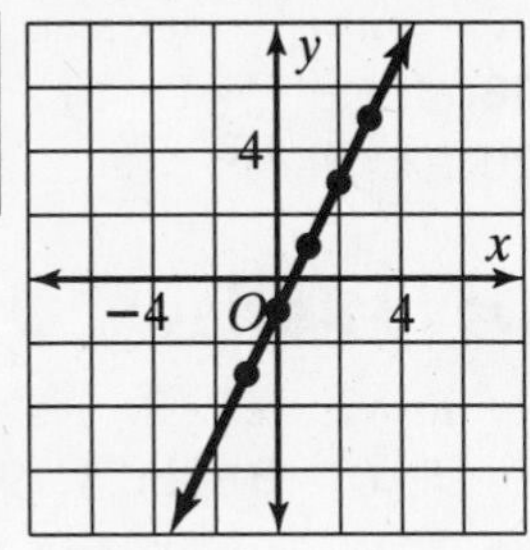

3. $(-4, 3)$ **4.** $(-2, 5)$ **5.** $(-3, 0)$ **6.** $(1, 2)$
7. $(-1, -3)$ **8.** $(-5, -4)$ **9.** $(4, -5)$
10. $(3, -1)$ **11.** $(0, -2)$ **12.** $\frac{1}{3}$ **13.** $\frac{x}{8}$ **14.** $\frac{15m}{14}$
15. 14 **16.** $\frac{y}{5}$ **17.** $\frac{7}{8r}$ **18.** $125a^3b^3$ **19.** $\frac{16}{x^2y^8}$
20. $\frac{m^9n^{12}}{8}$ **21.** 1.2 mL **22.** 0.9 mL
23. 1.1 mL

Daily Review 7-4

1.

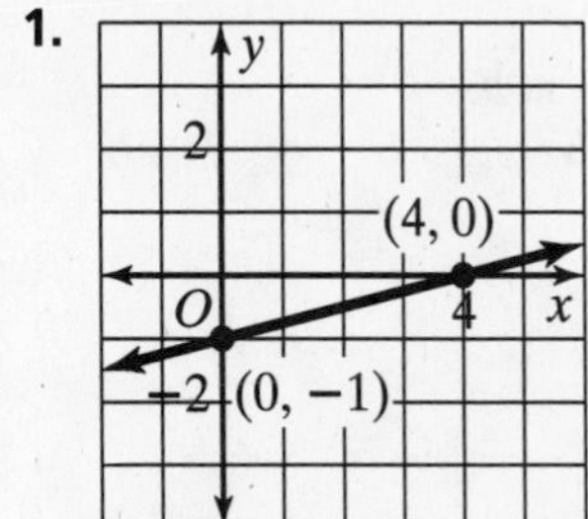

2.

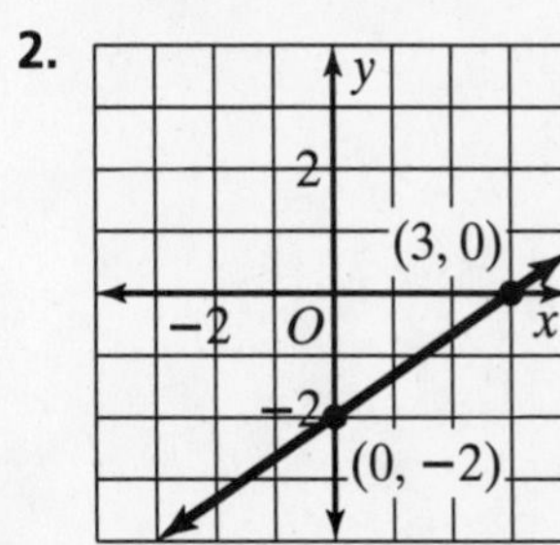

3. no **4.** yes **5.** yes **6.** no **7.** $19n$
8. $h - 16$ **9.** $\frac{m}{n}$ **10.** $2y + 7$ **11.** $5(x + 9)$
12. $\frac{1}{2}a - 15$ **13.** $x(3x - 14)$
14. $5(2x^2 - x + 7)$ **15.** $8mn(n - 5mn + 9m)$
16. $y(9y - 23)$ **17.** $7(3n^2 - n + 4)$
18. $6x^2y(2xy - y + 7)$ **19.** $(x - 10)(x + 10)$
20. $(3x + 11)(3x - 11)$
21. $y^2(6y + 5)(6y - 5)$ **22.** $(n + m)(n - m)$
23. $(4y - 7)(4y + 7)$ **24.** $7(3x - y)(3x + y)$

Daily Review 7-5

1. 2 **2.** $\frac{1}{3}$ **3.** 2 **4.** $\frac{4}{3}$ **5.** $-\frac{3}{4}$ **6.** −6

7. y x −2 O 2 −2

8.

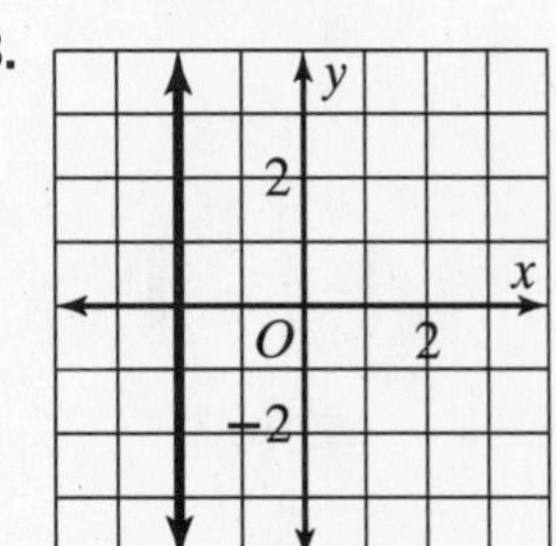

9.

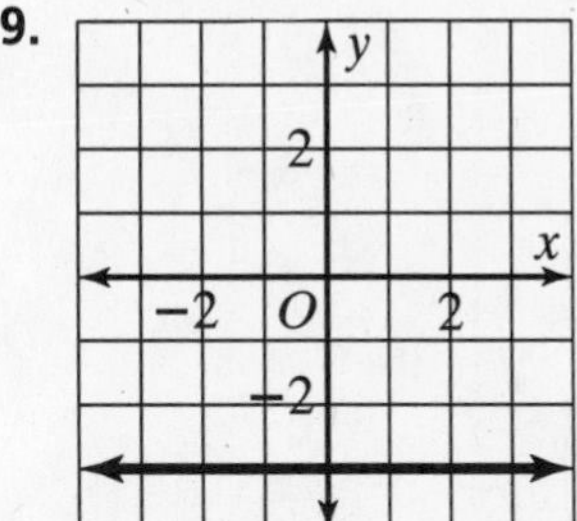

10. −17 **11.** 22 **12.** −11 **13.** 3 **14.** −6
15. 6 **16.** $x = \frac{y - b}{m}$ **17.** $m = \frac{y - 3}{x - 2}$
18. $y = m(x - 8) - 7$
19. $a = 4A - b - c - d$ **20.** $x = \frac{y + 8}{3}$
21. $y = 2x + 10$ **22.** $x^2 + 16x + 63$
23. $15y^2 - 24y$ **24.** $2x^2 + 7x - 30$
25. $x^2 - 15x + 44$ **26.** $48x^2 + 28x$
27. $24x^2 - 5x - 1$

Daily Review 7-6

1. $\frac{7}{4}$ **2.** −9 **3.** $\frac{2}{5}$ **4.** $-\frac{2}{3}$ **5.** $\frac{1}{3}$
6. −2 **7.** $-\frac{1}{2}$ **8.** $\frac{1}{3}$

Daily Cumulative Review Answers (continued)

9–17.

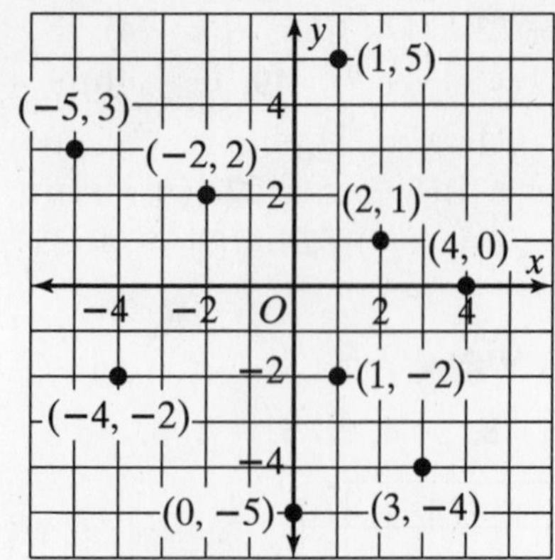

18. $(3x - 2)(x + 7)$ **19.** $(5x - 1)(2x + 3)$
20. $5(2x - 1)(x + 4)$ **21.** $(7x - 1)(x - 2)$
22. $(3x - 5)(x - 4)$ **23.** $7(2x + 9)(x + 1)$
24. $(n^2 + 9)(n + 3)(n - 3)$
25. $5(x - 8)(x + 8)$ **26.** $8(x - 2)^2$

Daily Review 7-7

1. $y = 3x - 10$ **2.** $y = -5x + 7$
3. $y = \frac{2}{3}x - 6$ **4.** $y = x - 9$ **5.** $y = -\frac{3}{4}x + 7$
6. $y = \frac{4}{5}x + \frac{33}{5}$
7.

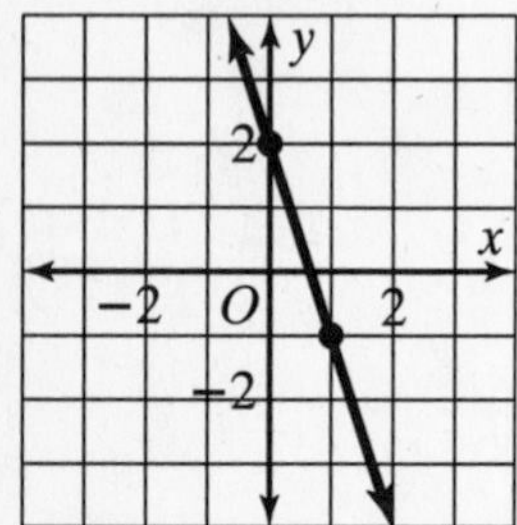

8.

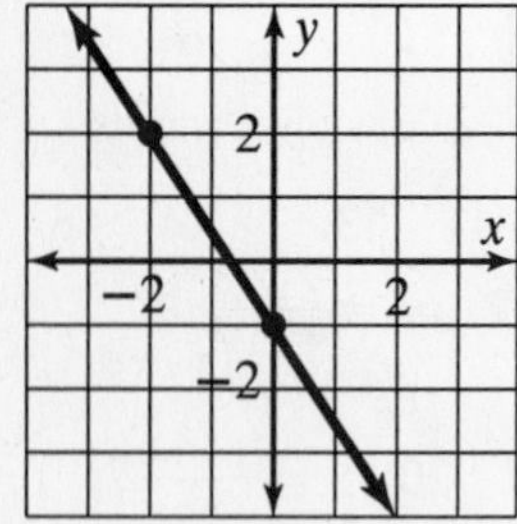

9. -99 **10.** 60 **11.** -7.7 **12.** 1 **13.** -1
14. -1 **15.** $x < 8$ **16.** $y < -12$ **17.** $x \geq 7$
18. $y \geq 0.9$ **19.** $x > 18$ **20.** $y \leq -16$
21. $x \leq 6$ **22.** $x < 6$ **23.** $y > -12$
24. $-11, 12$ **25.** $-7, 3$ **26.** $-\frac{2}{3}, 5$

Daily Review 7-8

1. \$5125 **2.** \$66.27 **3.** $y = x - 4$
4. $y = \frac{2}{3}x$ **5.** $y = -\frac{1}{2}x + 7$ **6.** $y = 5x + 12$
7. $y = \frac{3}{4}x + 6$ **8.** $y = \frac{5}{3}x - 1$
9. Commutative property of multiplication
10. Symmetric property **11.** Additive inverses
12. Associative property of addition
13. Commutative property of addition
14. Distributive property of multiplication over addition
15. $9x^4 + 5x^3 - 4x^2 - 12x + 5$
16. $x^2y - 10xy + 5y - 11$
17. $-m^2n^2 - 8m^2n - 12mn^2 + 17mn$
18. $4(x - 6)(x - 5)$ **19.** $10(x + 4)^2$
20. $(x^2 + 7)^2$

Daily Review 7-9

1. no **2.** yes **3.** yes **4.** yes **5.** no **6.** yes
7. \$85.60 **8.** \$2125 **9.** p^{12} **10.** a^8 **11.** m^8
12. a^5b^7 **13.** y^3 **14.** m^3n **15.** x^{20} **16.** $\frac{y^{12}}{16}$
17. $\frac{9x^6y^4}{16}$ **18.** b^{21} **19.** $\frac{a^{14}}{64}$ **20.** $\frac{25x^8y^{10}}{36}$

Daily Review 7-10

1. By definition, the x-intercept of a line is the x-coordinate of the point where the line intersects the x-axis. All points on the x-axis have y-coordinates of zero. Therefore, the x-intercept of $ax + by = ab$ is the value of x when $y = 0$.
$ax + by = ab$
$ax + b(0) = ab$ Substitute 0 for y.
$ax = ab$ Simplify. $x = b$
Therefore, the x-intercept is b.
2. yes **3.** no **4.** yes **5.** yes **6.** no **7.** no
8.

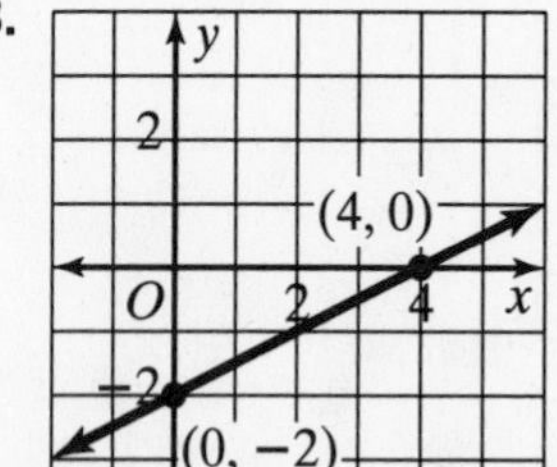

9.

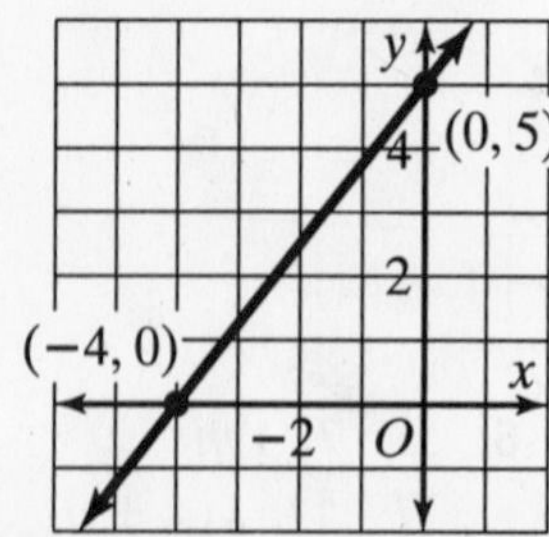

10. yes **11.** no **12.** no **13.** yes

Daily Cumulative Review Answers (continued)

14. $x^2 + 3x - 88$ **15.** $x^2 - 18x + 81$
16. $10y^4 + 3y^2 - 18$

Daily Review 8-1

1. 15 m **2.** 25 loads
3. $y = mx + b_1$; $y = mx + b_2$
4. $y_0 = mx_0 + b_1$
5. If (x_0, y_0) is on the second line, then $y_0 = mx_0 + b_2$. But this can only happen if $mx_0 + b_1 = mx_0 + b_2$, which implies $b_1 = b_2$. We already know $b_1 \neq b_2$, so it cannot be true that (x_0, y_0) is on the second line. Therefore the lines are parallel.
6. 3, −9 **7.** 5, −4 **8.** 9, 0 **9.** $x(x + 4)^2$
10. $(3 - 2y^2)^2$ **11.** $(m + 13)^2$ **12.** x^5
13. $27a^5b^5$ **14.** $16y^8$

Daily Review 8-2

1. (3, 2);

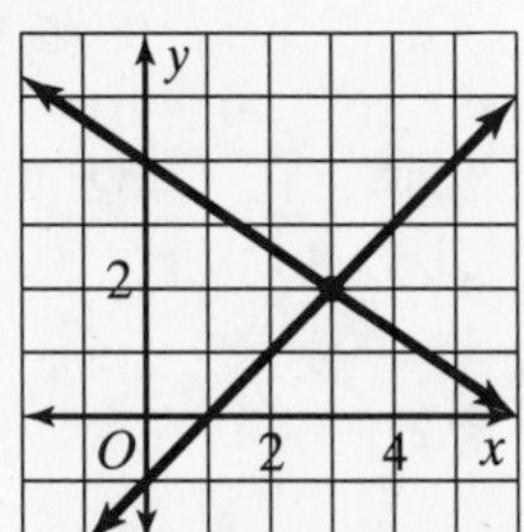

2. (1, −3);

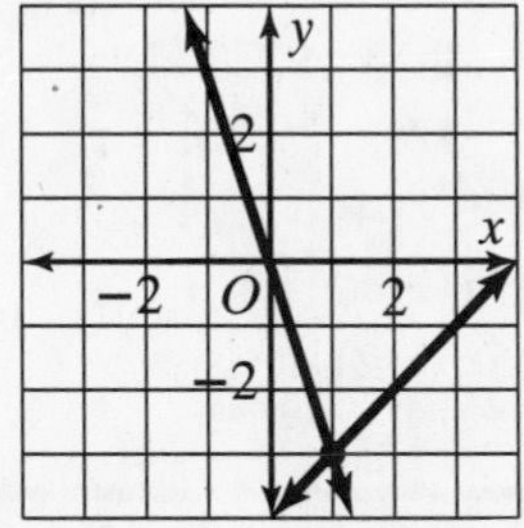

3. (−2, 4)

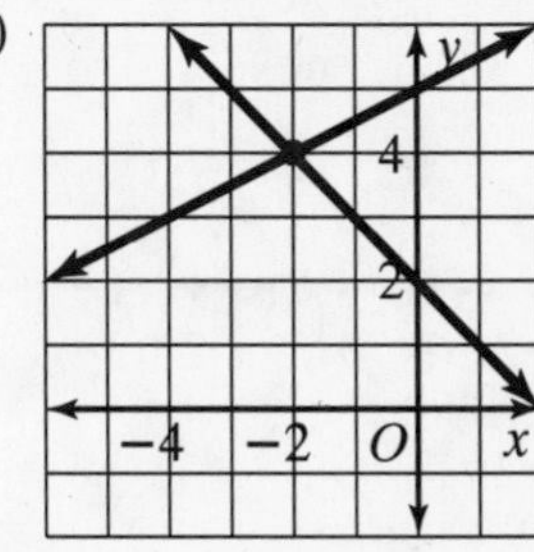

4. 390 **5.** 28 **6.** $n^4 + 10n^2 + 25$ **7.** $x^4 - 1$
8. $6y^3 - 24y^2 + 15y$ **9.** a^2b^2 **10.** x^9
11. $x^3y^2z^4$ **12.** $x - 5$ **13.** $3y - 2$
14. $-5a + 3b$ **15.** 13 **16.** 1 **17.** −7

Daily Review 8-3

1. (2, −6) **2.** (3, 1) **3.** (−4, −5) **4.** (−3, 5)
5. (1, 5) **6.** (−1, −5)
7. (2, 4);

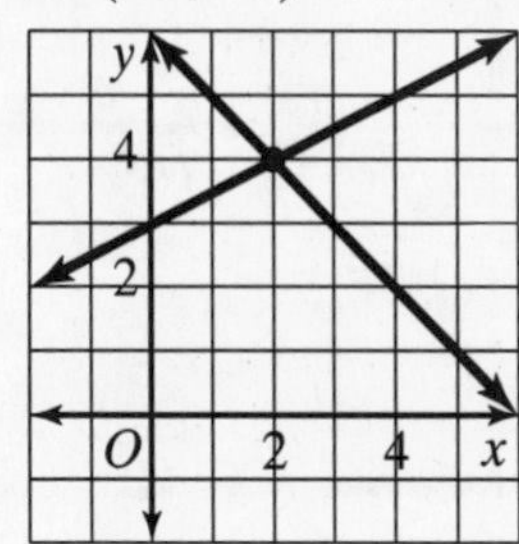

8. (1, −4);

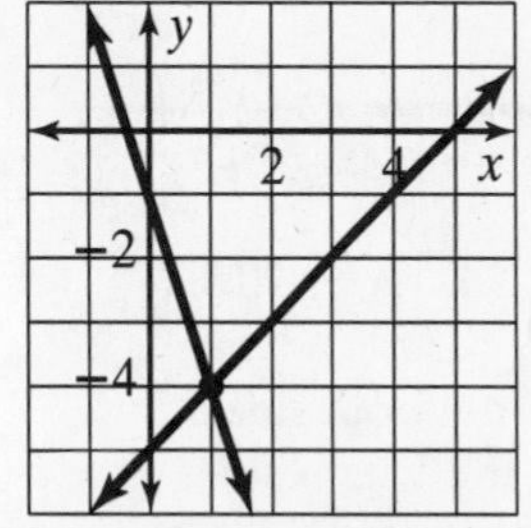

9. (−3, 2);

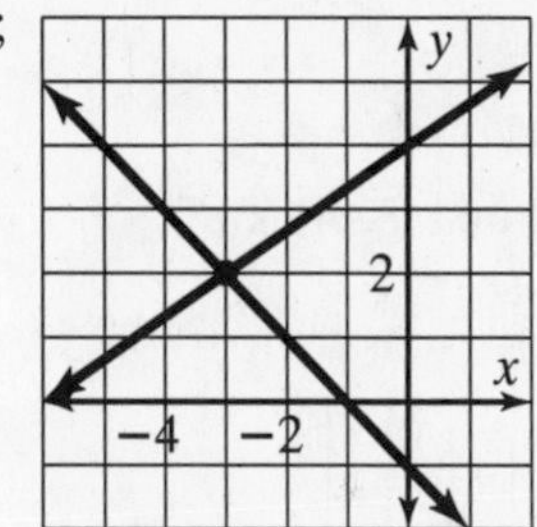

10. $-\frac{1}{2}$ **11.** $\frac{1}{2}$ **12.** $\frac{2}{5}$ **13.** $3(x + 5)(x - 5)$
14. $(3y + 7)(3y - 7)$
15. $(0.8m + 1.3)(0.8m - 1.3)$
16. 3 **17.** 9 **18.** −3

Daily Review 8-4

1. (5, 3) **2.** (6, −2) **3.** (−2, −5) **4.** (3, 6)
5. (−5, 9) **6.** (2, 1) **7.** (−21, −17) **8.** (8, −3)
9. (5, 1) **10.** (−8, −4) **11.** (3, −9) **12.** (4, 9)
13. $y = 2x - 5$ **14.** $y = -\frac{5}{2}x + 3$
15. $y = -3x - 4$ **16.** $(2x + 5)(x - 3)$
17. $(m - 8)(3m + 2)$ **18.** $3(2y + 3)(3y + 2)$
19. 1.0×10^4 **20.** 3.5×10^{-6} **21.** 1.92×10^2
22. −72 **23.** 5 **24.** 81

Daily Review 8-5

1. $J = \frac{1}{2}S$, $J + S = 150$; $J = 50$, $S = 100$
2. $b + 3f = 3.86$, $5b + 2f = 6.43$;
$b = 0.89$, $f = 0.99$

Daily Cumulative Review Answers (continued)

3. $J = 2R,\ J - 4 = 3(R - 4) + 1;$
$J = 14, R = 7$
4. $(5, -3)$ **5.** $(2, 9)$ **6.** $(-6, -3)$ **7.** $(4, 3)$
8. $(-6, 2)$ **9.** $(-8, -3)$
10. $x > 16;$

10 11 12 13 14 15 16 17 18 19 20

11. $y > \frac{1}{12};$

12. $n < 15;$

10 11 12 13 14 15 16 17 18 19 20

13. $-6x + 15$ **14.** $8x - 20y + 4$
15. $15x + 30y - 75z$
16. Subtract 5 from both sides.
17. Subtract 10 from both sides.
18. Multiply both sides by 5.

Daily Review 8-6

1. 2.5 h **2.** 120 mi **3.** 40 km/h
4. $n + d = 136,\ n - d = 52; n = 94, d = 42$
5. $c = 2d,\ c + 10 = 3(d - 5); c = 50, d = 25$
6.

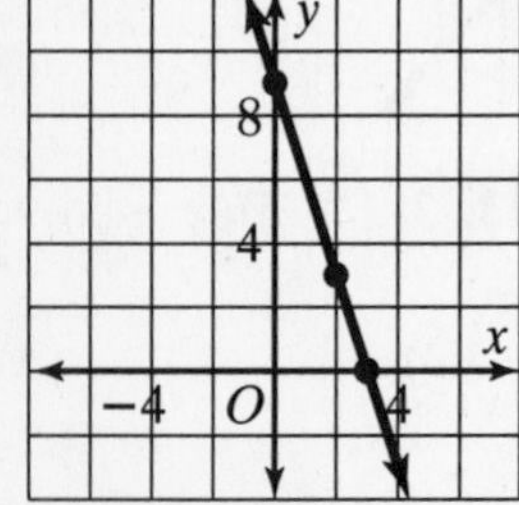

7.

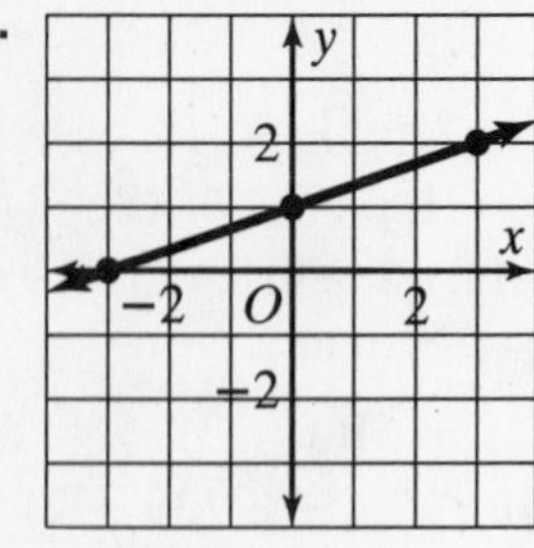

8.

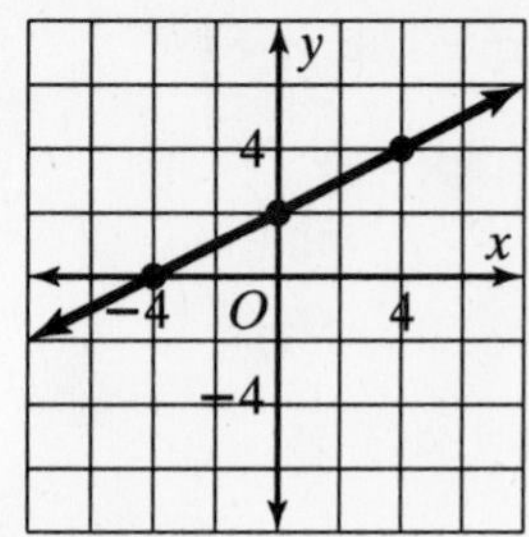

9. $x(3x + 5)$ **10.** $2n^2(9n^3 - 5)$
11. $x(x^4 - x^2 + x + 1)$ **12.** 8 **13.** -80
14. -51

Daily Review 9-1

1. $p + d = 125, 10d + p = 458; d = 37, p = 88$
2. $a + b = 12,\ 10a + b + 36 = 10b + a;$
$a = 4, b = 8;$ the number is 48
3. $a + s = 450,\ 5a + 3s = 1600;$
$a = 125, s = 325$
4. 8 h **5.** 10 miles **6.** $(3, -2)$ **7.** $(6, 5)$
8. $(-1, -8)$ **9.** 6.5×10^5 **10.** 9.03×10^{-4}
11. 1.5×10^1 **12.** 3.98×10^{-1} **13.** $\frac{d}{t}$ **14.** $\frac{I}{Pt}$
15. $\frac{C}{2\pi}$ **16.** 13 **17.** 25 **18.** 8

Daily Review 9-2

1. $\{0\}$ **2.** $\{0, 1, 2, 3, 4, 5, 6, 7\}$ **3.** $\{-2, -1, 0, 1, 2\}$
4. $\{-1, 0\}$ **5.** $\{-2, -1, 0, 4, 5, 6, 7\}$
6. $\{0, 1, 2\}$ **7.** $\emptyset$ **8.** $\emptyset$ **9.** 23 nickels; 56 dimes
10. 37 **11.** -2 **12.** $-\frac{1}{6}$ **13.** $-\frac{23}{11}$
14. $(x^5 + 1)(x^4 + 1)$
15. $(a + b + c)(a + b - c)$
16. $n(5n^2 + 2)(5n + 2)$
17. $n > -7;$

−9 −8 −7 −6 −5 −4 −3 −2 −1 0 1

18. $n < \frac{2}{3};$

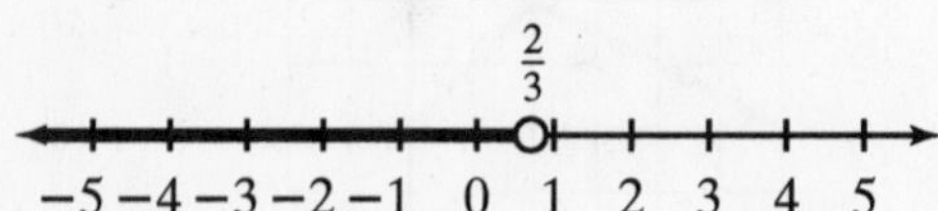

19. $n \geq \frac{1}{2};$

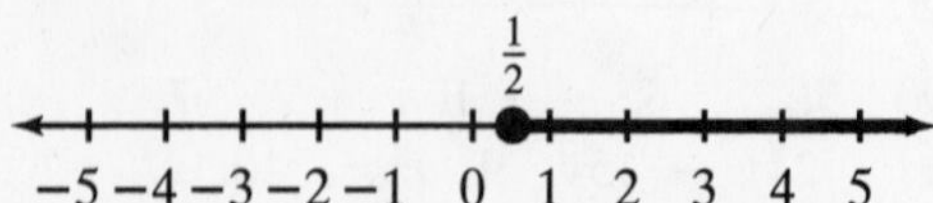

20. -23 **21.** -119 **22.** $-\frac{5}{6}$

Daily Cumulative Review Answers (continued)

Daily Review 9-3

1. 

2. −5 −4 −3 −2 −1 0 1 2 3 4 5

3. −2 −1 0 1 2 3 4 5 6 7 8

4. −6 −5 −4 −3 −2 −1 0 1 2 3 4

5a. $N = \{15, 14, 13, \ldots\}$
b. $N = \{x \mid x \text{ is an integer and } x \leq 15\}$
6a. $B = \{1, 3, 5, \ldots\}$
b. $B = \{x \mid x \text{ is an odd integer and } x > 0\}$
7a. $M = \{10, 15, 20, \ldots\}$
b. $M = \{x \mid x \text{ is a multiple of 5 and } x > 5\}$
8. no **9.** no **10.** yes **11.** $(x + 3)(x + 6)$
12. $(y - 8)(y - 5)$ **13.** $(x + y)(x - 2y)$
14. 15% **15.** 24% **16.** 62.5% **17.** 16.7%
18. $-\frac{16}{21}$ **19.** 0 **20.** −8

Daily Review 9-4

1. $\{-14, 4\}$ **2.** $\{-3, 9\}$ **3.** $\{1, 5\}$ **4.** $\{-8, 2\}$
5. $\{-5, 1\}$ **6.** $\{-3, 6\}$
7. $3 \leq x \leq 6$;
−2 −1 0 1 2 3 4 5 6 7 8

8. $-8 < x < 10$;
−10 −8 −6 −4 −2 0 2 4 6 8 10

9. $x < 2$ or $x > 5$;
−3 −2 −1 0 1 2 3 4 5 6 7

10. $x < -5$ or $x > 0$;
−7 −6 −5 −4 −3 −2 −1 0 1 2 3

11. $(3, 6)$ **12.** $(5, -2)$ **13.** $(-6, 0)$
14. $5x^2 - x$ **15.** $11y^2 + y - 3$
16. $xy^2 + x^2y + 5x^2$ **17.** −5 **18.** 6 **19.** −6
20. $3 \cdot 3 \cdot 3 \cdot 3$ **21.** $5 \cdot m \cdot m$
22. $y \cdot y \cdot y \cdot y \cdot y$ **23.** 6

Daily Review 9-5

1. $-3 < x < 3$;
−5 −4 −3 −2 −1 0 1 2 3 4 5

2. $-11 < n < 1$;
−12 −10 −8 −6 −4 −2 0 2 4 6 8

3. $-\frac{11}{2} \leq y \leq 4$;
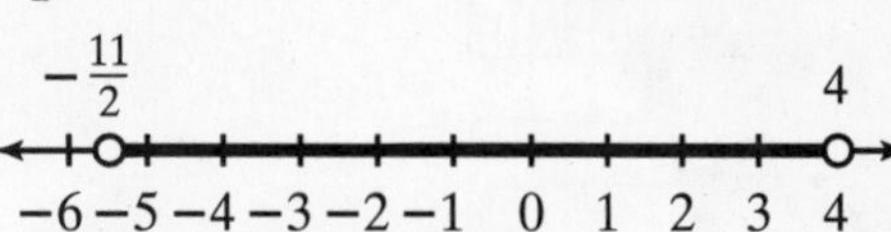

4. $-4 < y < 4$;
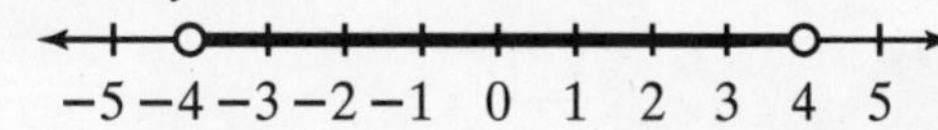

5. $x \leq -5$ or $x \geq 5$;
−5 −4 −3 −2 −1 0 1 2 3 4 5

6. $b < -2$ or $b > 8$;
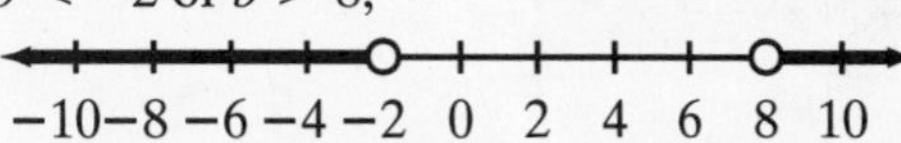

7. $\{-4, 14\}$ **8.** $\{-\frac{23}{3}, 5\}$ **9.** $\{-9, -7\}$
10. $\{-11, 1\}$ **11.** $\{-12, 7\}$ **12.** $\{-15, 7\}$
13. $(6, -3)$;
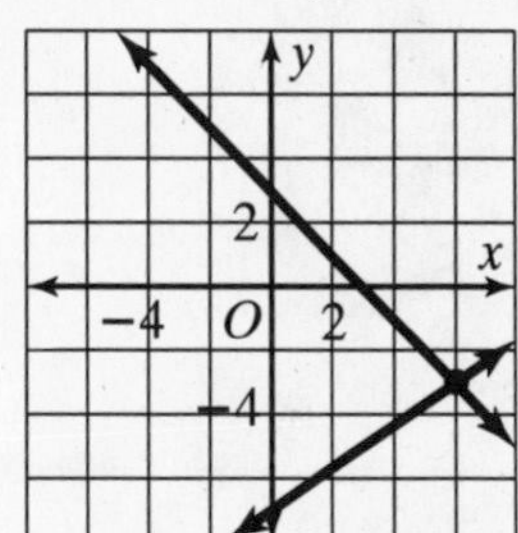

14. $(2, 7)$;
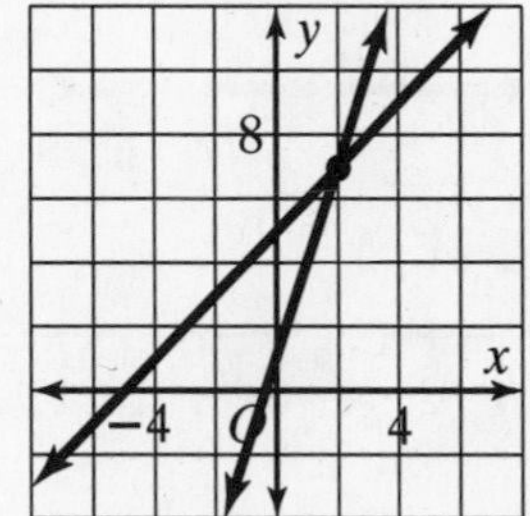

15. $(-3, 5)$;
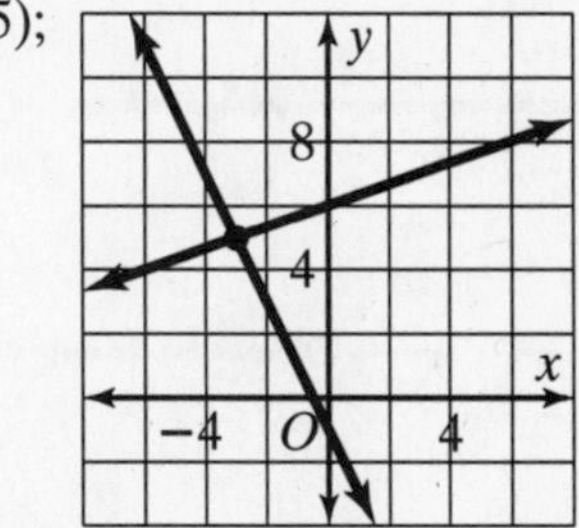

16. $(5x + 10)(5x - 10)$ **17.** $2x(x + 3)(x - 3)$
18. $(1.3x - 0.8)(1.3x + 0.8)$
19. $2x^5 + 8x^4 + x^3 + x$ **20.** $-4x^2y^3 + 5x^2y^2$

Daily Cumulative Review Answers (continued)

Daily Review 9-6

1. 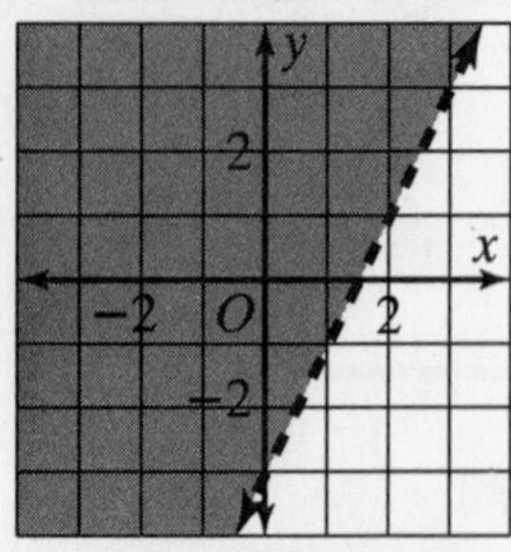

2. 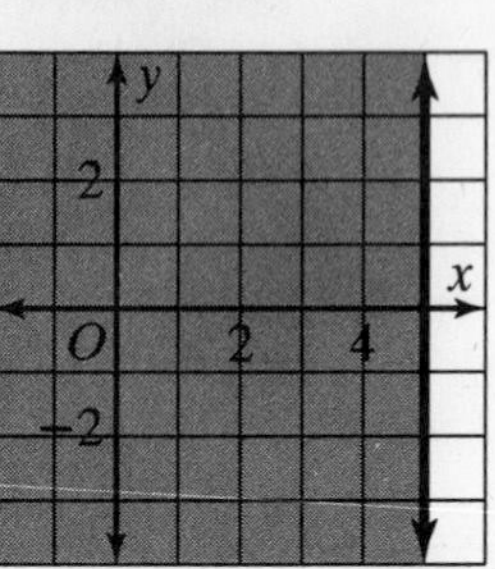

3. 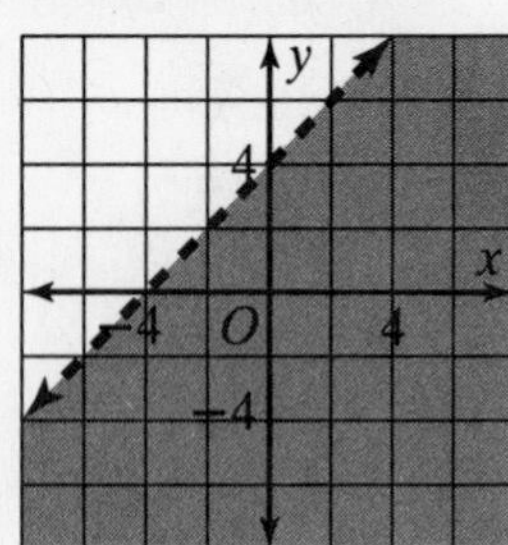

4. $x \le -6$ or $x \ge 6$;

5. $-8 < x < 8$;

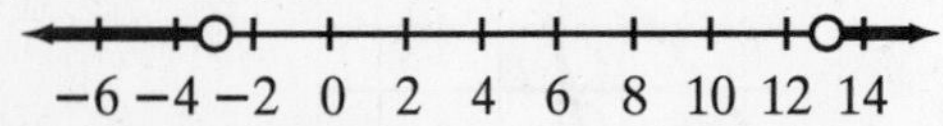

6. $y < -3$ or $y > 13$;

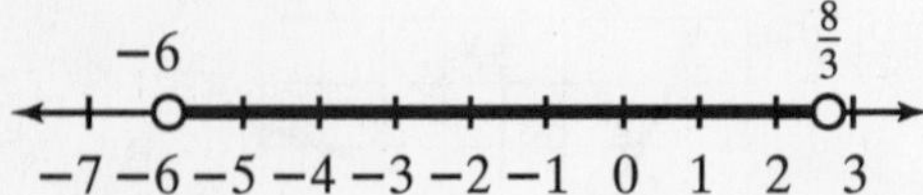

7. $-6 < n < \frac{8}{3}$;

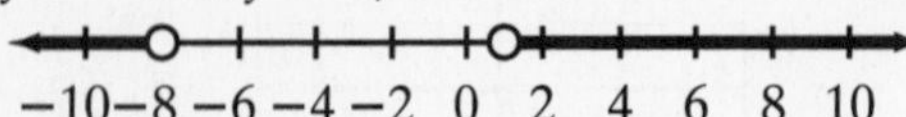

8. $y < -8$ or $y > 1$;

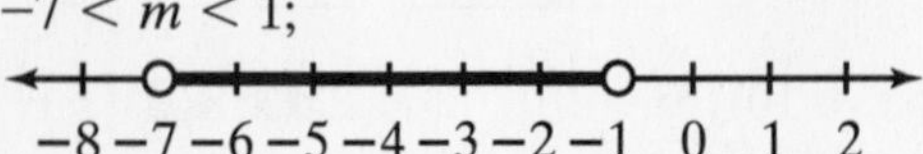

9. $-7 < m < 1$;

10. $y = 2x - 4$ **11.** $y = -\frac{1}{4}x + 4$ **12.** $y = \frac{3}{2}x$
13. x^{15} **14.** $81y^{20}$ **15.** $\frac{m^{16}}{n^8}$ **16.** 5 **17.** $7x + 1$
18. -38 **19.** -4 **20.** 10 **21.** 5

Daily Review 10-1

1. 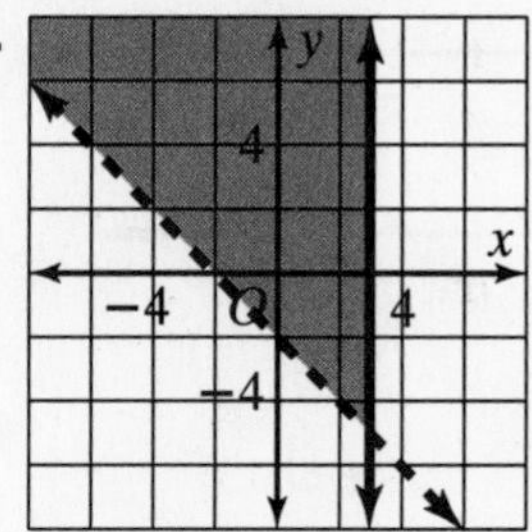

2. 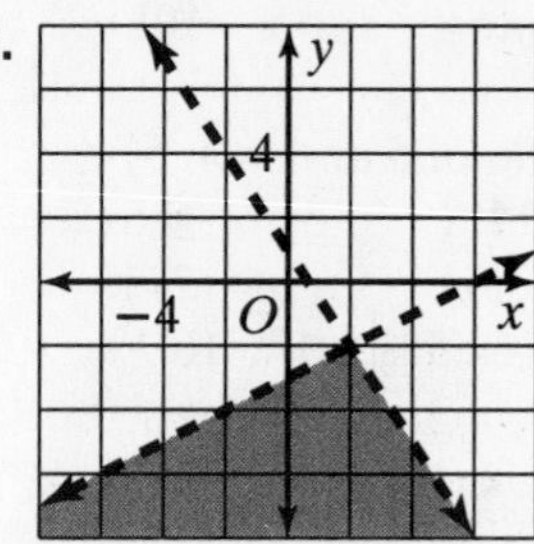

3. 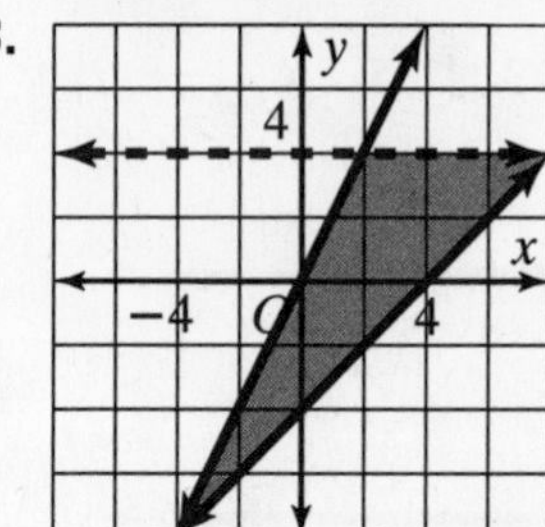

4. $y < x + 2$ **5.** $x \ge 1$ **6.** $y \le -2x + 3$
7. 5^2 **8.** k^4 **9.** s^2t^2 **10.** $a(a - 3)$
11. $6mn(m + 2n^2)$ **12.** $x(x^2 - 2x + 3)$
13. $(2, 1)$ **14.** $(3, 1)$ **15.** $\left(\frac{1}{2}, 5\right)$

Daily Review 10-2

1. $\frac{x^3}{2y^2}$ **2.** $\frac{x - 3}{x}$ **3.** $\frac{1}{z^3}$ **4.** $\frac{a^2 + 9}{a + 3}$ **5.** $\frac{m - 6}{m - 2}$
6. $\frac{r + 2}{r + 4}$ **7.** $y \ge -1, x < 2$ **8.** $y \le 0, y > 2x$
9. $y < -\frac{1}{3}x + 1,\ x > -3$ **10.** $-35x^3$
11. $15a^{11}b^9$ **12.** $-48c^9$ **13.** $(x - 3)(x - 5)$
14. $(y + 13)(y + 2)$ **15.** $(z - 7)(z + 5)$
16. $y = -5x + 23$ **17.** $y = -\frac{1}{2}x - \frac{5}{2}$
18. $y = \frac{1}{7}x - \frac{5}{7}$ **19.** $b > -2$ **20.** $n \ge \frac{1}{6}$
21. $q < 8$

Daily Review 10-3

1. $\frac{4}{x^2}$ **2.** $\frac{a+4}{16a^3}$ **3.** $\frac{d^2}{2}$ **4.** $\frac{n-8}{n+8}$

5. $\frac{y+3}{(y^2+5)(y-5)}$ **6.** $36x$ **7.** 3; 3

8. not defined; not defined **9.** not defined; 7

10. 7; 7 **11.** $4 \cdot \frac{1}{7}$ **12.** $a \cdot \frac{b}{1}$ **13.** $(2x-3) \cdot \frac{1}{5}$

14. $-\frac{1}{3}$ **15.** $\frac{5}{43}$ **16.** $-\frac{34}{5}$ **17.** $-\frac{9}{16}$

18. $\{-4, -2, 0, 1, 2, 3, 4\}$ **19.** $\{1, 3\}$ **20.** $\{0\}$

21. $\emptyset$ **22.** $\{-3, -1, 0, 1, 3\}$ or C

23. $\{-4, -3, -2, -1, 0, 1, 2, 3, 4\}$

Daily Review 10-4

1. $2x$ **2.** $\frac{8}{3}$ **3.** $\frac{2y-3}{3y+1}$ **4.** $\frac{a-4}{a+4}$

5. $\frac{x-3}{(x-5)(x+4)}$ **6.** $\frac{s-3}{s-2}$ **7.** $(u-v)(2v-3)$

8. $\frac{(b+2)(b-2)}{(b+1)(b-1)}$ **9.** $-3z$ **10.** $8x - 2y$

11. $3m + 3n$ **12.** $14p + 4q + 4r$ **13.** $-\frac{1}{3}a + b$

14. $-3.6c + 1.3d$ **15.** $3 + z$ **16.** $\frac{1}{2}x$

17. $y - 6$ **18.** 2 **19.** 28 **20.** 10 **21.** $\frac{2}{5}$

22. $-\frac{5}{2}$ **23.** $\frac{7y}{2x}$

Daily Review 10-5

1. $\frac{9x+1}{x+1}$ **2.** $\frac{3-c}{c+4}$ **3.** $2x + 1$

4. $-\frac{(p+3)(p-1)}{2p+5}$ **5.** $\frac{a+3}{a-3}$ **6.** $\frac{m+3n}{m-3n}$

7. $\frac{1}{x^3(x+4y)}$ **8.** $\frac{1}{(r+s)^2}$ **9.** $-8, 2$ **10.** $-12, 40$

11. 3, 9

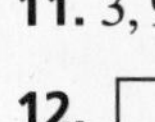
12.

x	y
−2	−3
−1	0
0	1
1	0
2	−3

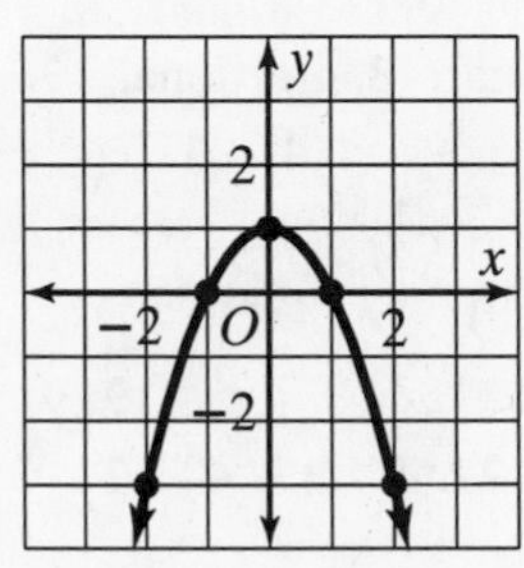

13.

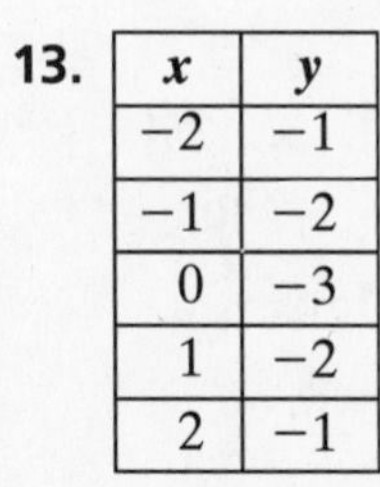

x	y
−2	−1
−1	−2
0	−3
1	−2
2	−1

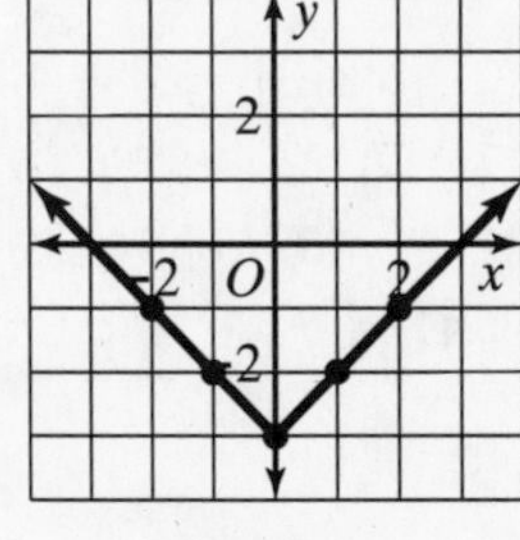

14. $(a^2+3)(a-1)$ **15.** $(b-3)(4b^2+5)$

16. $(m-n)(p+6)$

Daily Review 10-6

1. $\frac{5x+7}{x^2}$ **2.** $\frac{a(2a+9)}{a+4}$ **3.** $\frac{1}{s(s-1)}$

4. $\frac{-y-25}{(y+5)(y-5)}$ **5.** $\frac{7a+6}{c-3}$ **6.** $\frac{(b+6)(1-2b)}{4b+7}$

7. $\frac{m+1}{3m-1}$ **8.** $\frac{k+2}{2k-9}$ **9.** $y^3 - 8$ **10.** $m^4 - 1$

11. $a^4 - 4a^2 - 4a - 1$

12. $x^{10} - 4x^6 - 12x^4 - 9x^2$

13. 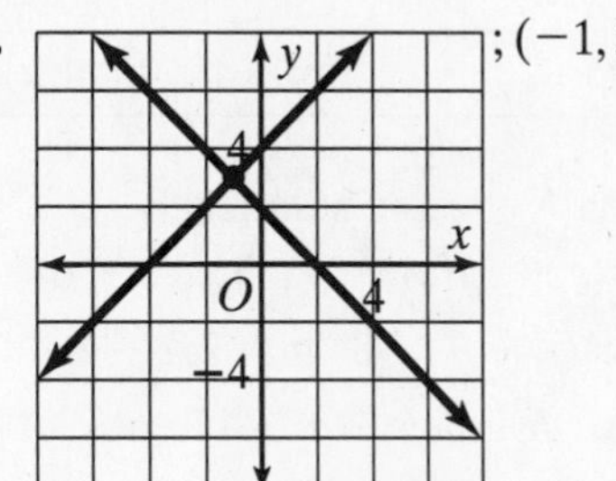

; $(-1, 3)$

14. 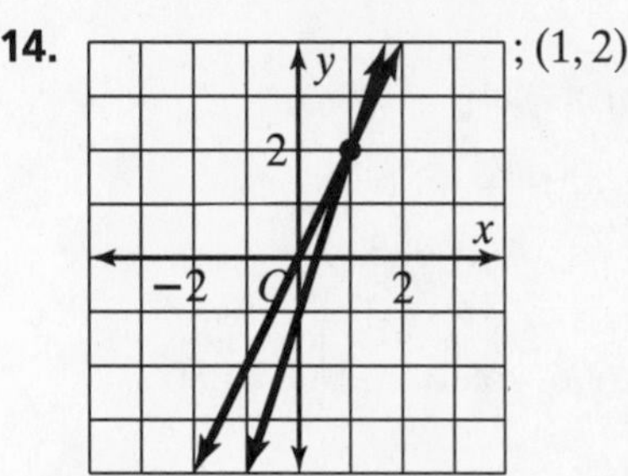

; $(1, 2)$

15. 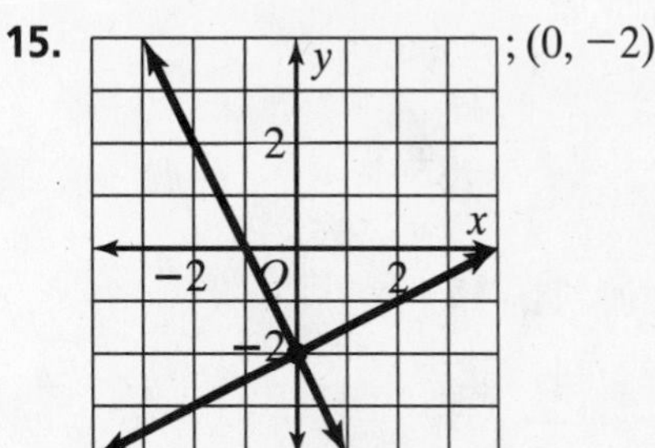

; $(0, -2)$

Daily Review 10-7

1. $-1, -5$ **2.** $\frac{23}{2}$ **3.** 19 **4.** no solution **5.** $\frac{2}{5}$

6. $-\frac{5}{28}$ **7.** $9(2-z)$ or $9(z-2)$

8. $(w+10)(w-10)$

9. $(x+4)(x-4)(x+5)$

10. $(y-3)(3y+1)(3y-2)$ **11.** $3n - 5$

12. $\frac{1}{5}(n-10)$ **13.** $\frac{9}{n} + 7$ **14.** A and C

15. B and C **16.** $x \leq -2$

Daily Review 10-8

1. $1\frac{1}{5}$ h **2.** 50 mi/h; 70 mi/h **3.** -15

Daily Cumulative Review Answers (continued)

4. no solution **5.** $0, -\frac{3}{4}$ **6.** $-1, 1$ **7.** 6th year
8. $c + 3c$ or $4c$ **9.** $\frac{1}{2}a + \frac{1}{3}(5 - a)$ or $\frac{5}{3} - \frac{1}{6}a$
10. \$3750 **11.** \$1000

Daily Review 10-9

1.

	Amount of solution	Percent acid	Amount of acid
Solution A	x	70%	$0.70x$
Solution B	$1 - x$	40%	$0.40(1 - x)$
Final solution	1	50%	0.50(1)

2. $\frac{1}{3}$ gal of solution A, $\frac{2}{3}$ gal of solution B **3.** $1\frac{1}{2}$ h
4. $11\frac{1}{4}$ min **5.** $4(s - 3)(s + 3)$ **6.** $t(t + 6)^2$
7. $(u - 4)(u + 4)(u - 1)$ **8.** $a = 2A - b$
9. $m = \frac{y - b}{x}$ **10.** $b^2 = c^2 - a^2$ **11.** no
12. yes

Daily Review 10-10

1. $3t^2 - \frac{3t}{2} + 2$ **2.** $t^2 + 5t + \frac{8}{3}$
3. $2a^2 - \frac{7}{2}ab - 6b^2$ **4.** $x - 3$
5. $v^2 - v + \frac{1}{v + 1}$ **6.** $3s^2 + 1$
7. $\frac{2}{3}$ L of 50% alcohol solution, $1\frac{1}{3}$ L of 80% alcohol solution
8. 2 lb of peanuts, 1 lb of cashews **9.** -3
10. $-\frac{4}{3}$ **11.** 2 **12.** 15 triangles
13. $3x^3 - 12x^2 + x + 7$
14. $6y^4 - 4y^3 + 3y^2 - y + 13$

Daily Review 10-11

1. $\frac{10}{3}$ **2.** $x^2 + x$ **3.** $-\frac{8}{25}$ **4.** $\frac{1}{b - 1}$ **5.** $\frac{a^2b + a}{ab^2 - b}$
6. v **7.** $2x + 2 + \frac{-3}{x + 2}$
8. $a^2 + 6 + \frac{19}{a^2 - 4}$ **9.** $r^3 - r^2s + rs^2 - s^3$
10. Tami, Jose, Denison, Karenna, Ely
11. $-7x^2 + 56x$ **12.** $5x^2 + 27x - 18$
13. $9x^2 - 16y^2$ **14.** $\frac{21}{1}$ **15.** $\frac{13}{10}$ **16.** $\frac{-33}{100}$
17. $\frac{13}{3}$ **18.** $\frac{6}{-1}$ **19.** $\frac{-7}{5}$ **20.** yes **21.** yes
22. no **23.** no

Daily Review 10-12

1. Division theorem **2.** Division theorem
3. Substituting $a \cdot \frac{1}{b}$ for $\frac{a}{b}$ and $d \cdot \frac{1}{c}$ for $\frac{d}{c}$
4. Associative and commutative properties
5. Reciprocal theorem **6.** Division theorem
7. Transitive property of equality
8. $\frac{a - b + 1}{a^2 - 2ab - b^2}$ **9.** $\frac{s^2 - s + t^2 - t}{st}$
10. $\frac{2x^2 - x - 1}{x^4 + x^3}$ **11.** 4; 12 **12.** 10 cm; 5 cm
13. 28 **14.** 93 **15.** 2 **16.** $-\frac{3}{2}$

Daily Review 11-1

1. 96 cherries **2.** 72
3. Multiplication property of equalities
4. Division Theorem **5.** Commutative property
6. Associative property
7. Definition of reciprocal
8. Multiplicative identity
9. $-3xy$ **10.** $\frac{n - 6}{n + 6}$ **11.** $\frac{b - 6}{b - 4}$
12. $-8 \le x < 4$;

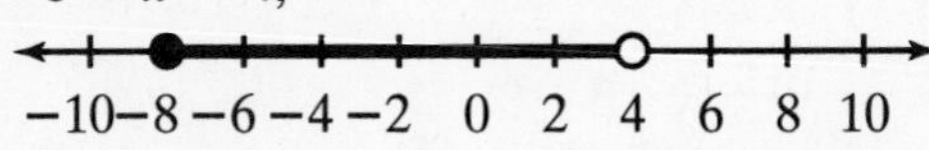

13. $-2 < x < 7$;

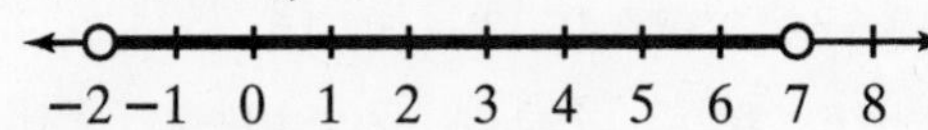

14. $-2 \le x \le 6$;

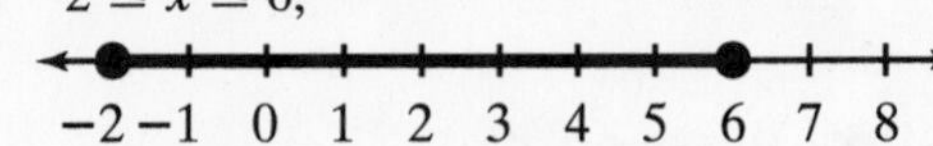

15. 0.0048 **16.** 7,005,000

Daily Review 11-2

1. irrational **2.** rational **3.** irrational
4. rational **5.** irrational **6.** rational
7. irrational **8.** irrational **9.** 6 **10.** 194 cards
11. $\{x \mid -7 \le x \le 4\}$ **12.** $\{x \mid -2 < x < \frac{10}{3}\}$
13. $\{x \mid x \ne -\frac{1}{2}\}$ **14.** $(-3, 2)$ **15.** $(6, 9)$
16. $(3, -8)$ **17.** $4x^4 - 9$
18. $9x^2 - 12xy + 4y^2$ **19.** $9x^2 - \frac{1}{4}$ **20.** -9
21. -7 **22.** 9 **23.** 49 **24.** 3 **25.** 54

Daily Review 11-3

1. $5|x|$ **2.** $|b + 3|$ **3.** 8 **4.** $\frac{14}{n^4}$ **5.** $125|x^3|$
6. $|y - 13|$ **7.** 22 **8.** -8 **9.** -1 **10.** -17
11. 41 **12.** 3 **13.** 25 **14.** 49 **15.** $\frac{y + 4}{y + 3}$
16. $\frac{x^2}{x + 2}$ **17.** $\frac{3}{4}$

Daily Cumulative Review Answers (continued)

18.

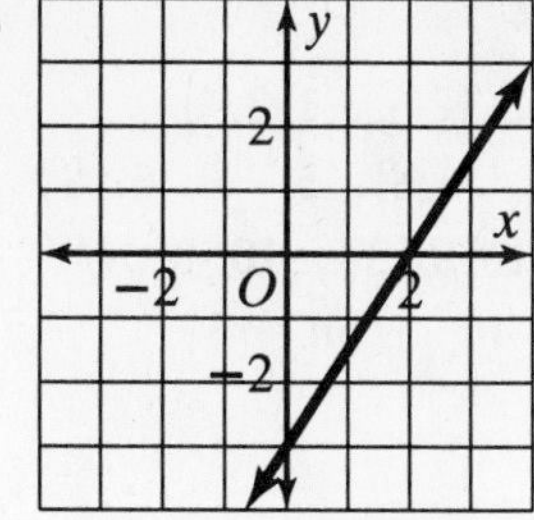

19.

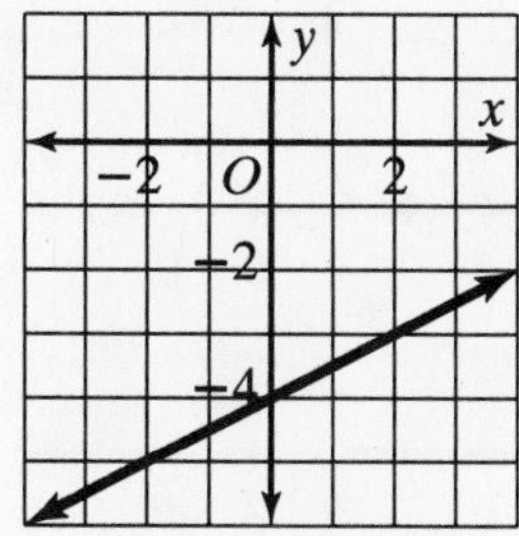

20.

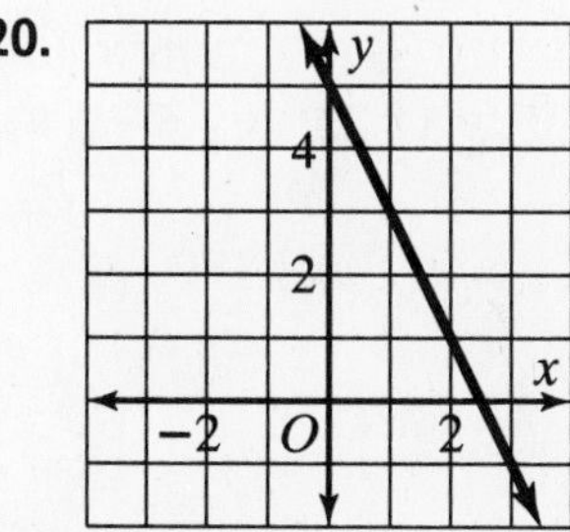

21. $0, \frac{3}{2}$ **22.** $6, -3$ **23.** $x \leq \frac{1}{9}$ **24.** $x > 3$

Daily Review 11-4

1. $3\sqrt{7}$ **2.** $2t\sqrt{3t}$ **3.** $3s\sqrt{3}$ **4.** $\sqrt{21}$
5. $2\sqrt{10}$ **6.** $3b^2\sqrt{b}$ **7.** $(x + 3)\sqrt{3}$
8. $2(x + 2y)$ **9.** $10(x + 3)^3\sqrt{2(x + 3)}$
10. $5x^2$ **11.** $2a^2$ **12.** $(2a^2)^2$ **13.** $2(y^2 + 1)^3$
14. $\frac{3|s|}{4t^4}$ **15.** $\frac{1}{|u^5|}$ **16.** $\frac{|x^3|}{2}$ **17.** $\frac{x^4}{2}$ **18.** $\frac{|d^5|}{|c^5|}$
19. -32 **20.** 65 **21.** -14 **22.** 4 **23.** -3
24. -1 **25.** $(x - 3)^2$ **26.** $(3y + 4x)^2$
27. $(z^2 + 4)(z - 2)(z + 2)$ **28.** II **29.** IV
30. I **31.** II

Daily Review 11-5

1. 4 **2.** $4\sqrt{2}$ **3.** $2x^2y\sqrt{3y}$ **4.** $2ab^2\sqrt{5abc}$
5. $7st^3\sqrt{2}$ **6.** $x\sqrt{x}$ **7.** $\sqrt{15}$ **8.** 3 **9.** $\sqrt{6}$
10. 0 **11.** $2\sqrt{6}$ **12.** $3\sqrt{6}$ **13.** 3^3 **14.** 7^2
15. 2^7 **16.** 5^1 **17.** -6 **18.** 12 **19.** -3
20. $\frac{-3r^3}{r - 3}$ **21.** $\frac{s + 5}{9s}$ **22.** $\frac{t - 6}{t + 6}$ **23.** $1.00; $.45
24. 10 calories per minute; 5 calories per minute

Daily Review 11-6

1. $\frac{5}{9}$ **2.** $\frac{1}{7}$ **3.** $-\frac{5}{3}$ **4.** $\frac{5}{7}$ **5.** 2 **6.** $\frac{1}{3}\sqrt{15}$ **7.** $\frac{\sqrt{2}}{2}$
8. $\frac{5}{x}\sqrt{x}$ **9.** $\frac{1}{yz}\sqrt{6xz}$ **10.** $x + x^2$ **11.** $0.1s^n\sqrt{s}$
12. $2(x + 1)^2\sqrt{x + 1}$ **13.** $u^2\sqrt{2} - 2\sqrt{u}$
14. $5x^4 + x^3 + 5x^2 + x - 11$
15. $-8x^5 - x^4 - x^3 + x + 6$
16. $9x^2 + 3x^2y - 5y - 5x$
17. $15x^2y^2 - 24xy^2 - 5x - 3y$ **18.** $\frac{15}{8}$
19. $-9, 9$ **20.** no solution **21.** 2.5 h
22. 468.75 mi/h; 31.25 mi/h

Daily Review 11-7

1. $-5\sqrt{10}$ **2.** $5\sqrt{2}$ **3.** $6\sqrt{2}$ **4.** $\sqrt{2}$ **5.** 0
6. $2\sqrt{3}$ **7.** $5\sqrt{2}$ **8.** $\frac{\sqrt{x}}{x^3}$ **9.** $\frac{\sqrt{6}}{3}$ **10.** $\frac{\sqrt{2}}{2}$
11. $\frac{3}{4}\sqrt{3}$ **12.** $\frac{\sqrt{2}}{4}$ **13.** $c = 4A - 3a$ **14.** $\frac{d}{b} = \frac{c}{a}$
15. $x = \frac{z}{1 + y}$
16. $-10y^8 + y^6 - 11y^4 + 13y^3 - y + 3$
17. $8z^7 - z^6 - 7z^5 + z + 15$

18.

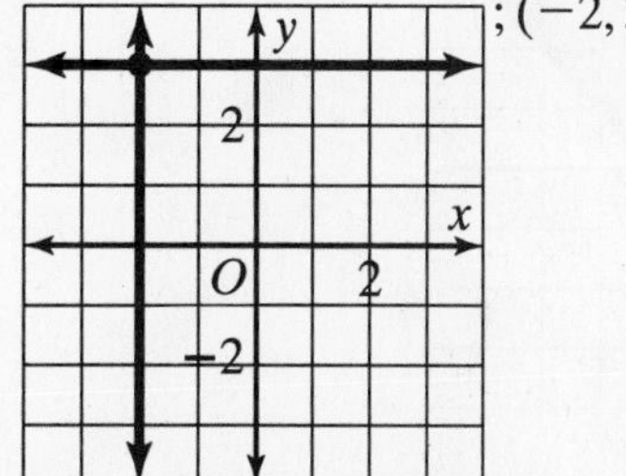

; $(-2, 3)$

19.

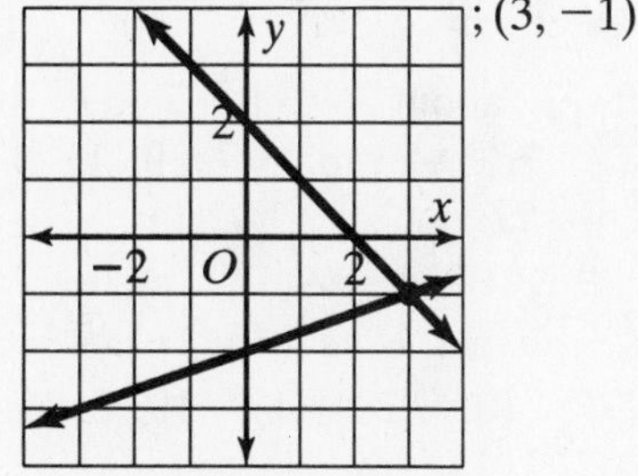

; $(3, -1)$

20.

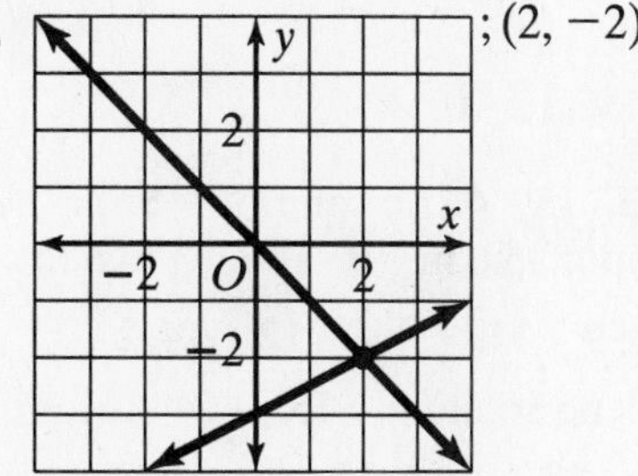

; $(2, -2)$

Daily Review 11-8

1. 12 **2.** 3 **3.** $2\sqrt{11}$ **4.** $4\sqrt{5}$

5. $(1 - x)\sqrt{x + 1}$ **6.** $(2ab - 6b + 1)\sqrt{3b}$
7. $(1 + 3x^2)\sqrt{2 + x^2}$ **8.** 140 booths **9.** 11
10. 42 **11.** 5
12.

13.

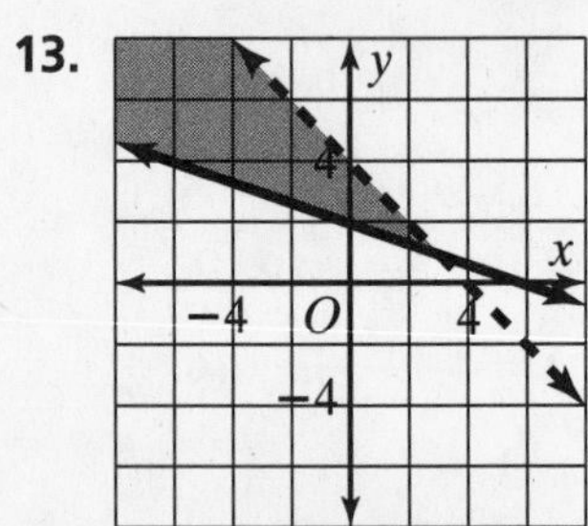

14.

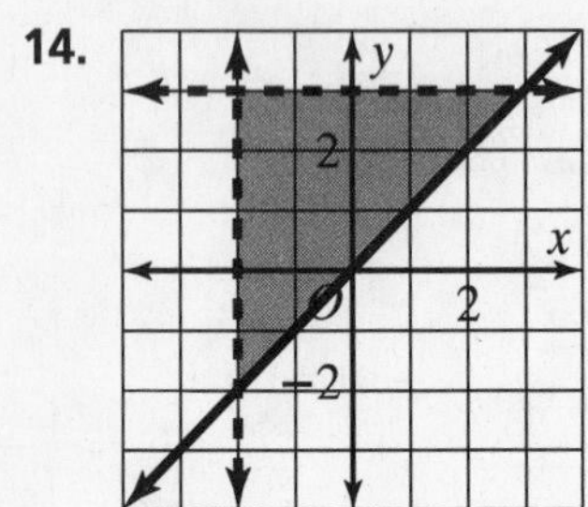

Daily Review 11-9

1. about 796.9 ft **2.** about 269.3 ft **3.** 39 **4.** 6
5. $2\sqrt{3}$ **6.** $2\sqrt{2}$ **7.** $5\sqrt{3}$ **8.** $\sqrt{7}$ **9.** 17
10. 7 **11.** $5 + y$ **12.** yx
13. $yx + 5$ or $5 + xy$ or $5 + yx$
14. $ba + c$ or $c + ab$ or $c + ba$ **15.** $-2x^5$
16. $3n^6$ **17.** $42y^6$ **18.** $-20, -17$ **19.** 3, 8
20. $-\frac{2}{5}, 1$

Daily Review 12-1

1. 225 **2.** 26 **3.** 18 **4.** no solution **5.** 7
6. 2, −2 **7.** about 15.6 m **8.** about 116.6 m
9. $\frac{3x^2}{2}$ **10.** $x + 9$ **11.** $\frac{x + 2}{x + 5}$ **12.** −4, 2
13. −10, 3 **14.** no solution **15.** −2 **16.** $\frac{1}{2}$
17. $\frac{3}{2}$ **18.** $\frac{x^4}{16y^4}$ **19.** $\frac{a^3}{b^{12}c^3}$ **20.** $\frac{32z^{10}}{x^5}$
21. $11x + 5y$ **22.** $4p^2 + 5z$ **23.** $3x^2 + 5xy$

Daily Review 12-2

1. $\{-7, -5, -3, -1, 1\}$ **2.** $\{-6, -1, 2, 3\}$
3. $\{0, \frac{1}{2}, 2, \frac{9}{2}, 8\}$ **4.** $\{0, 2, 4, 6, 8\}$ **5.** $\frac{43}{2}$ **6.** 8
7. 3, −3 **8.** no solution **9.** 34 **10.** 1.69
11. $x - 3x^2 + x^4$ **12.** $4n^2 + 5n - 3$
13. $3x - 5y^3 + 2x^2y$
14. $-8 \le x < 0$;

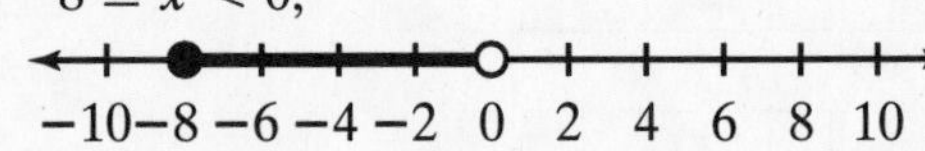

15. $-7 < x < 2$;

−8 −7 −6 −5 −4 −3 −2 −1 0 1 2

16. $-3 < x < 2$;

−5 −4 −3 −2 −1 0 1 2 3 4 5

17. 9.3×10^7 **18.** 3.81×10^{-1} **19.** 2.76×10^1
20. 3.0001×10^{-3} **21.** 5, −5 **22.** 6, −6
23. 4, −4

Daily Review 12-3

1.

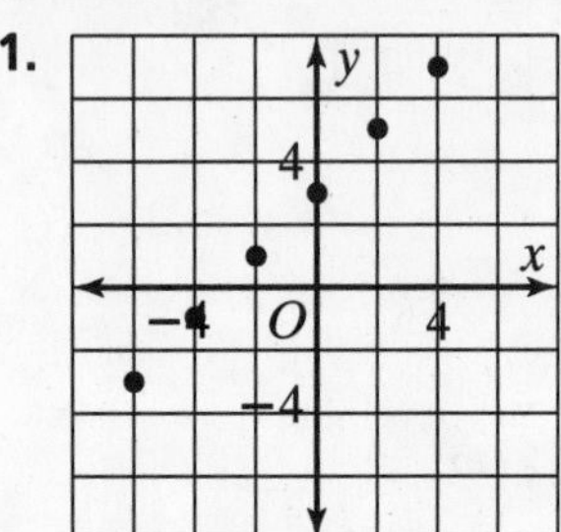

2.

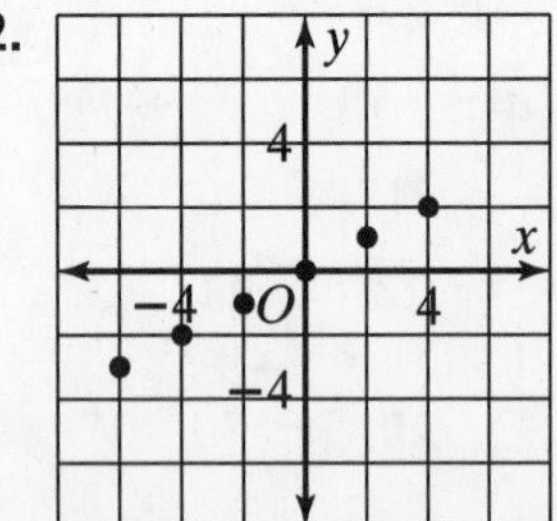

3.

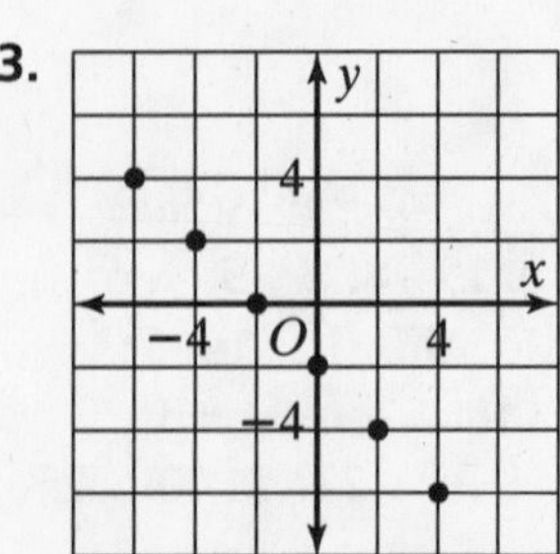

4. 68°; 41°; 32° **5.** 72 km/h; 88 km/h; 104 km/h

Daily Cumulative Review Answers (continued)

6. $\frac{1}{11}\sqrt{22}$ 7. $\frac{\sqrt{3cm}}{m^2}$ **8.** $\frac{1}{b}\sqrt{ab}$ **9.** $\frac{m-4}{2}$
10. y^2 **11.** $\frac{x-3}{x+3}$ **12.** $(-2, 5)$ **13.** $(6, 9)$
14. $(2, -8)$ **15.** $3(2x+5)(x-3)$
16. $4(x+3)(x+8)$ **17.** $(6-n)(5+2n)$

Daily Review 12-4

1. $g(w) = 50 + 20w$; $g(52) = \$1{,}090$
2. $f(m) = 35 + 0.25m$; $f(400) = \$135$
3. 

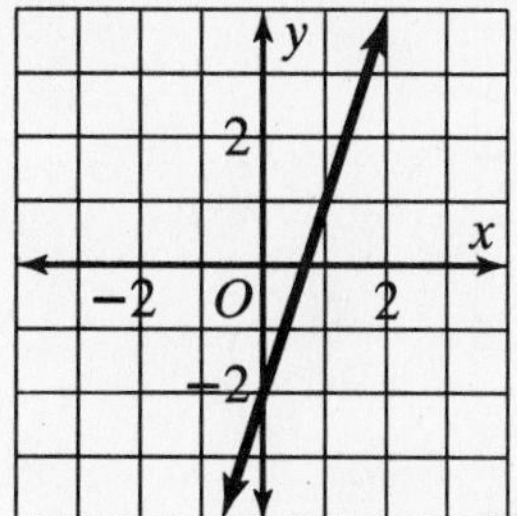

4. 

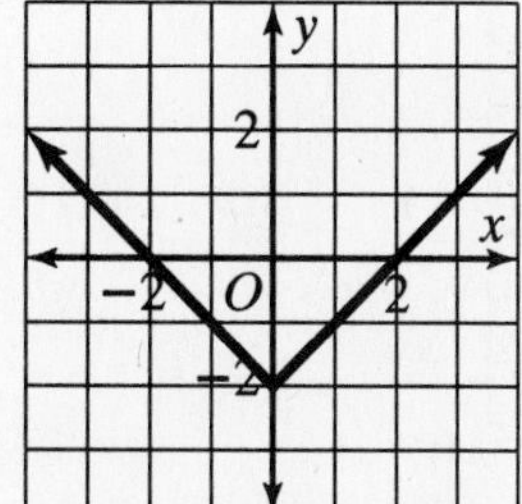

5.

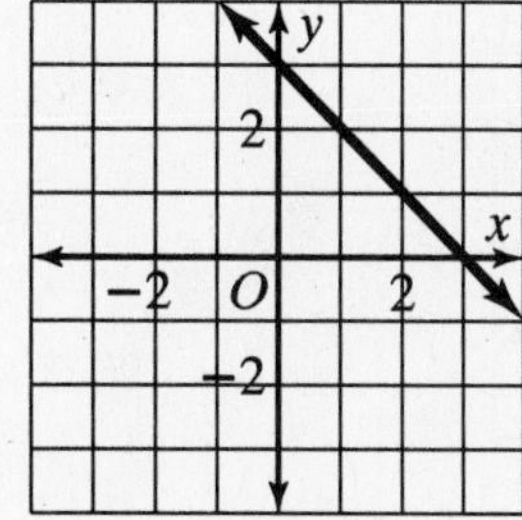

6. $x \geq 0$ **7.** $n \geq 5$ **8.** $y \geq \frac{5}{2}$
9. any real number
10. $-5 < x < 5$;

−5 −4 −3 −2 −1 0 1 2 3 4 5

11. $-3 \leq x \leq 3$;

−5 −4 −3 −2 −1 0 1 2 3 4 5

12. $x < -5$ or $x > -1$;

−9 −8 −7 −6 −5 −4 −3 −2 −1 0 1

13. $(9+y)(9-y)$ **14.** $3(3x+2)(3x-2)$
15. $x^3(x+3)(x-3)$ **16.** 0.1 **17.** 0.95
18. 1.5 **19.** 0.005

Daily Review 12-5

1.

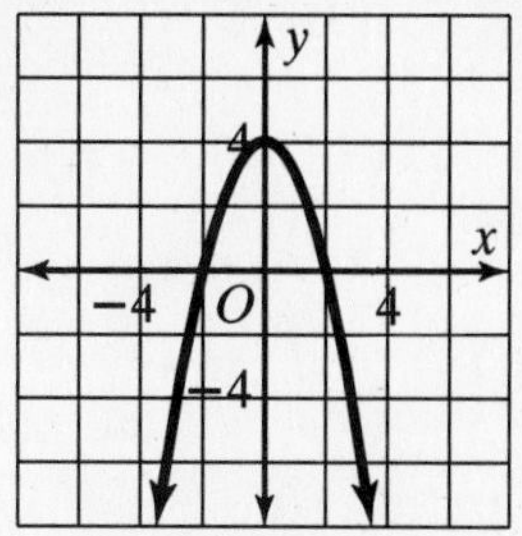

2.

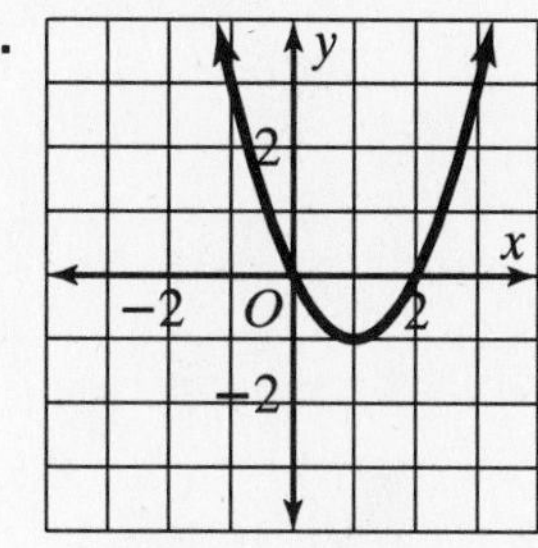

3.

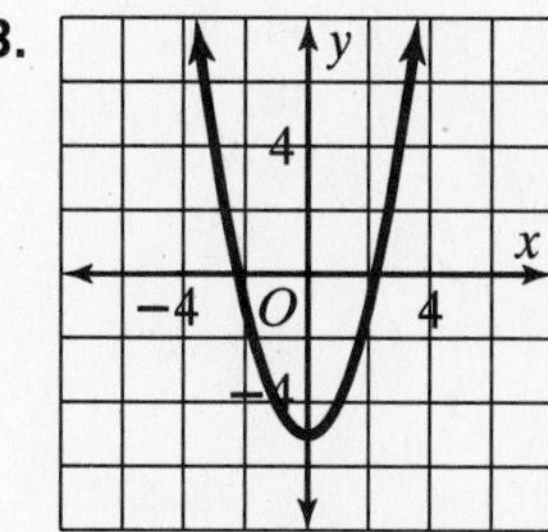

4. $c(m) = 0.25 + 0.07m$; $c(23) = \$1.86$
5. $c(h) = 2.5 + 4.5h$; $c(5) = \$25$ **6.** 15 **7.** −21
8. −17 **9.** 9 **10.** $(x+3)(x-5)$ **11.** $3n^2m^2$
12. $(x+3)(x+3)(x-3)$ **13.** yes **14.** no
15. yes **16.** 3, 1, 0; 3 **17.** 3, 3, 1; 3
18. 4, 3, 1, 0; 4

Daily Review 12-6

1. $y = 2.5x$ **2.** $y = 0.6x$ **3.** $y = 3x$
4. $y = \frac{5}{6}x$ **5.** $y = 12x$ **6.** $y = 3.25x$
7.

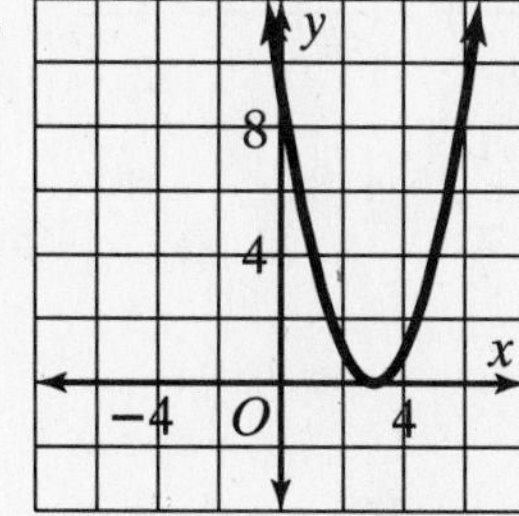

8.

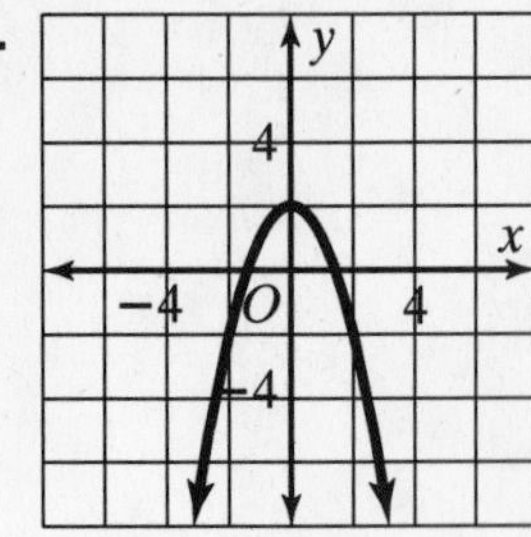

9.

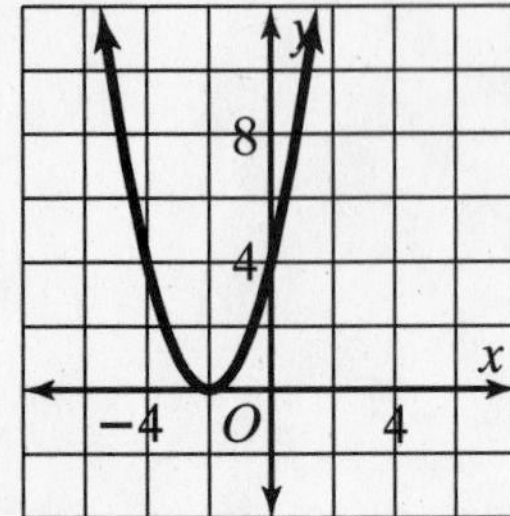

10. $3\sqrt{2}$ **11.** $2x\sqrt{3}$ **12.** $10\sqrt{5}$
13. $(x + 2)\sqrt{2}$ **14.** 45 dimes, 30 nickels
15. $-3, \frac{5}{2}$ **16.** $5, -4$ **17.** $7, -2$ **18.** $x \le 12$
19. $y < -5$ **20.** $n > 2$ **21.** $-3(x - 5)$
22. $x(y - z + a)$ **23.** $n(y + 3)$

Daily Review 12-7

1. $y = \frac{30}{x}$ **2.** $y = \frac{4.5}{x}$ **3.** $y = \frac{1}{x}$ **4.** $y = \frac{4500}{x}$
5. $y = \frac{24}{x}$ **6.** $y = \frac{0.05}{x}$ **7.** \$31.50 **8.** 165 mi
9. x **10.** 3 **11.** $5\left(\frac{n+1}{n+2}\right)$ **12.** $y = -x + 3$
13. $y = \frac{4}{5}x - 8$ **14.** $y = -4x + \frac{5}{2}$
15. $y \ge -7$;

−9 −8 −7 −6 −5 −4 −3 −2 −1 0 1

16. $x < 15$;

−10 −5 0 5 10 15 20 25 30 35 40

17. $y \le -5$;

−8 −7 −6 −5 −4 −3 −2 −1 0 1 2

18. $-10x - 5$ **19.** $-3a + 5b + 8c$
20. $-5x + 3y - 18$

Daily Review 13-1

1. $a = \frac{2}{3}bc$; 54 **2.** $m = 0.7npq$; 168
3. $r = 2.5stv$; 25 **4.** $y = \frac{6}{x}$ **5.** $y = \frac{1}{x}$
6. $y = \frac{50}{x}$ **7.** $y = \frac{4.5}{x}$ **8.** 17 **9.** 5 **10.** $6\sqrt{2}$
11. 7 **12.** $\frac{3}{2}$ **13.** no solution **14.** 35, 14
15. $3(n + 5)(2n + 2)$ **16.** not factorable
17. $3x^2(x + 1)^2$

Daily Review 13-2

1. $0, -4$ **2.** $7, -2$ **3.** $2, -5$ **4.** $5, -\frac{3}{2}$
5. $-3, -\frac{5}{3}$ **6.** $0, 3$ **7.** $x = \frac{y}{2z}; \frac{7}{3}$ **8.** $m = \frac{5n}{4p}; \frac{5}{2}$
9. $4\sqrt{3}$ **10.** $6xy^2\sqrt{x}$ **11.** $3a^2b^7\sqrt{2ab}$

12.

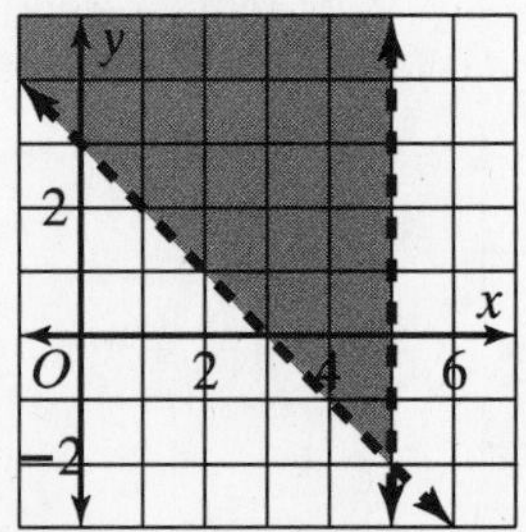

13.

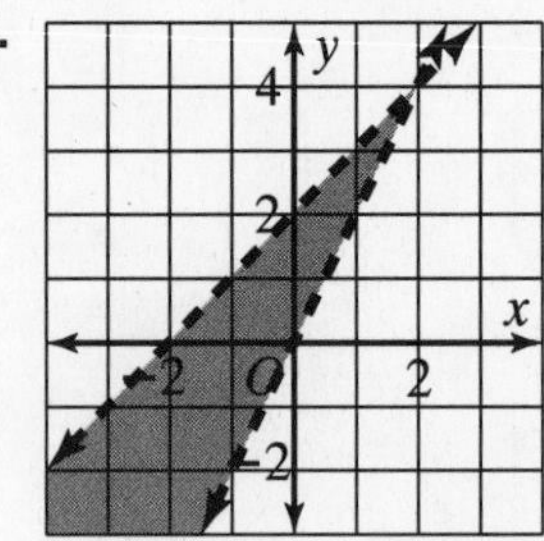

14.

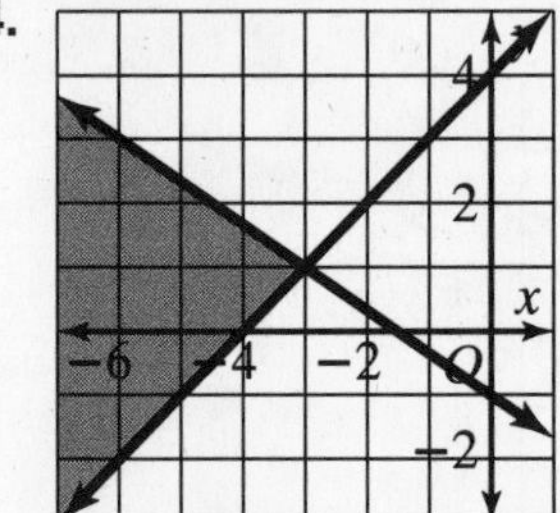

15. 9.002×10^{-3} **16.** 6.02×10^{9}
17. 3.298×10^{3}

Daily Review 13-3

1. ± 5 **2.** $1, -11$ **3.** $-4 \pm \sqrt{11}$ **4.** $9 \pm \sqrt{15}$
5. $1, -2$ **6.** $\pm \frac{3}{2}$ **7.** $0, -\frac{2}{5}$ **8.** $3, -5$ **9.** $3, \frac{5}{3}$
10. $-\frac{3}{2}, -\frac{3}{4}$ **11.** $0, -4$ **12.** $\pm \sqrt{6}$
13.

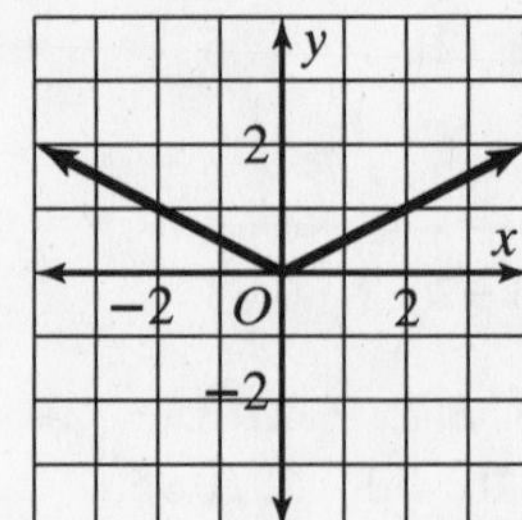

14.
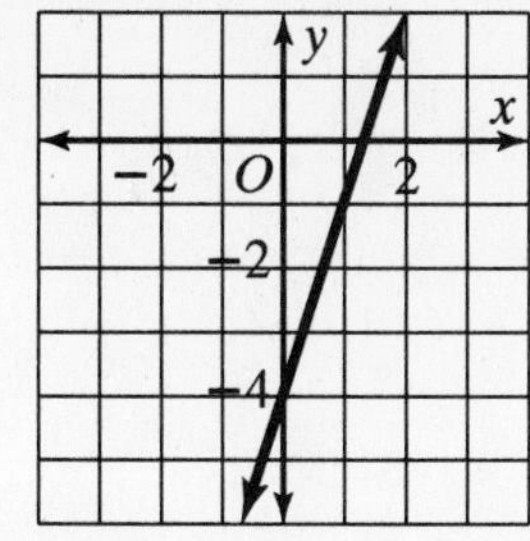

15.
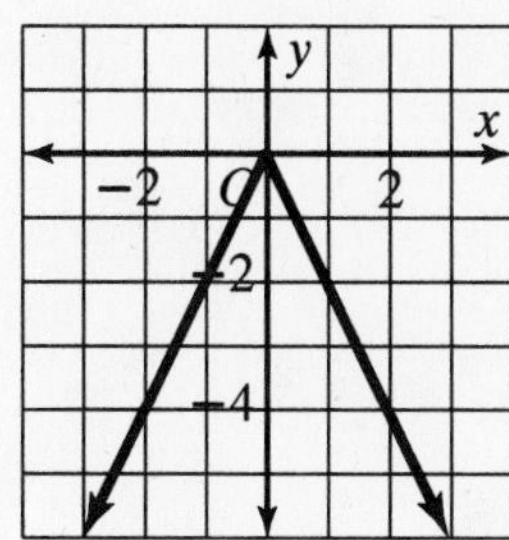

16. $-3\sqrt{x}$ **17.** $14\sqrt{2}$ **18.** $-13\sqrt{2}$ **19.** $(6, 11)$
20. $(-3, -8)$ **21.** $(5, -12)$

Daily Review 13-4

1. $-3, -5$ **2.** $8, -5$ **3.** $3 \pm \sqrt{7}$
4. $-5 \pm \sqrt{15}$ **5.** $\frac{7 \pm \sqrt{89}}{4}$ **6.** $\frac{-5 \pm \sqrt{33}}{4}$
7. $\pm 2\sqrt{2}$ **8.** $3 \pm \sqrt{15}$ **9.** $4, -14$
10. $-9 \pm \sqrt{17}$ **11.** $7, -1$ **12.** $\pm\frac{3}{4}$ **13.** $\frac{2\sqrt{6}}{3}$
14. $\frac{1}{2}$ **15.** $\frac{2\sqrt{mn}}{m}$ **16.** $\frac{\sqrt{5}}{3}$ **17.** $-6, -12$
18. $8, -48$ **19.** $6, 2$ **20.** $-\frac{5}{2}$ **21.** 4 **22.** $-\frac{3}{7}$
23. $-15x^8$ **24.** $32x^5y^{14}$ **25.** $-6n^{11}$

Daily Review 13-5

1. $8, -5$ **2.** $\frac{-1 \pm 3\sqrt{5}}{2}$ **3.** $\frac{5}{2}, -\frac{3}{2}$ **4.** $\frac{1}{3}, -2$
5. no real number solutions **6.** $\frac{4 \pm \sqrt{58}}{3}$
7. $x^2 - 7x + \frac{49}{4}$ **8.** $x^2 - 10x + 25$
9. $y^2 + 18y + 81$
10.
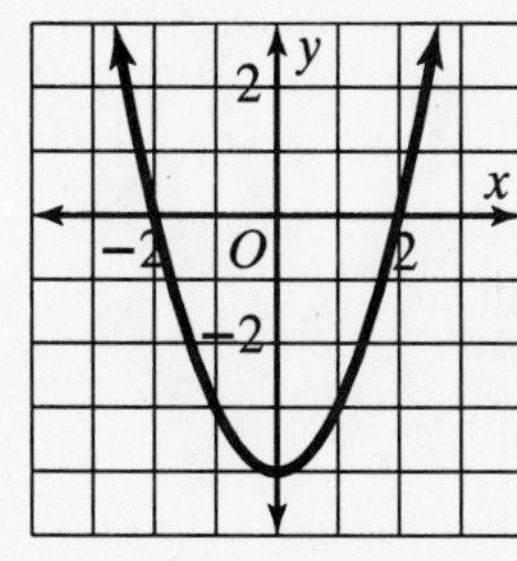

11.
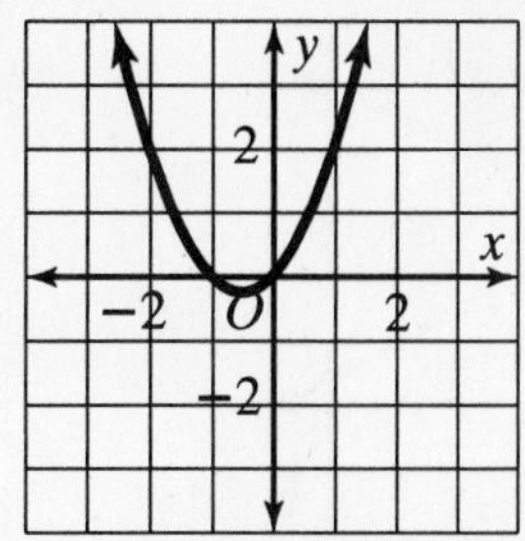

12.
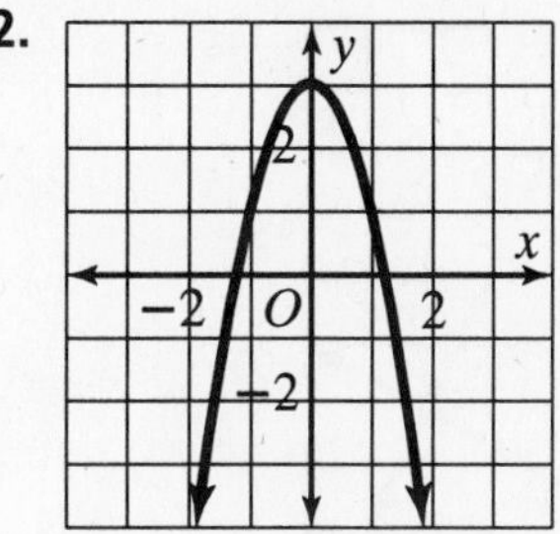

13. irrational **14.** rational
15. rational **16.** irrational
17. $-9 < x < 1$;

$-10\ -8\ -6\ -4\ -2\ 0\ 2\ 4\ 6\ 8\ 10$

18. $-6 \le x \le 3$;

$-10\ -8\ -6\ -4\ -2\ 0\ 2\ 4\ 6\ 8\ 10$

19. $-11 < x < 3$;

$-12\ -10\ -8\ -6\ -4\ -2\ 0\ 2\ 4\ 6\ 8$

20. $\frac{3}{2}$ **21.** -2 **22.** $-\frac{8}{11}$

Daily Review 13-6

1. $-4 \pm \sqrt{5}$ **2.** ± 5 **3.** $3 \pm \sqrt{10}$ **4.** 2
5. $6, -\frac{2}{3}$ **6.** no real solution **7.** ± 2.7
8. $1.5, -1.1$ **9.** $5.1, -4.1$ **10.** $1.8, -1.2$
11. $1.4, -6.4$ **12.** $-1, -\frac{1}{2}$ **13.** $x \ge 0$
14. $x \ge 5$ **15.** $x \ge -\frac{5}{3}$ **16.** any real number
17. $\frac{1}{x - 5}$ **18.** a^2 **19.** $\frac{y + 2}{y - 3}$
20. $(3, 4)$;
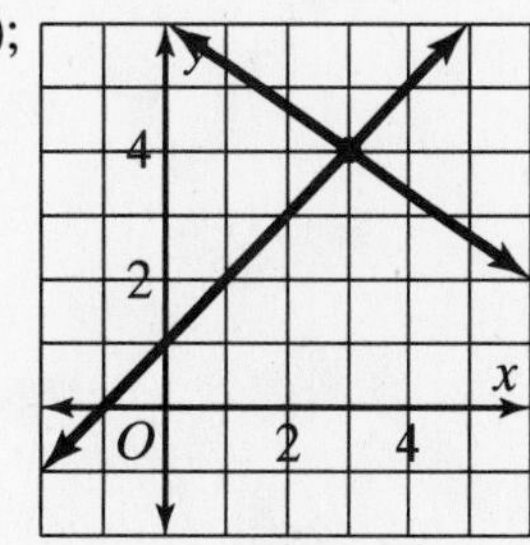

Daily Cumulative Review Answers (continued)

21. $(-5, 4)$;

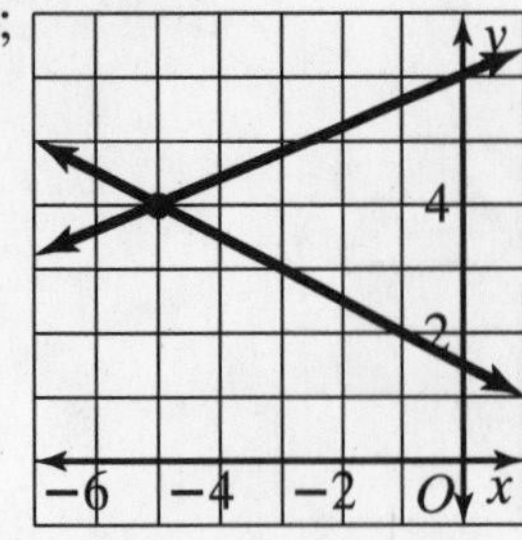

22. $(2, -4)$;

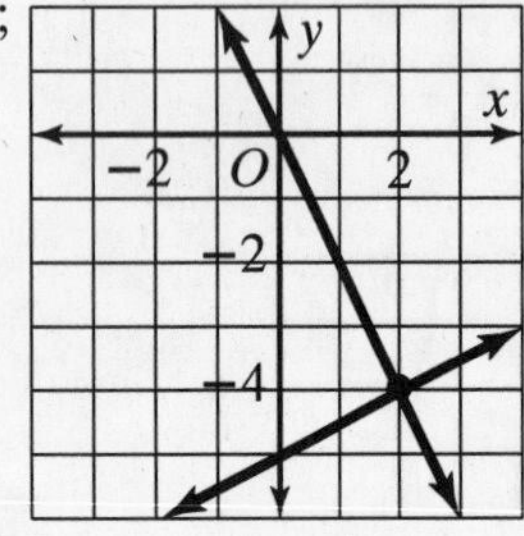

Daily Review 13-7

1. 25 **2.** 52 **3.** 36 **4.** $\frac{16}{3}$ **5.** 144 **6.** 8
7. $4 \pm \sqrt{2}$ **8.** 0 **9.** $3, -2$ **10.** $\pm\sqrt{7}$
11. $\frac{7 \pm \sqrt{73}}{2}$ **12.** $-2, -8$ **13.** $y = 5x$
14. $y = 2.25x$ **15.** $y = 5x$
16. $2x^4 + \frac{x^3}{3} + \frac{x^2}{6} - 3$ **17.** $x - 7$
18. $(x - y)(x - 7y)$ **19.** $(x - 13)(x + 8)$
20. $(n + 10p)(n - 7p)$ **21.** $4n + 7$ **22.** $\frac{n}{3} - 8$